"We've seen two years' worth of digital transformation in two months. From remote teamwork and learning to sales and customer service, to critical cloud infrastructure and security – we are working alongside customers every day to help them adapt and stay open for business in a world of remote everything."
– Satya Nadella, CEO, of Microsoft

THE ULTIMATE MODERN GUIDE TO CLOUD COMPUTING

- EVERYTHING FROM CLOUD ADOPTION TO BUSINESS VALUE CREATION -

ENAMUL HAQUE

First Printing: July 2020

ISBN: 9781447827597 and 9798666050637 (old)
Imprint: Lulu.com

Publisher:
ENEL PUBLICATIONS
London, United Kingdom

- THE BOOK AT A GLANCE –

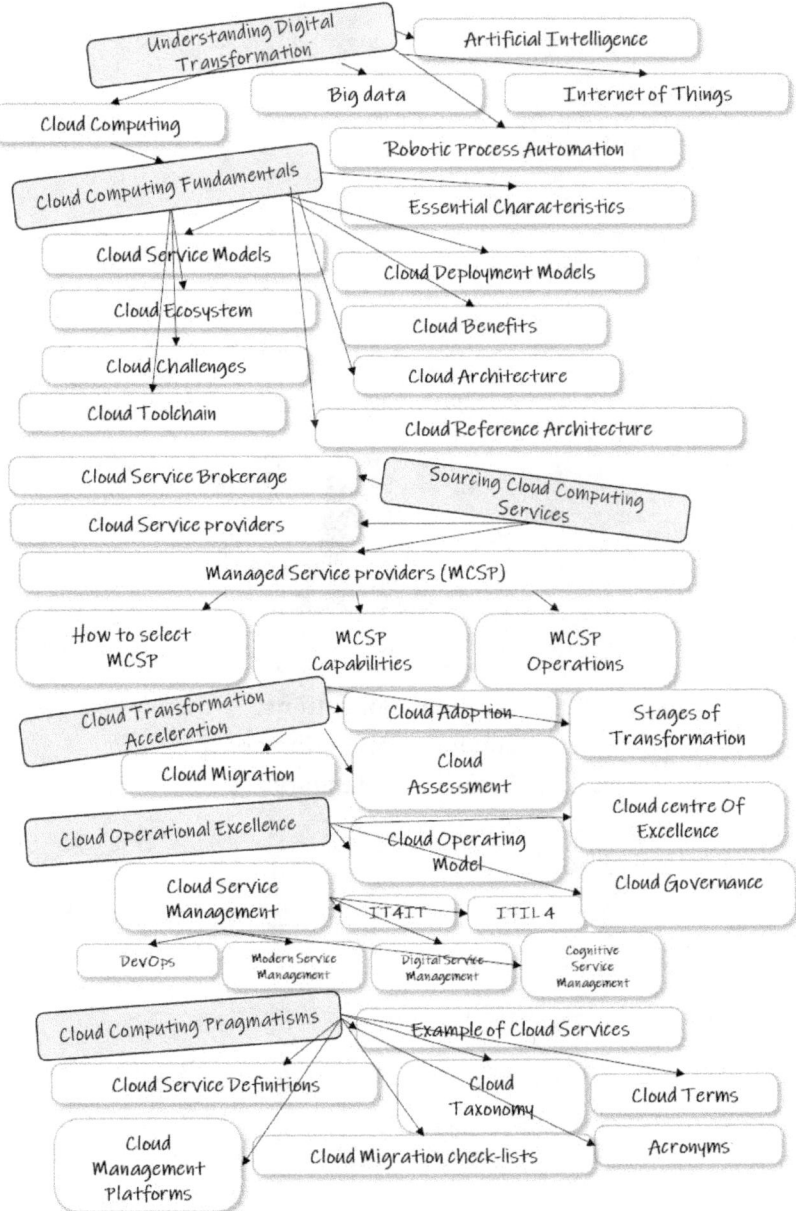

Enel Publications,
London, United Kingdom
Revision 8 – January 2023

CONTENTS

Preface

For the last eight years as Enterprise Digital Transformation Architect, I have been in the front seat of many prominent companies' most substantial technology shifts. I have worked with senior executives, talented cloud architects, data scientists and DevOps engineers on hundreds of global projects. I worked in large-scale cloud transformation projects and have treasured the value added to such conversions. All my books are the results of hands-on, proven, compelling work experiences captured in an immensely readable and straightforward way without ever being superficial.

As Dr Thomas Frankel, Professor and Department Head of International University in Geneva, Switzerland, wrote in the foreword section of my book *"Cloud Service Management and Governance"* – ***"Enam uniquely combines a strong academic background with management and consulting expertise for global leaders. The book is a must-read for all levels of management, including C-level executives and board directors since, in essence, cloud computing is about strategy: it can create a technology-based competitive advantage for companies of all sizes, from start-ups to large corporations."***

Honestly speaking, as a practitioner for over twenty-six years, I have seen how companies leverage technology. I have seen how technology revolutionised across all industries, significantly impacting business model refinement to match an ever-evolving human lifestyle.

Technology seems to be morphing at a pace like never before, and it won't stop. I have had the opportunity to witness a lot of changes in today's world which made me treasure more comprehensive knowledge of transition and transformation in the IT industry.

In recognition of my long-term exposure in the IT sector, I was invited by the University of Coventry to deliver a guest lecture for MBA students on *"Leveraging corporate know-how as a lucrative income source"*. There I had to give two talks on the same subject to two different groups of MBA students, together with university professors.

The professors and students found my storytelling very thought-provoking; what they heard came from a practitioner rather than someone who had just learned from books. I shared my experience as an industry practitioner from my fieldwork, learning by working. Their positive feedback was very encouraging to me.

I received encouragement from my vast network of family, friends, and colleagues and, most importantly, massive support from people who appreciated my work on different projects around the globe – the customers! Notably, I worked considerably in New York and Chicago on the projects. I received inspiration for writing a book considering the realistic approach I provided to complex challenges. My network supported me, saying my work would massively benefit a wider world.

My interest in cloud computing started to grow in 2006 when it was the hottest buzzword in technology. Clouds began to get known as the metaphor for the Internet. Cloud computing became a ubiquitous piece of jargon, yet many tech executives found it annoying; nevertheless, it was hard to avoid.

I have worked with Enamul on a global project designing a new target operating model for a cloud managed services. Not only is he a great communicator and has excellent knowledge across many areas (including service management, enterprise architecture and cloud), but he is also a smart person that is great to work with. I think he is one of the most insightful persons around service management and processes I ever met.

Jörg Veidt
Senior Manager Public Services at KPMG

My cloud computing engagement started nearly eight years ago as a Microsoft employee when we transitioned from Nokia to Microsoft as Microsoft Devices Group.

I learned about Azure. We were part of the IT Service Integration and Management team. We had ticketing tools on the cloud, and infrastructure was outsourced to a third party, where we were engaged and managing the operations. ServiceNow was the cloud solution; at that time, ServiceNow was only Software as A Service (SaaS).

Learning opportunities flourished at Microsoft. I had the chance to visit Microsoft Headquarters in Redmond, Seattle. It was a fantastic experience. I attended a few crucial workshops for transition planning, service desk integrations and IT Service Management (ITSM) process alignments. I took this opportunity to visit the employee shop, the Microsoft Museum and other art galleries. Once my interest in the cloud increased, I continued to develop my skills, focusing on cloud service integration, governance, and continuous improvements.

As a part of continuous learning and development, I got cloud architecture training on Amazon Web Services (AWS) and Microsoft Azure. I participated in cloud workshops, webinars and panel discussions. Using my own initiative, I took several Amazon cloud training courses from their training portfolio. I obtained certification in Cloud Essentials, DevOps, IT4IT, Cyber Security and Privacy, Artificial Intelligence and Big Data. And I never stopped learning. I have proactively shared knowledge with my colleagues and been an ambassador of mentorship initiatives, ensuring learning is transferred to future generations so it can be sustained. In parallel to my solution architect job, all these activities inspired me to write this book.

In my recent work with Capgemini as Managing Consultant in Cloud Infrastructure Services, I am working to help companies in their digital transition into the cloud world, assisting them in translating their "Cloud First" strategy into a realistic and meaningful outcome. As Managing Consultant, I design, develop, and implement digital solutions using technologies such as Cloud Computing, Big data, Artificial Intelligence (AI) and the Internet of Things (IoT).

- SOME PRAISES TO SHARE -

Enam produced a great deal of material to support this workstream in a short period, and this has enabled us to start engaging with the Airport around this politically sensitive piece of work earlier than anticipated. I think collectively it's been recognised that he is very much the go-to person when looking for an expert in this field, and he has been well received within the project team, both Capgemini, our project partners, and The Airport. He is a self-starter requiring very little management and is highly productive and reliable, meeting critical timeframes as promised. Lee B. Lead Cloud Architect, Capgemini

Enam is resourceful, dedicated and knows the value of appreciation and motivation. Within a few months of joining our team, he was geared up, performed exceptionally well to earn customer faith and appreciation. There have been so many challenging situations, and whatever you throw at Enam, he comes back smiling with a solution! Apart from the knowledge, he is a great mentor too and has been appreciated for exceptional training skills, organisation change management skills and ability to create a positive influence for better collaboration." – Tarun G. Global Head of SIAM, HCL technologies

Enam brings so much of experience, knowledge, driving implementation in parallel along with knowledge sharing sessions and always willing to work on new things and in a minimal amount of time he adopted a new style of working, coordinating with offshore teams, solving tough situation! while he is popular as a magnetic manager, his ability to drive integration projects as engagement lead has lately been much praised." – Vikrant I., Service Integration Architect, HCL America

I have worked with Enamul in project basis as well as on operational matters during several years at Nokia, he is a sharp person, has a clear focus and is very easy to work with. He is always willing to help and share information." – Minna B., Program Manager, Digital Manufacturing, Outokumpu

I have been impressed with Enam's general professionalism and his positive and helpful attitude. What has impressed me most is Enam's great breadth and depth of knowledge in so many areas especially Service Management, SIAM and the Cloud. – William S. – Director, Capgemini

Enamul has proven to be the state of the art when it comes to understanding challenges and opportunities implementing corporate Knowledge Management solution. Enamul has a world-class professional knowledge of the balance between common sense and rigid knowledge management system implementation. – Thomas D., Chief Advisor, Danske Bank

Introduction

I got feedback from many of my contacts from the wider professional network, working in the world's leading companies such as Microsoft, Apple, Google, Amazon, and Capgemini, that they wanted to see two distinct books from me out of my first book *"Digital Transformation Through Cloud Computing"*, with different levels of details. In fact, in that book, the first part was mainly focused on digital transformation and the latter on cloud computing. I heard them, so my new book *"Elements of Digital Transformation"* was born. I worked on this parallel, and yet another book, *"Cloud Service Management and Governance"*, was published recently. The book *"Cloud Service Management and Governance"* takes Cloud Service Management and Governance to the next level with smart Service Management in the cloud era. Towards the end of this book, I added details of all other titles that I have published so far.

The Ultimate Modern Guide to Artificial Intelligence:	Cloud Service Management and Governance:	The Ultimate Modern Guide to The Internet of Things (IoT):
ISBN-13: 979-8691930768	ISBN: 978171678-8352	ISBN-979-8574788950

WHY ANOTHER BOOK ON CLOUD COMPUTING?

As I received various certifications in cloud computing and Artificial Intelligence, I read many materials and extensively researched cloud computing and other emerging technologies. This, along with the inspiration to write books, lead me to navigate into the big data of cloud computing. Needless to say, my work driving digital transformation for the world's leading companies in different sectors, such as the world's largest airport, utility company, beauty industry, life sciences etc., endorsed practical value add to my expertise. I am a great admirer of knowledge sharing; also, I came across plenty of books written on cloud computing, too; these would include, *Ahead in the Cloud, Cloud Computing Fundamentals, The Basics of Cloud Computing, Cloud Computing: A Guide for IT Leaders, Cloud Computing Bible* – just to name a few of them. So, I wanted to focus on bringing something unique: write a book on cloud computing that can guide you from the point you understand digital transformation and all the technologies required to elevate that. Then eventually, grow the fundamental knowledge of cloud computing and advance without missing anything. That is needed to cultivate cloud adoption, and finally, once you have moved into the cloud, you start to create business value with cloud operational excellence.

WHAT IS VALUE CREATION?

Value is the perceived benefits, usefulness, and importance of something. The purpose of an organisation is to create value for stakeholders. Based on perception, whether on the service consumer or service provider organisation side. Value is co-created through collaboration between service providers and consumers, and it is not mono-directional or distant. Value = Utility + Warranty.

Value can come in many ways, such as increased productivity, reduced negative impact, reduced costs, the ability to pursue new markets, or a better competitive position. There are many ways cloud computing can create value for your organisation; this could be by increasing the productivity of your employees, being environment-friendly, which supports climate change-related initiatives, it can accelerate your IT modernisation and so on.

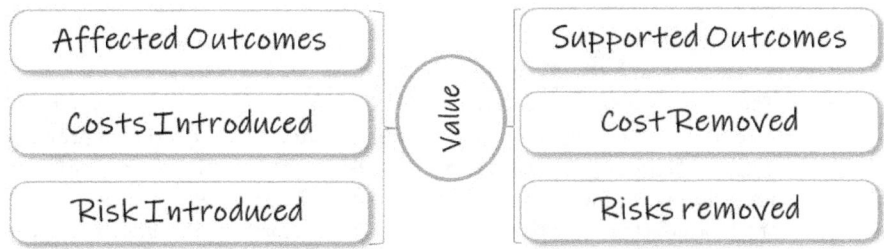

Figure 1 - Value Creation Explained

WHO IS THIS BOOK FOR

This book is for you if you are an executive at a large enterprise. Regardless of how far you may be on your cloud journey, you might face many of the same challenges that other executives have met, and this book will help you learn from their experiences.

If you are an IT leader, then the contents of this book will help you lead and reorganise your teams, influence your peers, and (ideally) rebrand "enterprise IT" from a cost centre to a revenue generator. Moving to the cloud is not just about changing your infrastructure. Cloud-native companies also adopt many related practices like DevOps, microservices, containerisation, etc. This book will tie all of these things together and add the experiences of leaders who have been there before.

Finally, plenty is here for you if you are merely interested in the cloud and its impact.

To make it easier, I have added vital cloud service management definitions to keep this handy. I also added cloud taxonomy, examples of cloud services, and a comprehensive glossary, so you don't need to navigate a big ocean of information while starving for knowledge. You will have the right and relevant information at your disposal when you will need it the most.

I hope you enjoy this book as much as I enjoyed constructing it. And please look for my other books through my profile on Amazon

(amazon.com/author/enamulhaque); who knows, you might find what you need to complete your transformation journey.

Chapter: 1
Understanding Digital
Transformation

*"Every kid coming out of Harvard, every kid coming out of school
now thinks he can be the next Mark Zuckerberg, and with these new technologies
like cloud computing, he actually has a shot."*
- Marc Andreessen

Digital Transformation

The core elements of digital transformation include migrating from on-premises systems to hybrid clouds, modernising financial and operational software, improving the customer experience using technology, and creating a more dynamic and flexible working environment. However, it is not only the disruptions caused by the emergence of new technologies but also the ability to keep business running during an outbreak of a disease that makes digital transformation almost mandatory.

In terms of the definition of digital transformation, it is the process that uses digital technology to transform business faster with ever-changing technology to create new or modify existing customer experience to meet shifting business and market requirements. Digital is more than technology, more than new ways of engaging with customers. It represents an entirely new way of doing business. It is less of a thing but a way of doing things, critically about understanding customer behaviour and expectations in today's world, and it is continually evolving. The essence of customer-centric digital transformation dictum comes clearer from this statement - *"Every digital transformation is going to begin and end with the customer, and I can see that in the minds of every CEO I talk to."* - Marc Benioff, Chairman and Co-CEO, Salesforce[1]

Cloud computing fuels this new paradigm of digital transformation. It supports a robust digital transformation framework. Cloud is synonymous with digital; not only is it cost-effective but also for more mature organisations; it is all about increased agility, dynamic scaling, speed to market and innovation. Agile organisations lead to agile IT to support an agile business.

Cloud computing empowers businesses to create solutions to connect to systems of engagement and to optimise enterprise applications by moving appropriate applications to the cloud. It can deliver compelling customer experiences and opportunities by rapidly creating and integrating cloud-based applications.

Fundamentally the IT industry is seeing a significant and growing spending shift by organisations from traditional on-premises deployments towards cloud infrastructure and services. 'Cloud-First' is, or will be, the de facto for future application deployments, with organisations failing to embrace the cloud, leaving them at a disadvantage.

Digital Transformation Enabling Technologies

In his book"Digital Transformation", Thomas Siebel clearly mentioned that the technologies that propel digital transformation are gamechanging. Still, we are in the very early stages of this new era. He suggested that organisations must learn new technologies to make well-informed decisions.

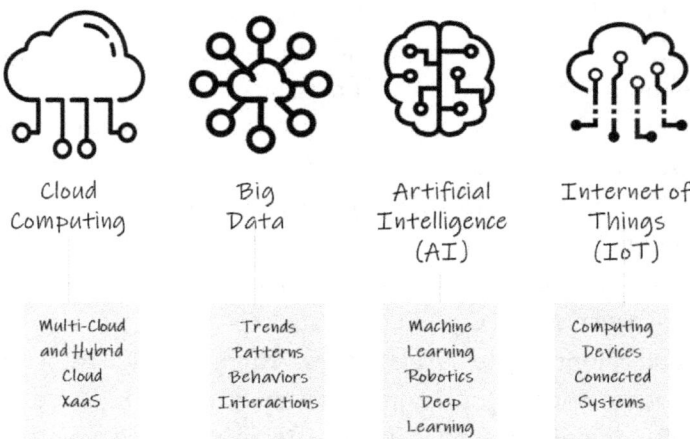

Figure 2 – Digital Transformation Enabling Technologies

According to Tom, there are four key technologies that both drive and enable digital transformation – Cloud Computing, Big data, AI and IoT. We will briefly touch on those areas in this section.

Cloud Computing

Cloud Computing is the first of the four technologies that drive digital transformation. Without Cloud Computing, digital transformation will be impossible. This is the main subject of this book.

Big Data

Big Data is considered the crucial second enabler of digital transformation. Big data has one or more characteristics: high volume, high velocity, or great variety. Artificial intelligence (AI), mobile, social and the Internet of Things (IoT) are driving data complexity through new forms and sources of data. For example, big data comes from sensors, devices, video/audio, networks, log files, transactional applications, web, and social media — much of it is generated in real time and at an enormous scale.[2]

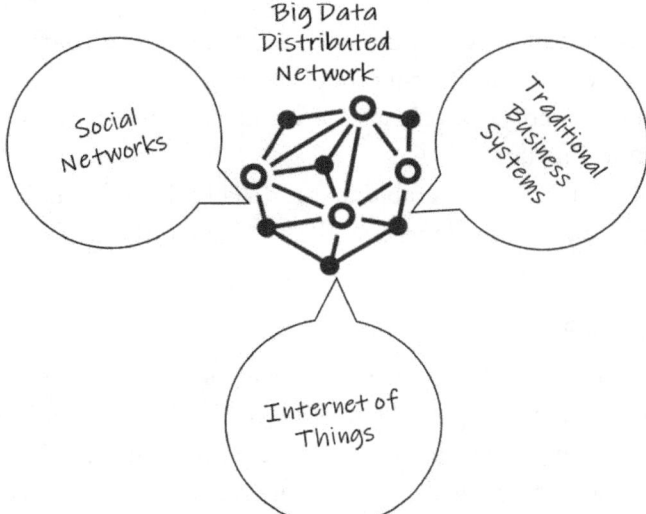

Figure 3 - Big Data Capture Networks

As computer processing and storage capacity is increasing significantly, it has become possible to process and store increasingly large data sets. Today, we can store and analyse all the data that we generate, regardless of its source, format, frequency and whether its structured or unstructured.

Big data comprises structured, semistructured, and unstructured data that has been gathered by organisations and can be mined for information and used in advanced analytics applications like predictive modelling and machine learning.

Big data enables businesses to make strategic changes that minimise costs and maximise profits. If a company doesn't adopt big data, its digital transformation isn't complete. If you know what customers and staff are doing today, you may anticipate their future behaviour and begin making changes to better meet their wants and objectives.

Data is becoming a vital asset that is more valuable than any physical asset, such as land, a house, or a luxury car.

Big Data refers to data that can be managed by Hadoop or distributed databases and kept on numerous computers. Small data is the term commonly used to describe data that is managed with Excel or R and fits in machine memory. Traditional warehouses and databases can no longer handle big data.

This data is so considerable that it doesn't fit in the main memory. Moreover, it enters the algorithm like a substantial stream. Big Data is classified based on the resources it is coming through:

Social Networks

The data is loosely structured and ungoverned and serves as a record of human experience that was formerly recorded in books and is now preserved through photographs, audio, or video (As an illustration, consider the data produced by Facebook, Twitter, Instagram, blogs, comments, Picasa and Flickr images, YouTube videos, internet searches, text messages from mobile phones, etc.)

Traditional Business Systems

Database systems are typically used to store highly structured and process-mediated data using tables, transactions, and relationships (For instance, the information generated by government agencies, health records, commercial activities, banking, online shopping, and credit cards)

Internet of Things

Well-structured machine-generated data that is suitable for computing processes, but its speed exceeds that of conventional methods. As an illustration, information from sensors, home automation, traffic and pollution sensors, mobile sensors, mobile phone location, automobiles, satellite photos, logs, and computer system weblogs.

The volume of data that has been processed is unrestricted. Throughput refers to the amount of data transported from one point to another over a predetermined time frame. Performance is typically measured in bits per second (bps), megabits per second (Mbps), or gigabits per second (Gbps). The productivity of the computer processor was assessed using throughput, which was measured in millions of instructions per second. The definition of what constitutes big data is not set in stone. It is challenging to establish a limit on the exponential increase of data. Yes, there aren't many restrictions on using big data. One of them is how to handle data that isn't digitally accessible. Processing this kind of data is challenging, almost unachievable undertaking.

Why "Big Data" for Digital Transformation

For digital transformation to be successful, data and analytics must be considered strategic priorities. Data analytics could be as helpful as it could even work as a competitive weapon.

Gartner predicts that by 2022, 90% of corporate strategies will explicitly mention information as a critical enterprise asset and analytics as an essential competency. "A company's ability to compete in the emerging digital economy will require faster-paced, forward-looking decisions," says Douglas Laney, distinguished VP analyst at Gartner. "Data and analytics leaders must assert themselves into corporate strategic planning to ensure that data and analytics competencies are incorporated within the highest-level public-facing enterprise plans."[3]

Jason Hiner, of ZDNet[4], in his article on Big Data Analytics, clearly states, "You may have heard the phrase, "data is the new oil." It's actually a pretty good metaphor because oil doesn't have any value on its own; it has to be refined into something like gasoline or plastic. Similarly, we're all inundated with a ton of data, but that data must be refined into business insights to have real value. As a result, we'll look at how big data drives digital transformation."

Jason gives a significant example of how big data can become a refined oil to prosper. He claims that a century-old business urged its data team to use big data to develop more accurate sales forecasting techniques. For decades, the business's forecasting methods simply compared the number of products sold in the current month to those sold in the same month a year prior.

However, the data team began analysing Twitter sentiment and what users were saying about its brands and products. In order to determine the most popular brands and items, it also looked at Google Trends. It then compared that data to its actual sales to determine whether it was predictive and discovered that it was indisputable.

To generate a much more accurate forecast, it now mixes unstructured data (sentiment analysis from Twitter and Google Trends) on top of structured data (how many automobiles it sold last month and a year ago this month). Additionally, if it wished to become even more intelligent, it might perform sentiment analysis on all of the names and goods of its rivals. The bottom line is that the company can plan sales, promotions, and marketing activities far more successfully, thanks to big data.

Melvin Greer[5], Chief Data Scientist, Americas, Intel Corporation, wrote in his article, Data: *The Fuel Powering AI & Digital Transformation*. – "Data is driving the customer experience, and analytics, machine learning and AI running on advanced hardware platforms empower companies to look at data as a strategic enabler, not an output product. A few examples include the hyper-personalisation of retail experience, location sensors that help companies route shipments for greater efficiencies, more accurate and effective fraud detection, and even wearable technologies that provide detailed information about how workers are moving, lifting or their location to reduce injuries and increase safety. And that's just the beginning. Advanced algorithms are analysing genetic information to help to detect disease earlier than ever to save lives."

How Big Data Works

Big Data is everywhere, and it is imperative to preserve the generated data, so something should not be missed. It is challenging to store that huge amount of data any company produces. Traditional computing techniques are not able to handle such large datasets. Processing data frequently makes use of artificial intelligence and machine learning. The term "big data" initially appeared in the mid-1990s.

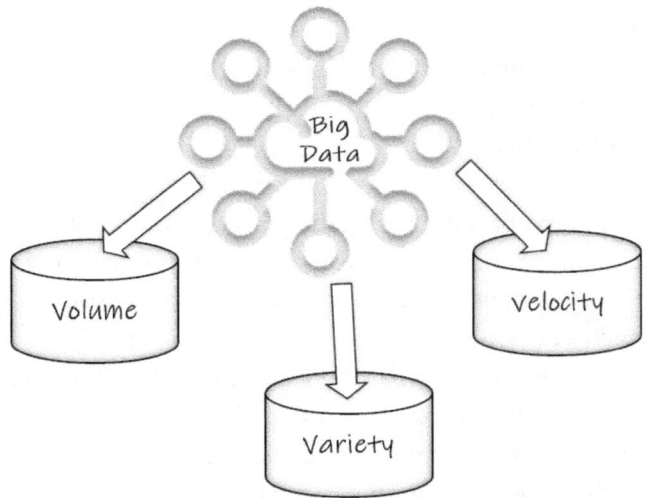

Figure 4 - The three dimensions of the Big Data

In 2001, an analyst 'Doug Laney' expanded the notion of Big Data. He explained that Big Data includes an increased variety of data being generated by an organisation and the velocity at which the data was created and updated. Later in 2005, 'Gartner' popularised the 3Vs of the Big Data concept. 3Vs are three big problems related to Big Data. 3Vs of Big Data are Volume, Velocity and Variety. Common issues associated with Big Data are Volume of the data, velocity, variety, veracity, complexity, and variability. Figure 4, can better explain the volume, variety, and velocity of the data:

Volume:
- A large volume of data
- Terabytes or petabytes
- Size, records, transactions, or tables

Velocity:
- Frequency of data updates
- Real-time or streams
- Batch Processing

Variety:
- Number and type of data sources
- Structured
- Unstructured

Coming to the part of the question 'how it works', will be explained with the following example. Suppose your Facebook account is open, it is very often that you only see videos or pictures or even posts in your newsfeed in which you are interested/you viewed frequently. It is because Facebook analyses the data by observing the videos/pictures/posts on which you hit the like button. As a result, they appear in your newsfeed. Patterns and trends are scanned and then established by social media sites. From the different amounts of data sets, only those are selected in which viewers are interested.

Benefits of Big Data[6]

360° View of the Customer

Big data is often used by businesses to create dashboard applications that offer a 360-degree perspective of the customer. These dashboards compile information from many internal and external sources, analyse it, and then provide it to customer support, sales, and/or marketing staff in a way that aids in their job performance.

Fraud Prevention

One of the most well-known big data applications for credit card customers is fraud protection. Credit card issuers have been employing rules-based systems to assist them in identifying possible fraudulent transactions even before advanced big data analytics became widespread. Therefore, a customer care representative may contact to verify that the cardholder is on vacation and that the card hasn't been stolen, for instance, if a credit card was used to rent a car in Hawaii, but the consumer lived in London.

Security Intelligence

Organisations are also utilising big data analytics to assist them in fighting hackers and cyber attackers related to criminal activity issues. A corporate IT department's daily operations produce a vast amount of log data. Information about cyber threats is accessible from outside sources, such as law enforcement or security companies. To prevent, detect, and mitigate threats, many organisations now turn to big data solutions to help them aggregate and analyse all of this internal and external data.

Data Warehouse Offload

Removing some of the burdens from data warehouses is one of the simplest and perhaps most cost-effective methods for organisations to start utilising big data capabilities. It is customary to have a data warehouse that supports your business intelligence (BI) operations, even among the few organisations that haven't yet started experimenting with big data analytics.

Price Optimisation

Setting prices to maximise revenue is the aim of every business. Businesses selling to both businesses and consumers (B2C and B2B) embrace big data analytics to optimise the pricing they charge their clients. They will sell fewer things and make less money if the pricing is too high. They might, however, leave money on the table if the price is too low.

Operational Efficiency

Big data analytics can assist businesses in identifying additional chances to improve operational efficiency or increase profits in addition to helping them optimise their pricing. This specific big data use case frequently falls under the jurisdiction of BI or financial analysts.

Recommendation Engines

Speaking about the recognition, the recommendation engine is among the most well-known applications of big data. You probably now take it for granted that the website will propose related things that you might love when watching a movie on Netflix or shopping for stuff on Amazon. Of course, using big data analytics to analyse past data is what allows us to make such recommendations.

Social Media Analysis and Response

One of the most blatant examples of big data is the deluge of posts circulating across social media platforms like Facebook, Twitter, Instagram, and others. Today, businesses must keep an eye on what their consumers are saying about them on social media and respond correctly; otherwise, they risk losing customers.

Preventive Maintenance and Support

Retail and financial companies are a common theme in the big data use cases discussed so far. However, big data can also be useful for companies in the economy's industrial, energy, construction, agricultural, and transportation sectors. In many instances, employing big data to enhance equipment maintenance may provide some of the most significant benefits.

Internet of Things

Additionally, businesses across all sectors are starting to recognise the potential of the Internet of Things (IoT). Similar to the preventive maintenance example, they are utilising sensors to gather data that can be analysed to produce insights that can be used. They might maintain tabs on the weather, watch the security camera footage, or follow the movement of customers or products.

Artificial Intelligence (AI)

AI is number three among the four key enablers of digital transformation. A system is claimed to have "artificial intelligence" if it can simulate human intelligence and mental processes. There are many types of AI, including robotics, computer vision, machine learning, and natural language processing. As a result, the abbreviation "AI" is widely used to refer to any computers that imitate our cognitive processes, such as "learning" and "problem-solving" in general. The most reliable working definition is the study of creating systems that can simulate human intelligence and mental processes, which take numerous forms.

According to Accenture, "AI could double the annual economic growth rate by 2035 and boost labour productivity by up to 40 percent"

Data drives the customer experience, and analytics, machine learning and AI running on advanced hardware platforms empower companies to look at data as a strategic enabler, not an output product.

As per a report from International Data Corporation (IDC), worldwide spending on the technologies and services that enable digital transformation is likely to reach $1.97 trillion in 2022. Similarly, Gartner's CIO Survey found that AI implementation grew by a massive 270 percent in the last four years.[7]

Artificial intelligence makes the machine think, and AI's final goal is to create an AI application such as a self-driving car, instant machine translation, etc.

An application that uses machine learning and deep learning within the app is an AI application. AI has two subsets, Machine Learning and Deep Learning.

Machine Learning

Machine learning provides us with statistical tools to explore the data. There are three different approaches to machine learning

1. *Supervised Machine Learning* – This term explains when you have some labelled data, such as past data, which is then used to make

predictions for the future. Which is also known as predictive analytics, so it requires past labelled data.

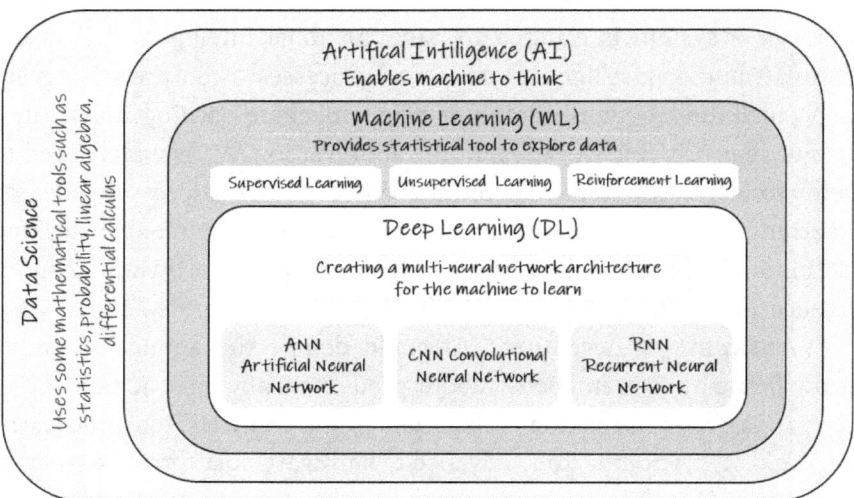

Figure 5 - AI, ML, DL and Data Science Relationships

2. *Unsupervised Machine Learning* – When we don't have any past labelled data, with this, we solve the clustering type of problem. There are many different clustering techniques, such as hierarchical clustering and K-Means clustering, so basically, the machine will group the data based on the similarities.

3. *Reinforcement Learning* – This term is used when the machine learns from past data, and with the help of new data when it comes in, it produces learning paradigms alongside supervised learning and unsupervised learning. The most crucial part is we need to have data. So, we have a statistical tool to explore and analyse the data.

Deep Learning

Deep Learning is a subset of machine learning. Also known as deep structured learning or differential programming. The idea behind deep learning is that the machine can learn how we humans learn things using our brain.

Therefore, in deep learning, we create multi-neural network architecture. So, we are using multi-neural architecture to develop deep learning neural network. So, the main idea behind deep learning is to make machines imitate the human brain, as we spotted earlier in this chapter. To let machines learn things the way the human brain learns things. It is deep learning; there are different techniques, such as:

- **ANN** - Artificial Neural Network – solves number-related problems
- **CNN** - Convolutional Neural Network – it is designed to map image data to an output variable
- **RNN** - Recurrent Neural Network – heavily used in Natural Language Processing (NLP)

Data Science

Data science is a technique applied to all the above parts such as machine learning and deep learning. It also uses some mathematical tools such as statistics, probability, linear algebra, and differential calculus. Hence, data science will work based on the user cases with mathematical tools, deep learning, and machine learning.

AI in Digital Transformation

Machine learning can be precious for an organisation seeking to bring about a digital transformation. Organisations often don't realise that digital transformation and machine learning together can help achieve complete digital transformation when they go hand in hand. There are several advantages to taking a complementary approach.

A survey-based report[8] by Indian IT giant Infosys titled Human Amplification in the Enterprise found that 98 percent of respondents who used AI-supported activities for digital power transformation reported that it had generated additional revenue for their organisations and raised their bottom line by at least 15 percent. The report states that the biggest impact came from machine learning since it helped drastically reduce the average time spent on executing day-to-day activities and has assisted in making more informed decisions with less room for errors.

Digital transformation or customer experience enhancement must be the foundation of any investment in new technology or business processes. Achieving digital transformation is not just a technical, abstract concept but a necessary tactic for retaining and acquiring clients. There are hundreds, if not thousands, of examples of happy customers generated by the most successful digital transformation programmes.

Following is a few of the ways that AI can improve digital transformation's success rate:

- Better customer personas, used from the outset of digital transformation projects, can be created with the assistance of AI.
- To better forecast which customers will take advantage of a bundle or pricing offer, AI-based algorithms can be used to develop propensity models by persona.
- To succeed in the modern marketplace, businesses need customer-focused, AI-powered digital transformation frameworks.
- Companies are rethinking their IT architecture and integration considering AI findings in order to grow client experiences more effectively.
- Supply chains are frequently digitised as part of digital transformation programmes, allowing for timely performance based on AI-gleaned insights.
- As identity theft and other cybercrime become increasingly common, AI is reshaping how businesses implement digital security policies.
- By 2025, Gartner anticipates that businesses in the customer service industry that integrate AI into their customer engagement centre platforms will see a 25 percent boost in operational efficiencies, which will radically alter the industry.
- By tracing purchases back to campaigns by channel and understanding why certain personas purchased while others did not,

AI is increasing digital transformation's success rate in marketing and selling effectiveness.

- In the post-COVID-19 era, when transparency is increasingly defined by it, track-and-traceability that has been strengthened with AI-based prediction algorithms is now an absolute must.

One method to gain and maintain the confidence of your customers, workers, suppliers, and partners is to keep them updated on the development of your digital transformation activities. In these unstable times, businesses need to be as open as possible. The first step is to establish a system of communication.

Business Benefits of AI

The three areas where AI can bring substantial benefits to a business are the automation of business processes, insight gained through data analysis and engaging with customers and employees. If companies examine AI through the lens of business capabilities rather than technology viewpoints, these benefits will become clear.

Process Automation

Because the "robots" (that is, code on a server) in Robotic Process Automation (RPA) work like a human inputting and consuming information from numerous IT systems, it is more advanced than prior business-process automation solutions. In the book's final chapters, we'll go further into the topic at hand.

Cognitive insight

Predicting a customer's next purchase, spotting credit card and insurance claim fraud in real-time, analysing warranty data to spot manufacturing defects in cars and other manufactured goods, automating personalised digital ad targeting, and providing insurers with more accurate and detailed actuarial modelling are all examples of how such insights could be put to use.

Cognitive engagement

The primary purpose of cognitive engagement technologies is to facilitate communication between staff rather than with customers. That could change if businesses get used to relying on robots to connect with customers. For example, Vanguard is testing a smart agent to help its customer care reps with the most frequently requested inquiries. The goal is to have customers interact with the cognitive agent instead of human agents in the future. Amelia, a lifelike intelligent-agent avatar, is used as an internal employee help desk for IT support at SEBank in Sweden and the medical technology firm Becton, Dickinson in the United States. As part of a pilot programme to gauge interest and performance, SEBank has just made Amelia available to a select group of customers.

According to research by Thomas H. Davenport and Rajeev Ronanki (February 2018) and published in Harvard Business Review, "Through the application of AI, information-intensive domains such as marketing, healthcare, financial services, education, and professional services could become simultaneously more valuable and less expensive to society." Overseeing routine transactions, answering the same queries, and extracting data from countless documents are all examples of mundane business tasks that could be automated, freeing up human workers' time and energy to focus on more valuable endeavours. Cognitive technologies are a driving force behind developing other data-intensive technologies, such as driverless vehicles, the Internet of Things, and mobile and multichannel consumer technologies.

Robotic Process Automation (RPA)

A large-scale transformation towards a 'next-generation' IT organisation requires a robust digital transformation strategy. However, the main focus of such conversion will be on a sustainable reduction in the total cost of ownership for IT services. In any transformation, nearly all companies look to reduce cost, enable a flexible cost model and, above all, would like to have contractual flexibility as multi-supplier collaboration is the must-take these days.

Focus on automation as part of the delivery engine is required to realise the efficiencies. Across the board, efficiency gains, price stability, and faster service delivery times can be achieved by using an automated production facility. To seed data-driven culture and capability to support innovation, machine learning aptitudes must be applied. The automation technology that couples with machine learning are Robotic Process Automation or RPA.

Robotic process automation (RPA) is the automation of routine, high-volume processes that humans previously performed using software with AI and machine learning capabilities. RPA technology is becoming essential for organisations on their digital transformation journeys. These are software robots (bots) roaming inside virtual machines, safeguarding data integrity, e.g., reliably doing the right thing, conducting repeatable tasks, or mimicking a human worker. RPA bots can log into applications, enter data, calculate and complete tasks and then log out.

RPA technologies are categorised into three types: probots, knowbots and chatbots.

Probots

Probots are bots that process data according to straightforward, repeatable principles.

Knowbots

Probots are bots that process data according to straightforward, repeatable principles.

Chatbots

Virtual assistants, known as chatbots, can instantly react to client inquiries.

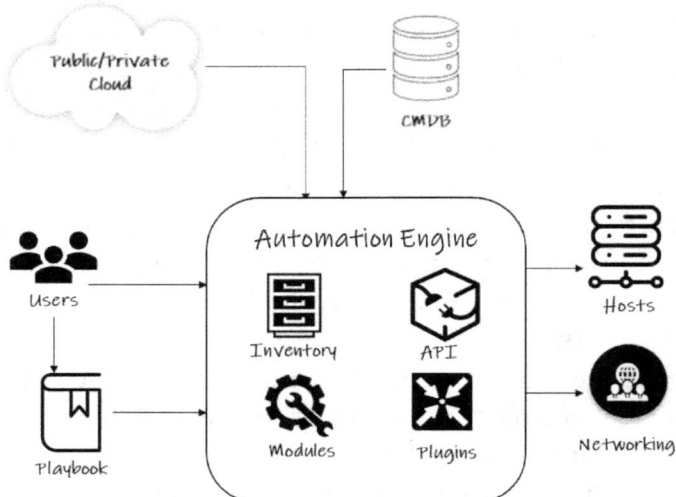

Figure 6 - Robotic Process Automation Architecture

Some of the highlights of chat-based operations:
- Increased collaboration
- Accelerated training and onboarding
- Workplace transparency
- Team building
- Support for distributed teams
- Employee engagement

RPA technology, when implemented efficiently, can benefit with:
- Assisted and automated remediation of incidents
- Coupled with using a short-lived dynamic password for the machine-to-machine communication
- Integration for collaboration, command, and control

- Reduced human involvement for mundane activities
- Operators spend time on intelligent analysis & actions
  - Reduced human error and fatigue

Internet of Things (IoT)

This is the fourth technology that is driving digital transformation. The term "Internet of Things" (IoT) is commonly used to describe the vast number of devices currently capable of connecting to the internet and exchanging and receiving data. If it can be wired into a network and given instructions digitally, almost everything in the real world can be turned into an Internet of Things device. Gartner says: "We expect to see 20 billion internet-connected things by 2020. These "things" are not general-purpose devices, such as smartphones and PCs, but dedicated-function objects, such as vending machines, jet engines, connected cars and a myriad of other examples."[9]

Connected devices and objects with sensors send data to an Internet of Things platform, which processes the information and uses analytics to determine the most useful data to share with applications designed to meet individual requirements.

These advanced IoT platforms can determine which data is worth keeping and which can be disregarded. This data can be mined for insights that lead to actionable recommendations and the identification of potential issues.

An IoT system has four main parts that all collaborate to get the intended result. Let's break it down component by component to see how it works:

Sensors

To begin, tiny data is gathered from the surroundings by means of sensors or gadgets. Data acquired may be as basic as a location or as complicated as a patient's vital signs. For example, my smartwatch with a built-in GPS and heart rate sensor measures my daily activities. This includes counting the number of steps, stairs, calorie consumption, and sleep patterns; it then sends data to my associated app on my smartphone. Centralised data creates analytics for me, and at the end of the week, I receive my weekly activities report, that helps to check my gaps, and I can then plan catch-up activities for my wellbeing.

It is possible to combine multiple sensors into a single device that can do more than just sense things, allowing for detecting the tiniest of data changes. The cell phone, for instance, is a gadget that relies on several internal sensors (GPS, camera, accelerometer, etc.) to function.

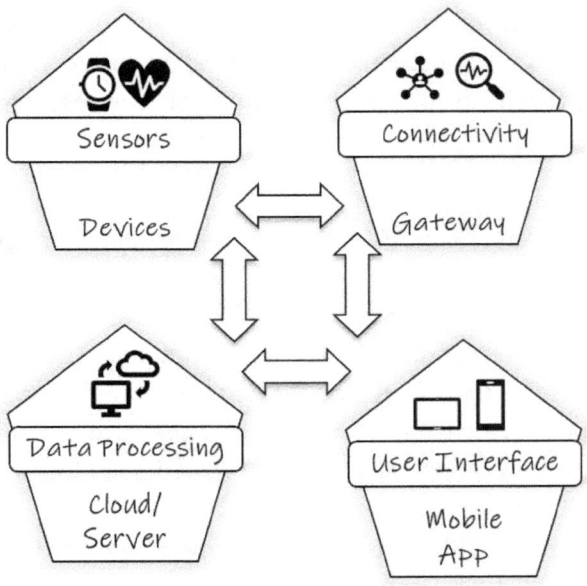

Figure 7 - Components of IoT

Connectivity

After the information has been gathered, it is transmitted to a cloud infrastructure, also known as an IoT platform. The ideal choice for transmitting data to the cloud is entirely dependent on the complexity level and specific requirements of an IoT application, although each of these connectivity solutions represents a trade-off between power consumption, connection range, and bandwidth. Bluetooth, Wi-Fi, Cellular Networks, LPWAN, Ethernet, etc., are just some of the many wireless and wired networking technologies that can be useful in these situations.

Data Processing

The Big Data Analytics Engine stores, analyses, and processes the data securely once it reaches the cloud infrastructure, allowing for more informed decision-making. This analysis can range from checking the temperature on a thermostat to recognising burglars using CCTV footage. As I've already mentioned in my explanation of my smartwatch, the processed data is subsequently used to conduct instant, intelligent actions that transform our regular physical devices into inventive technologies.

User Interface

Finally, the user is notified by an IoT app alert, whether it be via email, text message, notification, or audible signal. The user then can leave the automatically performed action as is, perform a proactive check in on their IoT system, or perform an action manually to backfire or alter the system, all of which depend on the system's complexity. If a user notices a temperature change in a room, for instance, he can make the adjustment from wherever he happens to be using an Internet of Things (IoT) app on his smartphone.

The Internet of Things (IoT) is a network of interconnected computing equipment, digital things, and people that collect, analyse and disseminate data in order to serve users better.

These advanced IoT platforms can determine which pieces of data are worth keeping and which may be disregarded. This data can be mined for insights that lead to actionable recommendations and the identification of potential issues.

Benefits of IoT

- **Data Analytics**: Collecting data from the network and analysing it with sophisticated methods might help you find new avenues for growth and savings in your business operations thanks to the Internet of Things (IoT). The Internet of Things enables process monitoring, control, and optimisation, raising productivity and efficiency across the board.

- **Better Tracking and Management**: IoT simplifies monitoring and administration for businesses across all sectors.
- **Efficient Resource Utilisation**: The Internet of Things allows for the effective management of resources in any setting, whether a private residence, commercial establishment, hotel room, or personal vehicle. An IoT system improves process efficiency and reduces the need for human intervention by harnessing the power of machine-to-machine interaction to gather data in real-time with the aid of sensors and actuators.

Figure 8 - Benefits of IoT

- **Automation and Control**: We urgently require automation, and the Internet of Things is well-known for providing just that. Most IoT devices communicate with one another using wireless networks, allowing them to function with minimal human oversight.
- **Comfort and Convenience**: The Internet of Things responds to our fast-paced modern society, when individuals are too preoccupied to

remember to execute mundane tasks like turning lights on and off or checking their energy usage. Thanks to the IoT system's seamless interoperability and centralised data storage, you have complete command over all of your connected devices.

- **Cost-saving**: To do more in less time, IoT is predicated on automating routine processes and minimising the need for human participation.
- **Improve Monitoring**: With the Internet of Things, a network of physical items may be monitored and controlled through sensors and intelligent devices.
- **Improve control of operation processes:** The Internet of Things (IoT) can be thought of as a means to better and more refined controls, in addition to the aforementioned additional capabilities.
- **Reduction of Human errors**: The Internet of Things allows for eliminating human error from routine or repeated processes.

Internet of Things in Digital Transformation[10]

There are many ways that the IoT is enabling successful digital transformation today. Here are a few of them:

- **Improved business insights & customer experience**: Connected equipment in manufacturing, aviation, the supply chain, agriculture, healthcare, and many other industries, is creating more data streams and analytics potential, meaning that companies are gaining much higher insights into their business operations and how their customers use their products or services.
- **Cost & downtime reductions**: One of the benefits of these new insights is often a reduction in operational expenditure and downtime.
- **Efficiency & productivity gains**: By connecting a business's key processes, leaders can more easily identify ways to boost efficiency and productivity. Thanks to these gains, businesses expect the Industrial IoT to increase revenues by $154 million, according to a recent Inmarsat report.[11]

- **Asset tracking & waste reduction**: The drive to reduce waste is closely linked to efficiency and productivity, to which IoT tracking is integral.
- **New business models**: While the most obvious use cases for the IoT revolve around efficiency, productivity, and process monitoring, we're increasingly seeing companies recognise its scope to provide them with information about their customers and how they use their products.

These are just some of the gains from implementing IoT technology as part of a wider digital transformation strategy. When combined with other emerging technology, such as AI, VR, AR, robotics, and blockchain (in terms of smart contracts and supply chains), businesses can unlock previously untapped revenue, gain new competitive advantages, create new training methods, and produce higher quality products and services.[12]

Smart devices

Here is a list of smart devices that are dominating the IoT world:

Home Devices:

1. Amazon Echo Dot (3rd generation) - smart speaker
2. Google Nest Mini - smart speaker
3. Google Nest Hub - smart display
4. Amazon Echo Show 8 - smart display for Alexa
5. Google Nest Wi-Fi - mesh router
6. TP-Link Kasa Smart Plug Mini - smart plug
7. Philips Hue White LED - smart light bulbs
8. Ecobee smart thermostat - smart thermostat
9. Arlo Pro 3 - home security camera
10. SimpliSafe - security system
11. Nest Hello - video doorbell
12. August Wi-Fi Smart Lock - smart lock
13. Arlo Pro 3 Floodlight Camera - outdoor floodlight camera

14. Kuri Mobile Robot – home robot specifically designed for entertainment
15. Belkin WeMo - smart light switch
16. Footbot - air quality monitor

Wearable devices you must know

Smartwatch

Smartwatches are wrist-worn computing devices with enhanced communication features. The majority of current smartwatches connect to your smartphone via Bluetooth. Some function by linking with a user's smartphone, providing an extra screen to display information like incoming calls, texts, and calendar events. With the addition of accurate and sensitive inertial sensors, smartwatches may now be used to record and analyse hand motions like smoking and other actions. Waterproof cases, global positioning system (GPS), and health/exercise tracking apps are just a few of the new features that manufacturers are incorporating into their wares.

Smart Eyewear

A wide variety of wearable devices, smart glasses, or smart lenses are utilised by the fields of optical head-mounted displays (OHMDs), head-up displays (HUDs), virtual reality (VR), augmented reality (AR), mixed reality (MR), and smart lenses. Despite their varied features and aesthetics, smart glasses can be broadly classified into two categories: those that require a smartphone pairing to view smartphone images and those that can display distinct images without a pairing but a wired connection to the source device. Monocular displays for smart glasses show one image to each eye, while binocular displays show two images at once.

Fitness Tracker

The wrist, chest, and ear are the most typical locations for fitness trackers, which were developed to monitor and track outdoor sporting activities and gym-related parameters including running speed and distance, breathing rate, heart rate, and sleep patterns. Several activity trackers have been studied to see how accurate and reliable they are in counting.

As a consequence, it was determined that while certain trackers are more suited to outside activities, others are just as effective when used indoors. Researchers believe that by giving users more control over their health, trackers can motivate children to exercise more. Adidas' miCoach activity tracker was widely used by European and American professional soccer teams to monitor and analyse player fitness levels and output.

Smart Clothing

Smart clothing encompasses a wide variety of wearables, including but not limited to chest straps, medical apparel, wear monitoring, uniforms for the military, and e-textiles. Shirts, socks, yoga pants, shoes, concealed cameras, bow ties, helmets, and caps are a few common types of intelligent clothing.

Sports organisations in fields as varied as golf, soccer, athletics, racing, basketball, and baseball are already harnessing the power of wearable smart biometric sensors to track their athletes' health and performance in the heat of competition. Firefighters, construction workers, and commuters all stand to benefit significantly from the development of smart clothes.

Wearable Camera

Wearable cameras gained popularity because to their portability, versatility, and user-friendly interface, all of which set them apart from traditional cameras. The fact that first-person video and stills can be created in real time with these cameras is quite exciting. Small cameras that can be attached to clothing or even worn in the ear and larger cameras that include attachments for clothing or helmets are employed. Some studies have demonstrated the usefulness of wearable cameras for observing the environment and detecting falls.

Wearable Medical Device

For disease prevention and early diagnosis, a wearable medical device often includes one or more biosensors. In order to capture useful patient health data using non-invasive device sensors, digital health-wearable equipment is typically paired with other types of wearable equipment, including activity monitors, smart clothing, and patches.

IoT Technology Stack

IoT consists of several technological layers that all play a role in the route from directly connecting 'things' and IoT devices to building applications that serve a clear goal, whether for consumer applications or industry-grade IoT projects.

Taking advantage of the Internet of Things requires a new technology solution connecting edge devices, IoT platforms, and the enterprise.

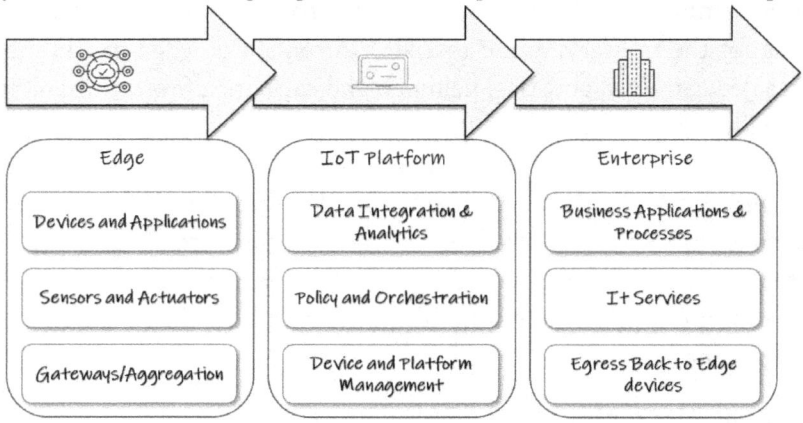

Figure 9 - Connecting Edge to the Enterprise

IoT Applications

In order for connected and intelligent gadgets to function, they require software that can operate on their internal processors.

SmartHome IoT applications

Smart houses are anticipated to become as prevalent as smartphones and have become a revolutionary step in the residential ladder.

Wearables

The sensors and software built into wearable devices are used to track and record user activity and data. This information will be preprocessed in the future so that crucial user insights can be gleaned from it.

Connected Cars

Vehicle interiors have been the primary target of digital technology's efforts to improve automobile. However, recent years have seen a shift in focus toward improving the time spent behind the wheel.

Cars with internet connectivity and onboard sensors can improve driving experience, vehicle upkeep, and occupant convenience.

Industrial Internet

GE Electric CEO Jeff Immelt has called the Internet of Things a "beautiful, valuable, and investable" asset. A central tenet of IoT is the idea that data exchanged between intelligent devices can be more reliable and precise than between humans. And this information can aid businesses in identifying inefficiencies and issues at an earlier stage.

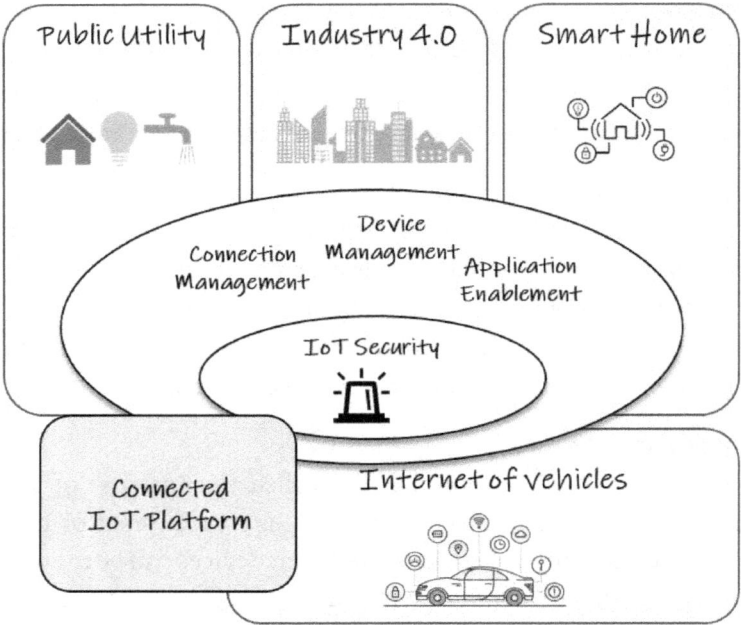

Figure 10 - IoT Driving Digitalisation

Smart Cities

IoT's other potent use, the smart city, is piquing people's interest around the globe. The internet of things has several uses for cities, including improved surveillance, automated transportation, smarter energy management systems, water distribution, urban security, and environmental monitoring.

IoT solutions

The many devices, sensors, networks, and platforms that make up the Internet of Things can be more efficiently delivered and managed with the aid of IoT solutions. Thanks to IoT solutions, companies can quickly and easily reap the benefits of the Internet of Things (IoT) as a reliable, secure, and potent grid of interconnected devices, buildings, and infrastructure.

- IoT Solutions would include:
- Home Automation
- Smart City

- Smart grid
- Wearable Technologies
- Industrial Internet of Things
- Retail

Figure 11 - Internet of Things in a Connected World

CHAPTER 2:
Cloud Computing Fundamentals

"The first rule of any technology used in a business is that automation applied to an efficient operation will magnify the efficiency. The second is that automation applied to an inefficient operation will magnify the inefficiency."
- Bill Gates

Understanding Cloud Computing

So, what is the definition of the "Cloud"? In fact, there are many definitions available of the cloud. The most popular one is "cloud is a metaphor
for the internet". However, there is a distinction between "The Cloud" and
"Cloud Computing". More literally, "The Cloud" refers to the Internet in
general. Network diagrams have long used a cloud to represent the neb-
ulous nature of the public Internet at large and everything outside of a
company's network borders.

The thing is that "The Cloud" is just the latest buzzword to describe
something people have been doing for at least a few decades. One could
argue that the very first e-mail and Internet servers put up at the dawn of
the Internet back in the late sixties were, in fact, "Cloud Services" and indeed, online services like Yahoo, Hotmail and Gmail are "in the cloud" by
definition and have been around since the late nineties.

The cloud is often referred to as "storage" by those in the know. Thor-
oughly explained, cloud storage saves files to a remote server instead of a
local hard drive. The term "cloud storage" can be used interchangeably
with "Google Drive," "DropBox," or "iCloud." You will be required to up-
load information to remote servers in the cloud. Once your data is stored
in the cloud, you or the people you grant access can access it from any
Internet-connected device.

On the other hand, cloud computing uses shared pools of configurable computer system resources and higher-level services that can be
swiftly delivered with low administration work, generally via the Internet. It's the automation of highly virtualised environments. A basic
definition of cloud computing is using the Internet for your tasks on your
computer. From a user point of view, a good definition of cloud computing is using web applications and server services that you pay to access
rather than software or hardware that you buy and install on your own
computing devices.

The National Institute of Standards and Technology's (NIST[13]) definition of cloud computing is widely recognised. NIST's definition is:

"Cloud computing is a model for enabling ubiquitous, convenient, on-demand network access to a shared pool of configurable computing resources (e.g., networks, servers, storage, applications, and services) that can be rapidly provisioned and released with minimal management effort or service provider interaction."

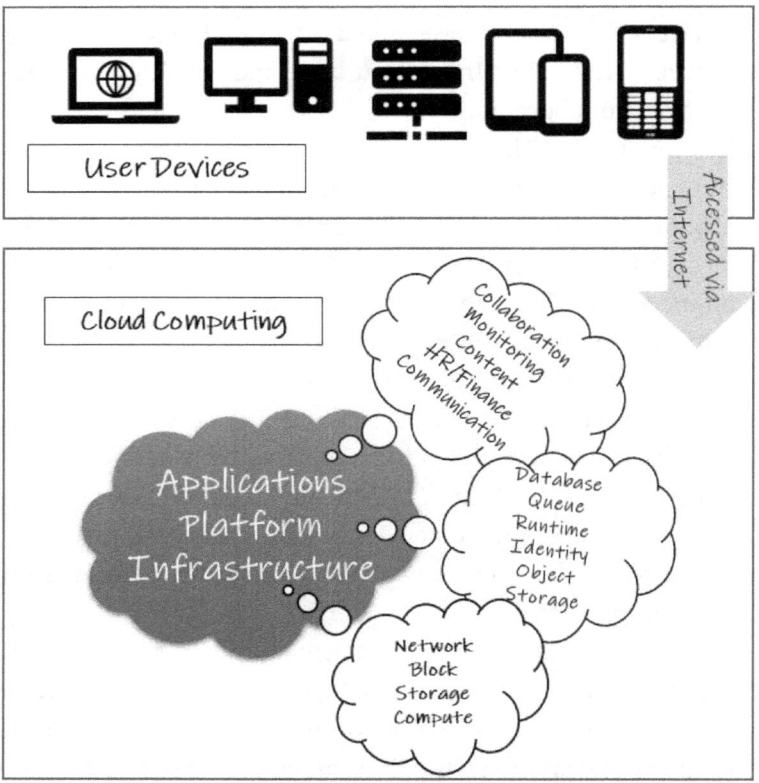

Figure 12 - Overview of Cloud Computing

According to Microsoft, "The definition of the cloud can seem gloomy, but essentially, it's a term used to describe a global network of servers, each with a unique function. The cloud is not a physical entity but instead is a vast network of remote servers around the globe linked together and meant to operate as a single ecosystem. These servers are designed to either store and manage data, run applications or deliver content or a service such as streaming videos, web e-mail, office productivity software or social media. Instead of accessing files and data from a local or personal computer, you are accessing them online from any Internet-capable device – the information will be available wherever you go and whenever you need it".[14]

There are a few other popular definitions of cloud computing that I would like to add here for the record:

"Cloud computing is a style of computing where massively scalable IT-related capabilities are provided as a service across the Internet to multiple external customers" – Gartner

"Cloud computing: A pool of abstracted, highly scalable, and managed infrastructure capable of hosting end-customer applications and billed by consumption." – Forrester.

"Cloud computing is Web-based processing, whereby shared resources, software, and information are provided to computers and other devices (such as smartphones) on-demand over the Internet." – Wikipedia.

Gartner's definition focuses more on the characteristics of cloud computing, giving more importance to the key advantage of cloud computing which is rapid elasticity. We will investigate this more closely in the Essential Characteristics section. Forrester also emphasises scalability but also underlines the financial advantages of cloud computing. And Wikipedia looks into another key essential characteristic, "On-demand". All these definitions are meaningful and support a more comprehensive understanding of cloud computing.

To summarise, the cloud aims to empower organisations to accomplish their computing essentials in support of digital transformation to better manage their growth with optimal management of finance, culture and operational goals.

My definition is, "Cloud is the digital wonderland of the Internet of Things, powered by Artificial Intelligence and Big Data" why? Because today we understand the characteristics, we know the advantages, and we know that it is essential; we know the configurations required, but what we get out of the cloud at the end of the day matters to me the most. Users don't want to know how Amazon's Alexa answers their queries, where it gets the answers or how it works; that's too complex for them to understand how a machine learns, what language is used to program virtual assistants, how it connects to the cloud and brings the answers from them. They want the right solution at the right time for doing the desirable thing.

This cloud computing is composed of three essential paradigms: the characteristics, the service models, and the deployment models. We will look into them in the following few headings.

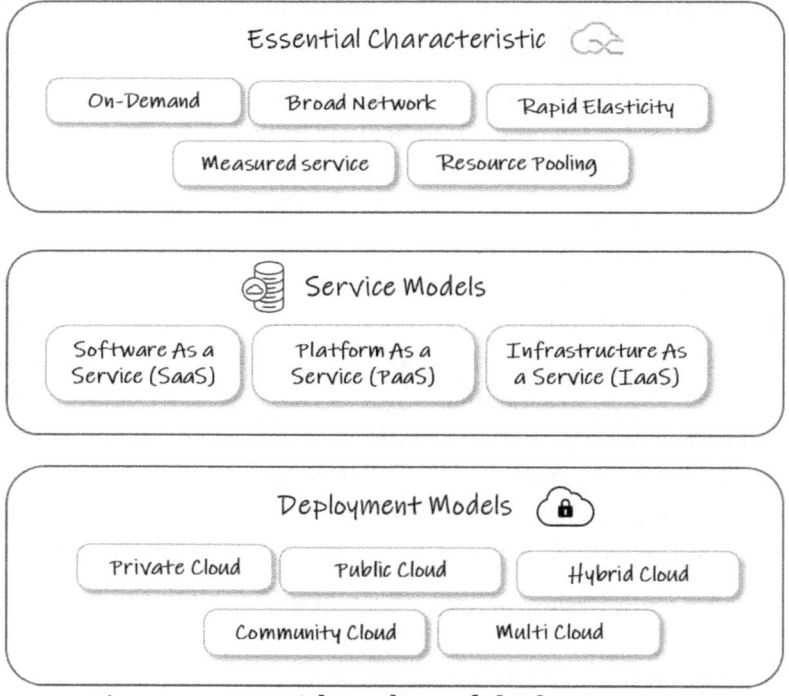

Figure 13 – 3 Essential Paradigms of Cloud Computing

The Essential Characteristics

Essential characteristics are the unique features that cloud computing can offer, for which it has gained massive acceptance and adoption as an integral part of digital transformation. There are five core attributes commonly known. Lately, more have been added to this list, such as automatics, security, availability etc.

On-Demand

This is one of the most important and valuable features of cloud computing. The cloud service consumer can adjust their need in self-service mode. They can consume storage and server time without intervening with the service provider. Organisations can use a "Self-Service" portal to control their usage, add or delete services, etc. Cloud service providers providing on-demand self-services include Amazon Web Services (AWS), Microsoft, Google, IBM and Salesforce.com. New York Times and NASDAQ are examples of companies using AWS (NIST). Gartner describes this characteristic as service-based.

Broad Network

In simplicity, it means capabilities of cloud computing are available over a more comprehensive network, e.g., you can use resources on the cloud by using any digital device such as mobile phones, tablets, or laptops from anywhere in the world where there is internet. You don't need to have your device physically connected to the network with a cable; for example, to watch a movie on Netflix, you can do that on-air using the internet to access the resources stationed in the cloud. In general, the connections are fast, there is no latency, and the quality of service (QoS) is excellent.

Resource Pooling

When resources are pooled, they are used to serve several clients simultaneously. In the cloud, resources are built to accommodate several users at once. With multi-tenancy, several users can share a single set of servers, applications, or other physical resources while yet maintaining individual control over their data. It's not unlike how apartment dwellers share common spaces like elevators and laundry rooms but enjoy individual space and security within the building. This is how cloud multi-tenancy functions.

Rapid Elasticity

This is one of my favourites and one of the critical characteristics of cloud computing. Finished are the days when you had to pay for a bigger capacity of servers but use only a fraction of it. Cloud computing can quickly provision resources in the cloud as organisations need them and just pay for that portion of consumption. With elasticity, you can scale cloud computing resources as per your need.

Cloud computing is characterised by its elasticity, which allows for the rapid provisioning and de-provisioning of resources. Storage, virtual machines, and even client apps might benefit from rapid provisioning and de-provisioning.

Measured service

Due to its significance in the billing process, this is yet another essential function. In order to automatically regulate and optimise resource utilisation, cloud computing takes advantage of its metering capability at a suitable level of abstraction for the service being used (e.g., storage, processing, bandwidth, and active user accounts). That's Service Level Management included. The manufacturing company is charged on a "pay as you go" basis, meaning that costs will fluctuate based on how many resources are actually used.

The Cloud Service Models

The services you get from cloud computing are divided into three categories: the services you get on-demand via the internet from a Cloud Computing provider's server. The three Cloud Service Models are Software-as-a-Service (SaaS), Infrastructure-as-a-Service (IaaS) and Platform-as-a-Service (PaaS). These three services comprise what Rackspace calls the cloud computing Stack, with SaaS on top, PaaS in the middle, and IaaS at the bottom.

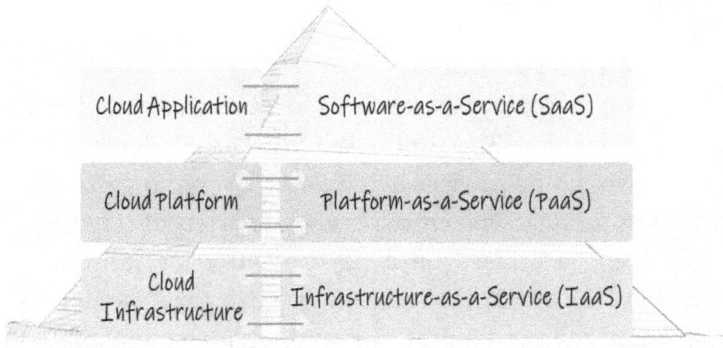

Figure 14 - Cloud Service Models

Infrastructure-as-a-Service (IaaS)

This base layer provides capabilities such as storage, networks, and other fundamental computing resources. AWS Elastic Computer Cloud (E2C), Azure Virtual Machines, IBM Cloud, and Google Compute Engine are the most protuberant examples of IaaS.

Platform-as-a-Service (PaaS)

This is the capstone of Infrastructure as a Service. In other words, this feature enables users to deploy applications built with programming languages, libraries, services, and tools that they've either developed or purchased into the cloud's underlying infrastructure. Examples of platform as a service include Amazon Elastic Beanstalk, Microsoft Azure Web App, and Google App Engine.

Software-as-a-Service (SaaS)

Adding this layer on top of PaaS enables the user to access and utilise the provider's cloud-based application suite. Thin client interfaces like web browsers (for example, web-based e-mail) or programme interfaces allow users to access the programmes from various client devices. Salesforce, Workday, ServiceNow, and Slack are well-known names in the SaaS sector. SaaS apps can also be found in companies like Microsoft, Adobe, SAP, Oracle, and Autodesk.

Anything as a Service (XaaS)

XaaS (Anything as a Service) is a fourth service paradigm becoming increasingly popular. The umbrella term "XaaS" describes many approaches to providing services in the cloud. Everything (X) as a service is what it refers to. XaaS encompasses a wide variety of cloud-hosted solutions that can be utilised on a pay-as-you-go or subscription basis. Instead of purchasing X as a solution, you can pay to access X's features through XaaS. You can think of it as renting the tech capabilities you use. You pay a regular price for as long as you require the service, but you never actually own the thing. In 'as-a-service' models, functionality is provided through remote access over the Internet. Thus, the degree to which the service provider is involved varies among the various XaaS computing models. For instance, the seller might merely supply the necessary infrastructure. Or, they may provide a finished programme with all the bells and whistles.

Cloud Service Consumptions

Whoever has an ongoing commercial engagement with and makes use of a cloud provider's services is considered a cloud consumer. The consumer is the service's most important constituent, and cloud providers design their offerings with them in mind. A cloud provider customer looks through the company's service catalogue, makes a service request, negotiates terms of service with the provider, and ultimately uses the service. The cloud service recipient may be charged for the service rendered and must make suitable payment arrangements.

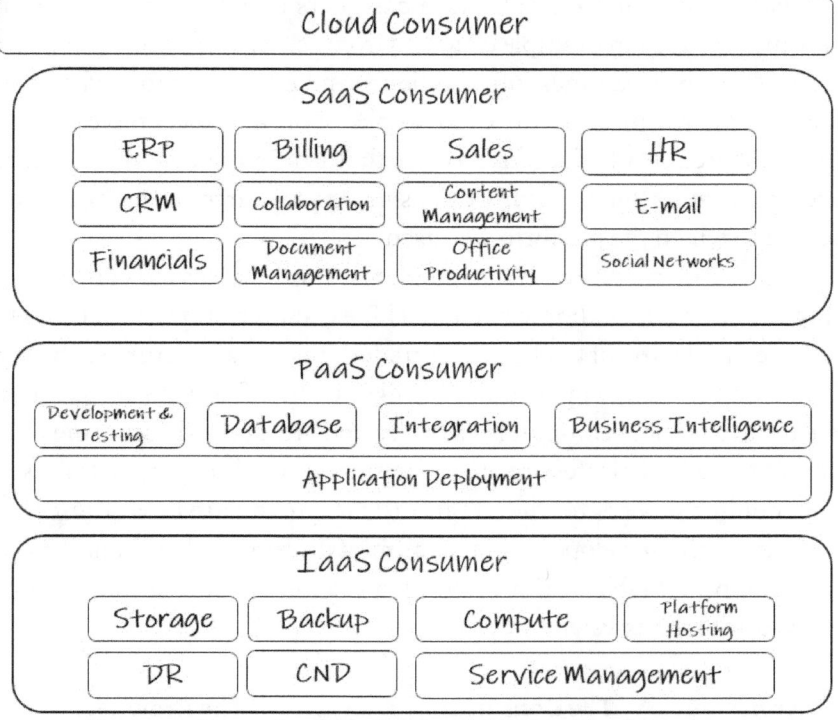

Figure 15 - Example of Services Available to a Cloud Consumer

Typically, SaaS applications are hosted and made available to users across a network to connect the various parties involved in the SaaS model. Organisations that offer their members access to software applications are one type of SaaS customer, as are end-users who run the programmes themselves and administrators who set them up for users. Users of the software as a service (SaaS) model get instantaneous access to the software and can be charged either by the number of users or by the number of services utilised. The latter might be evaluated based on how long it is used, how much data is saved, or how quickly it is accessed.

When using a PaaS, cloud users use the cloud provider's tools and execution resources to create, test, release, and administer cloud-based software programmes. Application designers and builders, testers who run and test apps in multiple cloud environments, application publishers who release programmes into the cloud, and administrators who set up and track performance metrics for applications are all examples of PaaS users. There are a few different ways that PaaS providers might charge their customers: by the number of users, the resources used, or the time period in which the platform was used.

Infrastructure as a service (IaaS) gives users access to core computing resources, including virtual machines, shared storage space on the internet, and parts of the Internet's underlying infrastructure so they can install and run any application they like. Users of an IaaS are given the means to use these computer resources and are charged according to the amount used. IT professionals who want to build, deploy, administer, and monitor services for their IT infrastructure can use IaaS. These users include system developers, system administrators, and IT managers.

The below table outlines the Cloud Service Model accountabilities more comprehensively:

Service Model	The Consumer	The Provider
Infra-structure as a	The consumer is responsible for installing the OS (where applicable) and	The Cloud Service Provider (CSP) provides server, storage, networking and other

Service (IaaS)	controls storage, database, middleware, and applications.	fundamental computing resources. Combinations of physical servers, virtual servers and servers with pre-installed OSs are available
Platform as a Service (PaaS)	The consumer does not manage the network, storage, servers, or OSs but does control the applications that run on it.	The CSP provides an environment that allows consumer-created or purchased applications to be deployed and operated.
Software as a Service (SaaS):	The consumer does not manage or control any of the underlying cloud infrastructure or the maintenance of the application. Limited configuration changes for the application may be available.	The software vendor provides an environment that allows the usage of the vendor's applications running on a cloud infrastructure.

Table 1 - Cloud Computing service model comparisons

The Cloud Computing Deployment Models

The location and ownership of the environment's supporting hardware and software determine the cloud computing deployment model.

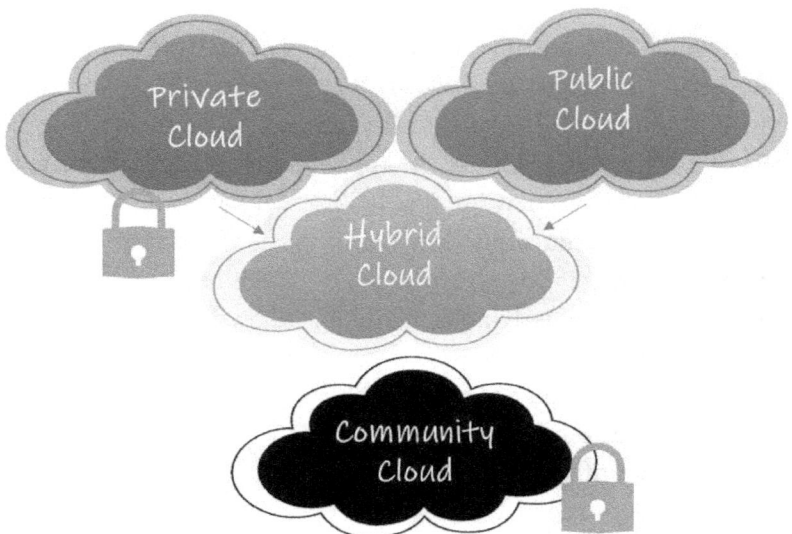

Figure 16 - Different Cloud Deployment Models

There are a variety of cloud deployment models available, and your organisation's needs will determine which model is best. Even more importantly, each cloud deployment option's value proposition and related expenses are unique. As a result, cost considerations may play a major role in helping you settle on a cloud deployment strategy. Any choice you make should be based on a thorough understanding of the factors at play in each setting.

The four deployment models are Private Cloud, Public Cloud, Hybrid Cloud and Community or Government Cloud. These are described below:

Private Cloud

As the name suggests, the cloud infrastructure, which is built and provisioned solely for the use of a single organisation privately, is called a "Private Cloud". It can be owned and managed by the organisation that uses it or by a third party and hosted on the owner's or consumer's premises. It can also be a dedicated platform in a public cloud environment for your organisation only. Due to the upfront cost of purchasing and maintaining private clouds, they are more expensive than public ones. Private clouds, however, are better equipped to meet modern businesses' privacy and security needs.

Public Cloud

The cloud infrastructure is built and provisioned for the use of any organisation or individual that wants to use it and agrees to the terms and conditions of use. Any business or publicly funded organisation can own and manage a public cloud.

Hybrid Cloud

The cloud infrastructure comprises two private, community, and public cloud types. Custom or standardised technology allows data and applications to run seamlessly on a single cloud type, across cloud types, or move from one to the other. An organisation uses interconnected private and public cloud infrastructure in a hybrid cloud. Businesses that need to expand their IT infrastructure often rapidly use this technique when adding more resources from the public cloud to an existing private cloud. To run its Web applications, an e-commerce site can turn to public clouds for more computing power, as one example, especially during the busy holiday shopping season.

Community or Government Cloud

The community of Government Cloud is a closed Private Cloud for a group of users. This is a cooperation between users who share concerns like security, application types, legislative issues and efficiency demands.

Community cloud environments are often only accessible to participating members.

Multi-Cloud

Organisations that do not want to depend on a single cloud provider may use resources from several providers to get the best benefits from each unique service.

According to Wikipedia, "Multicloud uses multiple cloud computing and storage services in a single heterogeneous architecture. This also refers to the distribution of cloud assets, software, applications, etc., across several cloud-hosting environments."

Gaia-X

The Franco-German project, born in 2018, aims to provide a secure data infrastructure while simultaneously allowing companies to move data across borders. Its overarching principle is to enable European nations to become digitally sovereign. To this end, they have drawn up the foundations for a federated, open data infrastructure based on European values, giving it the project name 'GAIA-X'. "Our goal is to join forces with other European countries to create the next generation of a federated data infrastructure for Europe, its states, companies and citizens; a data infrastructure which satisfies our highest aspirations regarding digital sovereignty while promoting innovations." – announces the project governance.[15]

Project "Gaia-X," named after an ancient goddess, aims to persuade businesses to choose domestic alternatives to "hyperscalers" like Amazon Web Services and Alibaba for data storage.

However, Gaia-X will not function as its own cloud service. France and Germany revealed at a conference that they had established a nonprofit in Belgium to serve as a platform connecting cloud-hosting services from dozens of corporations, allowing businesses to easily transfer data while having it secured by Europe's stringent data processing standards.

The Cloud Ecosystem

The three types of cloud services we saw in one of the previous pages have their intended customer types, from end-user to developers and system admins. But it's important to note that while customers may overlap between services, the service types don't overlap between customers.

Depending on the role of a service in an organisation, the user has a specific function in their use of that service. For example, a software developer may use a PaaS such as Google App Engine to build a product and then SaaS like Dropbox or even IaaS (Amazon Web Services) to store those project files. But while service use cases are specific, they are rarely exclusive. The very notion of "ecosystem" has a connotation that brings all these components – SaaS, PaaS, and IaaS – together into a single cohesive unit of tools for Cloud Computing.[16]

While you may pay for a service and subscribe to a container using an app, the service provider might use several other services to deliver your product. An example would be a Netflix user, who wants to watch a movie on the app on a selected device, and will not be interested in content delivery, which could be done by Amazon or the plus-in required for the video stream. Here Netflix will be a SaaS, the plug-in is PaaS, and the hosting service Amazon will be the IaaS. This is how the cloud ecosystem has been fully engaged while the end-user is delivered content.

In conclusion, a cloud ecosystem is a sophisticated system of interconnected parts cooperating to make cloud services possible. Everything in a natural environment, both living and nonliving, is interdependent and part of a larger system called an ecosystem.

Managing the many components of a company's end-to-end cloud adoption strategy can be complicated by the cloud ecosystem. CIOs have a harder time guaranteeing consistent performance, security, and control inside the multi-cloud ecosystem because they must now organise onboarding, management, and delivery of IT and business services from numerous portals and vendors. This has resulted in the necessity for a wide variety of jobs in cloud service delivery to ensure that IT needs are met across many clouds without compromising functionality or safety.

Within the cloud ecosystem, there are different roles, illustrated in the figure below, and descriptions are given after that.

Cloud Consumer

The entity that engages in commerce with and uses the services offered by Cloud Providers, Cloud Brokers, and Cloud Carriers is known as a Cloud Consumer. Before actually using a service, a cloud Consumer will look through a cloud Provider's or cloud Broker's catalogue of available services, request the desired service(s), and negotiate terms of service with the cloud Provider (directly or via a cloud Broker).

Cloud Carrier

A cloud Carrier links cloud Users with cloud Service Providers through the internet and other communication and computing infrastructure.

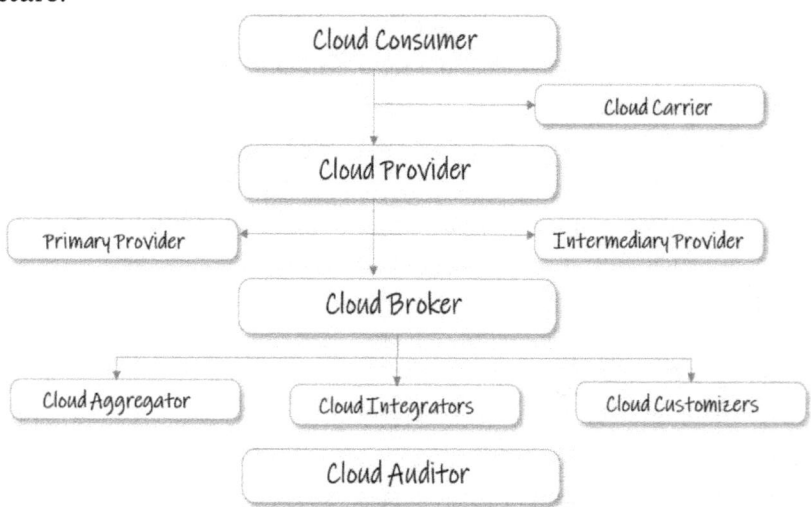

Figure 17 - Different Roles Within the Cloud Ecosystem

Cloud consumers can access services via desktops, notebooks, smartphones, tablets, etc., that are connected to the internet. Network and telecommunication Carriers, or transport agents, are usually responsible for disseminating cloud services. A transport agent is a company that facilitates the physical delivery of storage media like high-capacity hard drives.

Note that a cloud service provider will negotiate service level agreements (SLAs) with cloud carriers to ensure that cloud consumers receive service that meets or exceeds those requirements.

Cloud Provider or Cloud Service Provider (CSP)

According to NIST (same source as referred previously), the business that makes a service accessible to cloud users is known as the "cloud provider" (either directly or indirectly via a Broker).

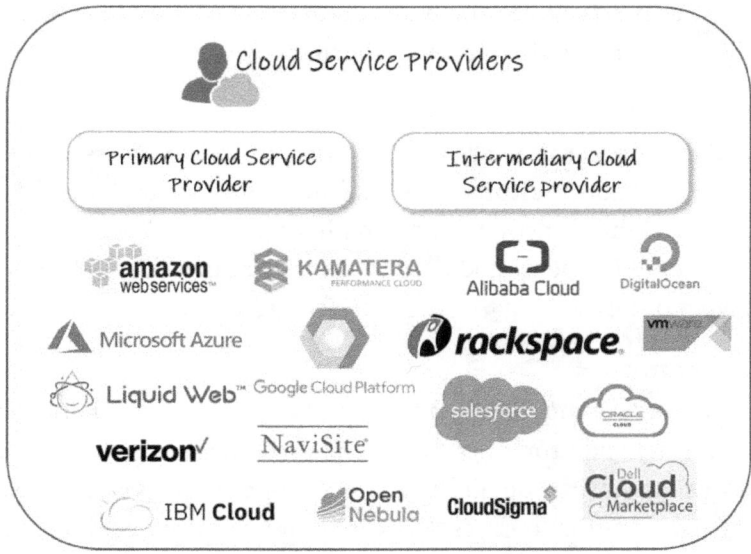

Figure 18 - Cloud Service Provider (CSP)

A cloud service provider (IaaS, PaaS, and SaaS) is responsible for acquiring and managing the necessary computing infrastructure to provide the services, running the cloud software that provides the services, and arranging the delivery of the services to cloud consumers via network access.

Primary cloud service providers (CSPs) and intermediate cloud service providers (CSPs) are the two main categories of CSPs.

Primary Cloud Service Provider

The company itself hosts services provided by a Primary Provider. Although a Primary Provider may distribute its services to end users via an intermediary (such as a Broker or Intermediary Provider), the latter does not outsource any of its operations to the former.

Intermediary Cloud Service provider

Without revealing any information about the Primary Provider, an Intermediary Provider can communicate with other cloud providers (s). An Intermediary Provider integrates the services of one or more Primary Providers into the service it offers to customers.

Cloud Broker

A Cloud Broker is an organisation responsible for overseeing cloud services' operation, performance, and distribution, as defined by the NIST Cloud Computing Reference Architecture. It mediates discussions between Cloud Providers and Cloud Users. Typically, cloud brokers offer three types of services: aggregation, arbitrage, and intermediation.

Cloud Auditor

An auditor in the cloud is a third party that evaluates cloud services independently and provides an opinion based on their findings. A cloud auditor can assess the quality of a cloud service in terms of safety, privacy, speed, and other metrics. By examining observable evidence, audits can confirm adherence to guidelines (as specified by regulations, the service contract, industry best practices, or other sources).

Cloud Reference Architecture

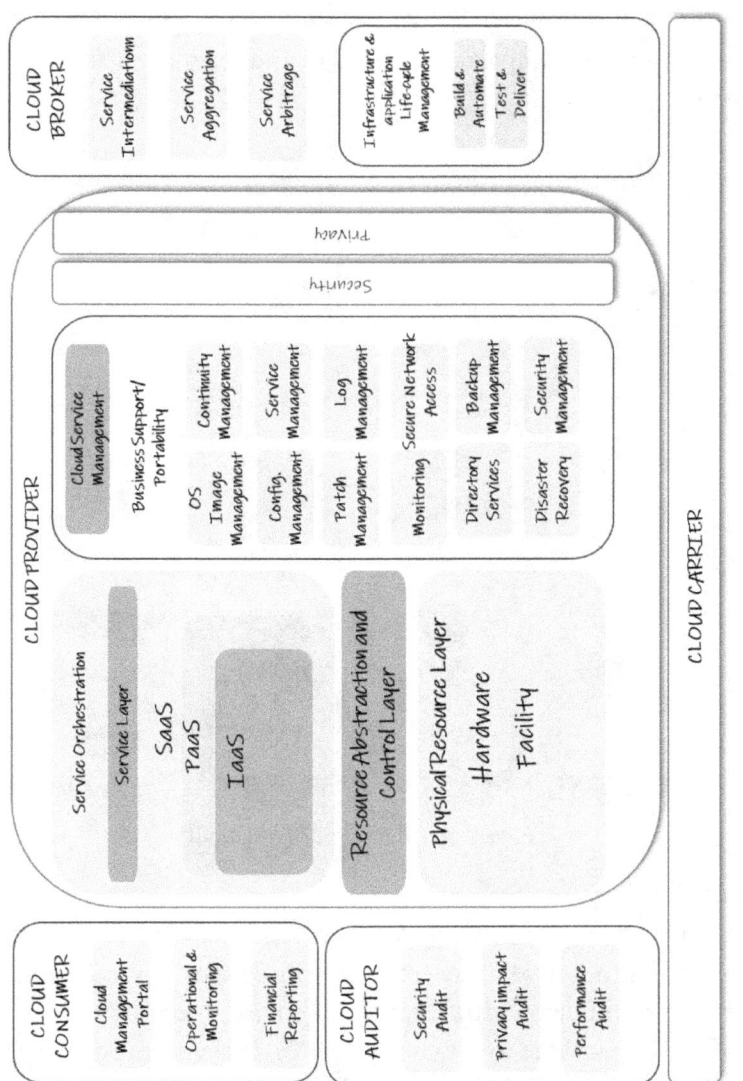

Figure 19 - Cloud Reference Architecture

Cloud Reference Architecture addresses the concerns of the critical stakeholders by defining the architecture capabilities and roadmap aligned with the business goals and architecture vision.

Benefits of The Cloud

There are many reasons that organisations choose to deploy in the cloud. I have chosen a few important ones here and tried my best to put them into context.

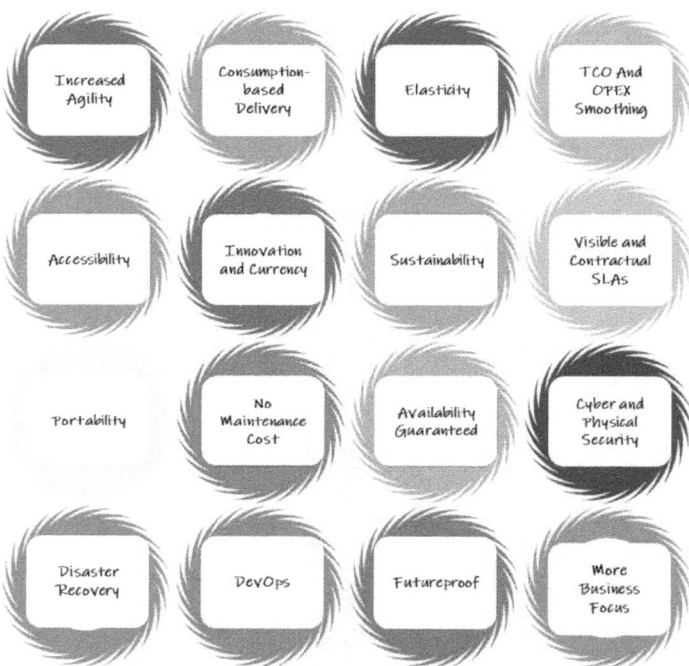

Figure 20 - Benefits of The Cloud

Increased Agility

Cloud services can be deployed and consumed very quickly, allowing organisations to derive value from new initiatives much more rapidly. One of the significant features of cloud environments is the speed and ease of access provided to the consumer. This provisioning feature delivers infrastructure and services whenever required without being governed by traditional purchasing cycles. It means that new concepts can be quickly tested, rejected, or taken forward to full development much faster. These features rely on deploying infrastructure/services as code, meaning a cloud service catalogue must be created and maintained. This was ranked as the essential benefit mainly to mitigate the threat of 'Shadow IT'"[17].

Consumption-based Delivery

Cloud-based services have no up-front costs and are charged as they are used. When combined with resource elasticity, organisations get an effective utilisation rate closer to 100%. Industry benchmarking has shown that a typical on-premises deployment runs at about 15%, whereas a typical cloud deployment runs at 65%. Usage metering by service allows full visibility of service costs to business units, making it simpler to make application cost vs benefit judgements.

Elasticity

Applications can be designed to 'burst' into the cloud to consume additional resources when needed and scale back down during 'normal' activity. Cloud environments can scale up and down rapidly (in many cases automatically) to handle workload volatility and imbalances in demand. When coupled with almost infinite supply, this rapid scaling means that organisations no longer need to worry about building infrastructure to meet peak demand only to see it standing idle for much of its lifetime.

TCO And OPEX Smoothing

Utilising cloud environments allows organisations to avoid the peaks and troughs of CAPEX-based purchasing cycles in preference for a more constant and predictable OPEX cost model. Up-front fees for new services can be dramatically reduced. This prevents the inefficiencies of having to size environments for future expansion; instead, cloud services can be 'right-sized' with the flexibility to dial resources up and down as required. Other on-premise costs associated with managing infrastructure and expanding data centres can also be offset.

Accessibility

Cloud environments are built for browser and mobile delivery, providing the flexibility of access and ease of use on almost any device from anywhere that has internet connectivity. Cloud also offers a more accessible federation with partners enabling organisations to deliver services to anyone that needs to consume them.

Innovation and Currency

Cloud services are automatically kept current by the provider and typically have much more frequent new features and function updates. This allows organisations to benefit from the latest innovations without the additional burden of traditional release, change and test management.

Sustainability

Hyper-Scale cloud service providers (AWS, Azure, Google) need to drive out energy efficiency in their data centres to be profitable, so they are typically much more efficient than on-premise equivalents. The sheer scale of CSP infrastructure means that any slight efficiencies deployed are much more likely to be cost-effective and therefore implemented. Cloud deployment could provide an offset for many organisations looking to reduce or minimise their environmental impact.

Visible and Contractual SLAs

Cloud Providers have well-defined service levels associated with their services; these often include penalty payments when the provider misses these.

Portability

Applications are increasingly decoupled from the infrastructure and environments they run in. Containerisation and development of microservices also enable workloads to be portable between on-premise and cloud as well as between cloud providers. This allows consumers to look for the best 'deal' and helps protect against vendor lock-in.

No Maintenance Cost

Cloud Services from the public cloud require no hardware or software maintenance, and Cloud traders will do that for them.

Availability Guaranteed

High availability is, ultimately, the foundation of the cloud. Virtually all cloud providers use active data backup and restore solutions.

Cyber and Physical Security

Cloud Provider's extensive physical and cybersecurity investment makes the customer delighted. Organisations get a great benefit from CSP's vast security endowments. They also comply with different data privacy regulations, which we discussed in this book in the data governance section.

Disaster Recovery

Cloud Service Providers ensure cross-region replication and the ability to restore to points in time for comprehensive, reliable disaster recovery.

DevOps

Easier and faster development with Continuous Delivery and Continuous Integrations (CD/CI). The Cloud gives developers a more comprehensive range of opportunities. We discussed this more in the DevOps section.

Futureproof

Cloud-based SaaS provides seamless upgrades and patching for continuous health-improving features for an invincible future.

More Business Focus

Since CSP take away lots of burdens from the organisations for managing IT, its core resources can focus more on strategic issues, being more agile, serving customers and concentrating on business improvements.

Challenges of The Cloud

According to Henry Tucker, the technology writer for Intel Corporation, "Any digital transformation will be an iterative process, and it's unlikely to be a smooth one." Like many anything else, transitioning to the cloud and its associated services comes with its own set of challenges. I am describing a few prominent ones here:

Security

Security has always been one of the top challenges, especially regarding cloud-based services. Data security is a significant concern to most organisations and having complete control over where the data is and how it is protected is preferable for some over-trusting 3rd party controls. With various industry segments adapting to the cloud culture, data violation can create mayhem for end users. Whether public, private or hybrid, poly cloud or single cloud, a lack of security measures can directly hamper the organisation's work.

Compliance

One of the major difficulties of cloud deployments is the need to adhere to regulations and meet compliance requirements. In the section on data governance, I covered a similar topic. The term "cloud compliance" refers to abiding by the rules and regulations that govern cloud computing. In addition, you should think about interception regulations or access to information laws that could provide governments or others access to your cloud data.

IT Operating Model

Most IT organisations built around managing on-premise systems are ill-prepared for managing cloud-based services. A change to managing a hybrid environment is very significant and requires new skills, processes, policies and potentially new service partners. It represents a large-scale IT transformation for most organisations.

Service Assurance

Service Levels offered by cloud providers are, in most cases, fixed and may not be equivalent to internal service levels where there is more control over people, processes and deployed technologies. Even if they are equal, some organisations are concerned about the lack of flexibility to step up service levels if future demand warrants it.

Consistent Performance

In some cases, it may be challenging to guarantee the performance of cloud-deployed services, mainly where workloads are latency-sensitive or tight integration with on-premises deployed solutions is involved. It makes organisations wary of using mission-critical applications in the cloud as the tuning and optimising of services and resolving performance issues may be beyond their control.

Financials

The CAPEX to OPEX shift necessary for migration of services to the cloud does not suit the financial models of some organisations, particularly where the choice to 'sweat assets' based on current business performance is essential.

Integrations

For most organisations managing a traditional on-premise environment, the actual application estate has a complex set of combinations and inter-dependencies. Tearing these apart to enable the deployment of appropriate services in the cloud creates some technical challenges around legacy integration methods or data volume/latency that might not be supportable in the cloud.

Vendor Lock-in

Although Cloud Service Providers (CSP) provide many portable services, other services (particularly PaaS offerings) have exclusive features that are difficult to replicate elsewhere. Organisations may be concerned with providers increasing the consumption costs of these services over time with no simple option for moving these services to a cheaper provider.

Cloud Expertise

Industry analysts have warned us that the skills shortage in Cloud Computing can hamper digital transformation efforts. The research found that many HR leaders have noticed a problematic skills gap as many organisations attempt to digitalise their operations. 64% of managers don't think their employees can keep pace with future skill needs.

Senthil Ravindran, Global Head of xLabs at Virtusa, said that this projection should cause significant organisations great concern. "For all the money being invested into digital transformation projects, these investments will stand or fall on the talents and abilities of the workforce," he elaborated. There will be a lot of wasted money if nearly two-thirds of a company's employees can't keep up with emerging technologies. Firms need to ensure that every employee has a minimal level of competency when utilising technologies like cloud and AI, which will soon become as important to how we work as word processing or email were in the last decade."[18]

Change Management

Finally, we get to the topic of change management. To help members and other stakeholders adjust to a sponsor's new vision, mission, and systems, change management must also pinpoint the causes of resistance and take steps to lessen them.

Overcoming Cloud Adoption Challenges

On the cloud resourcing and skillset availability issue, Gary Thome, the Vice President and Chief Technology Officer for the Software-Defined and Cloud Group at Hewlett Packard Enterprise (HPE), said in an article in CIO magazine[19]: "For most organisations, growing expertise organically may not get you results fast enough. It takes time to get your employees up to speed. And as you try to speed past your competitors, time is probably a resource you don't have much of. Of course, you can hire new employees with expertise in these areas, but the needed skills are scarce. Many businesses seek the same unique set of skills, and pro-spective employees with these skills are hard to find. And when they are available, they are snapped up quickly. Most enterprises are finding that hiring outside experts is a better solution. You obtain the required skills quickly, and you get a variety of experts working with you for as long as you need them. The most important thing to look for when hiring hybrid cloud consultants is experience. Your consultant needs to have a long his-tory of deploying hybrid cloud solutions without a bias toward one particular public cloud offering. Remember, your business is unique and will require solutions tailored to your specific needs, so you want all op-tions on the table."

Seeking assistance from various technological solutions for cloud cost management, involving a Cloud Computing partner skilled and ex-perienced at cloud solution management and creating a centralised cloud team to look at the budget details can help mitigate issues with cloud ex-penses-related challenges.

Adopting best practices, such as performing research and training, can help overcome the challenges with cloud operations. Dynamically managing vendor relationships, redesigning processes to involve all stakeholders and cloud patterns, and integrating cloud solutions by var-ious service providers into one SIAM (Service Integration and Management) can be helpful.

To overcome the challenges of migrating the existing application to the cloud, performing pre-migration testing focusing primarily on mi-gration-related needs will be helpful. Setting a realistic project deadline and keeping in mind the migration budget would avoid many hassles. Training with much-needed knowledge about the cloud is highly recom-mended for organisational change management.

To overcome issues concerning organisational change manage-ment, especially to handle change resistance as it is a critical element of corporate change activities, organisations should focus on three crucial dimensions: cognitive resistance, emotional resistance, and behavioural resistance. Cognitive resistance occurs as the unit or individual perceives how the change will affect its likelihood of voicing ideas about organisational change. Psychological resistance occurs as the unit or individuals balance emotions during transition. Behaviour resistance is an integration of cognitive and emotional resilience that is manifested by less visible and more covert actions toward the organisational change.

"The end of 'Fashion-IT' — customers will only pay for value and not technology."
- Sunny Ghosh,
Director and CEO
Wolf Frameworks

Cloud Architecture

Cloud architecture refers to the different components and subcomponents of Cloud Computing. These are databases, software capabilities, applications, etc., which are concocted to control the abilities of cloud resources to solve business problems. The cloud technology architecture will consist of frontend and backend platforms. The cloud architecture defines the components as well as the relationships between them; for example, it is the responsibility of the backend to provide the security of data for cloud users along with the traffic control mechanism when the frontend provides user infrastructure for interactions which is done via middleware or by using a web-browser or virtual sessions.

The frontend platform examples are fat client, thin client, and mobile devices, and backend platforms are servers, storage and network. Combinations of all these make the Cloud Computing architecture.

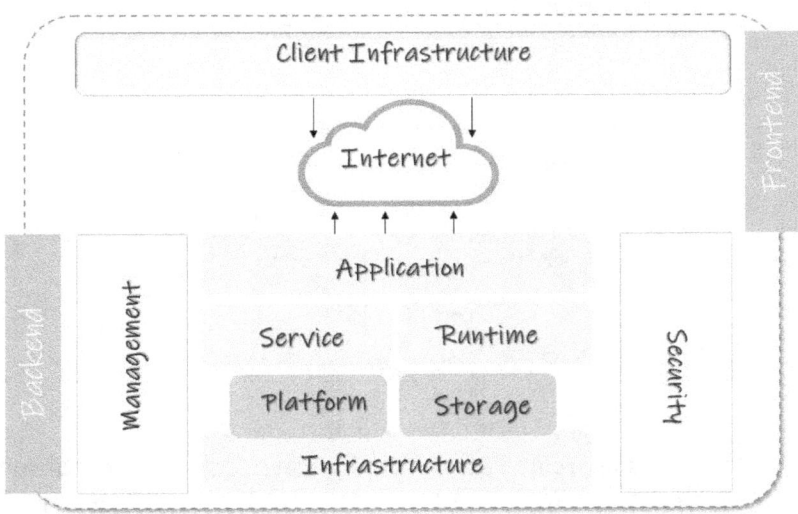

Figure 21 - Simplified Cloud Computing Architecture

According to Jason Bloomberg of ZapThink, the cloud-oriented architecture can necessarily be the building block of IoT in which anything can be connected to the internet. Cloud architecture is a combination of both services-oriented architecture and event-driven architecture. Therefore, cloud architecture encompasses all elements of the cloud environment.

IaaS Architecture

Infrastructure as a service, or IaaS, consists of a set of cloud-based hardware and software that can be used to build and deploy applications and manage workloads.

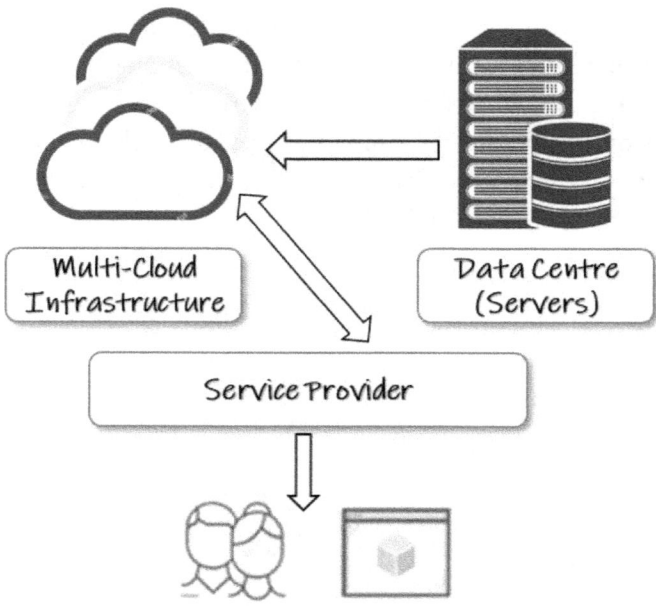

Figure 22 - IaaS Architecture

In most IaaS architectures, the physical infrastructure is abstracted from the end user and instead offered as a service. Infrastructure as a service includes computing, network, and storage. In this model, IaaS providers operate and maintain enormous data centres, often located in different parts of the world, that house the physical computers needed to run the multiple layers of abstraction on top of them and are made available to end-users over the web.

PaaS Architecture

PaaS does not typically replace a business's entire IT infrastructure. Instead, it incorporates various underlying cloud infrastructure components, such as operating systems, servers, databases, middleware, networking equipment and storage services. [20]

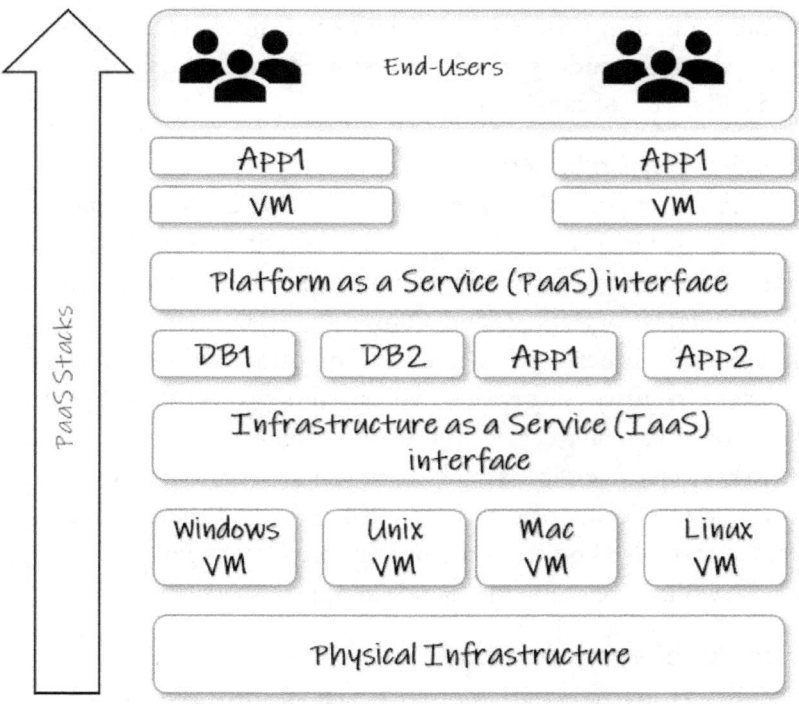

Figure 23 - PaaS — Origins and Architectures

A PaaS provider builds and supplies a flexible and optimised environment on which users can install applications and data sets. Each function is owned, operated, configured and maintained by the service provider. PaaS also provides additional resources, including database management systems, programming languages, libraries and various development tools. Users can focus on creating and running applications rather than constructing and maintaining the underlying infrastructure and services.[21]

SaaS Architecture

Service-oriented Architecture (SOA) is the software architecture that powers SaaS applications. SaaS is the methodology for providing computing services over the Internet. SaaS is also one of the main pillars of Cloud Computing; for many, it is known as the cloud as this is the interface where the end-user will connect with the cloud. SaaS platforms have a wide array of capabilities.

Cloud Security Architecture

When discussing the risks associated with Cloud Computing, the term "cloud security" is commonly used to describe the methods, mechanisms, and services employed to mitigate these dangers. This term typically relates to public Cloud Computing; however, the security requirements for other types of Cloud Computing are not dissimilar. In contrast to "security as a service," which refers to cloud-based protection for on-premises resources, "cloud security" refers only to those measures used to keep cloud services safe for their users. Security in the cloud must begin with the design of the cloud itself. Planning the cloud network's visibility part, also known as the performance management strategy, is essential while developing the Cloud Computing security architecture.

Service Architecture for XaaS

Today's Cloud computing providers enable organisations to access a range of resources "as a service," from infrastructure to software. With the expansion of the cloud, there has been a massive growth of various services and applications available for consumers to access on-demand over the internet as opposed to being utilised via traditional on-premise methods. "Anything-as-a-service" or "XaaS" is a term for all of these "as a service" components or services which allow organisations and users to source and consume their requirements, all on-demand. The Service architecture for a XaaS service can include the following key elements:

- **Service Chain Entity**: This will consist of the creator, provider, supporter, integrator, orchestrator, aggregator, consumer and payer.
- **Service Economics**: This is the cost management part which would include cost model, chargeback and showback.
- **Service Function**: Key components of the service architecture such as service name, function, description, utility, warranty etc.
- **Service Support**: Service Level agreements, resolver groups, service ownership, and so on.
- **Self-Service**: Self-Service would provide self-healing, knowledge management, how-to, automation etc.
- **Service Monitoring and Control**: Monitoring boundary, instrumentation etc.
- **Service Security**: Authentication, access control, authorisation, entitlement, usage permissions etc.
- **Service Usage and Billing**: This is the metering and billing part for unit measurement of service consumption.
- **Service Consumption**: Consumption components, methods, pre-requisite etc., make part of this.

Cloud Toolchain

DevOps Toolchain is a common name for these resources. A toolchain is a collection of interconnected tools used in software creation, distribution, and maintenance. A toolchain's efficacy is higher than the sum of its individual tool integrations because of its interdependence. Tools used in DevOps often have a home in one of the following categories, each of which is essential to the success of various DevOps projects: planning; developing; testing; packaging; releasing; setting up; monitoring; and modifying an existing code base.

Build Tools

These tools are configured to fetch dependencies, run unit tests, static analyses, and integration tests, and create artefacts with build tools such as Docker, Gradle, Maven, Bazel, Karma, Ionic, Xcode etc.

Cost Management

The tools that help in financial management for monitoring and analysing all cloud expenses across an organisation. For example, Cloudability

Cloud Optimisation

As the name says, they help optimise cloud usage so that organisations don't over-buy expectations for what is required. Tools in this category are: S3 Life-Cycle Tracker, EC2 Reservation Detector, RDS Reservation Detector

Cloud Integration

This software, like AtomSphere, facilitates the synchronisation of many cloud-based and on-premise software systems. CloudHub and Mule ESB, built on open-source technology, offer a prepackaged integration experience that enables rapid, dependable application connection without needing proprietary software or a commitment to a single vendor.

Cloud Infrastructure Management

They offer public, private, and hybrid cloud infrastructure management that can be fine-tuned to an organization's specific needs in terms of governance and security. An instrument like Enstratiu serves as an illustration.

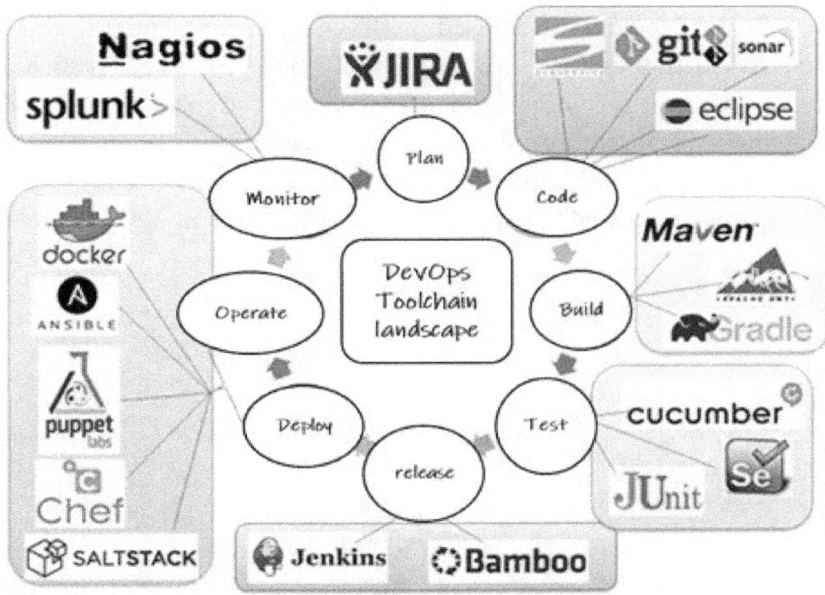

Figure 24 - DevOps toolchain Landscape

Cloud Data Integration

They can help reduce the risk of data breaches during application development and testing. Informatic is an excellent example of this category.

Cloud Configuration Management

Developed by Opscode and released under the Apache licence, Chef is a Ruby-based configuration management application. When managing cloud infrastructure, Puppet is also a popular choice.

Cloud Management

These tools provide configuration, monitoring, automation, and governance of Cloud Computing infrastructure and applications. For example, RightScale Cloud Management

Cloud Automation

The right tools must be used in DevOps environments to achieve faster application delivery. No single tool fits all your needs, such as server provisioning, configuration management, automated builds, code deployments, and monitoring. Many factors determine the use of a particular tool in your infrastructure. In this section, we looked into core tools which can be used in a typical DevOps environment.

"If you want to build a boat, do not instruct the men to saw wood, stitch the sails, prepare the tools and organize the work, but make them long for setting sail and travel to distant lands."
- Antoine De Saint-Exupery

CHAPTER 3:
Sourcing Cloud Computing Services

"He who can establish a monopoly in artificial intelligence, we are aware of the consequences – will rule the world."
- Vladimir Putin

Cloud Service Brokerage (CSB)

A cloud broker is a third party that facilitates transactions between buyers and sellers of cloud computing services. Cloud aggregators, integrators, and customisers are the three main categories of cloud brokers.

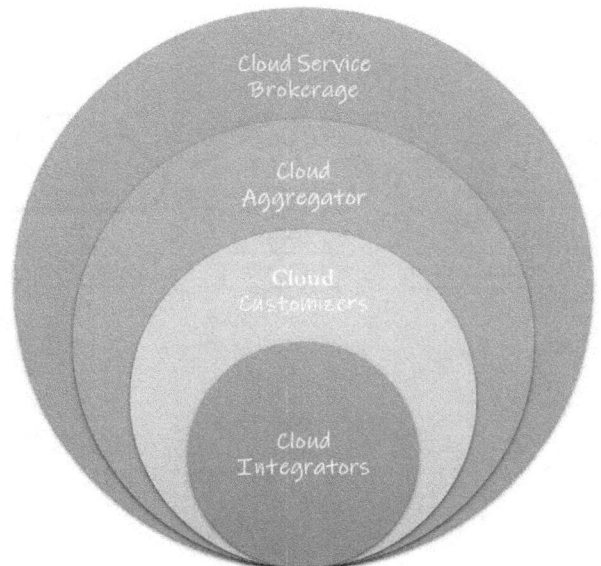

Figure 25 - Cloud Service Brokerage Types

Consumers of cloud services may find it increasingly difficult to handle the integration of cloud services as Cloud Computing develops. Instead of going directly to a cloud service provider, a cloud user can first contact a cloud broker to make a cloud service request. Cloud brokers allow users to access and administer many cloud services through a unified interface.

Cloud Aggregator

The cloud aggregator acts as a broker, bringing together a wide range of services under a single roof. The broker facilitates integration and guarantees data security when moving information between a cloud user and different cloud service providers. The cloud aggregator model is preferred because it saves the customer money and time compared to buying the services they need one by one.

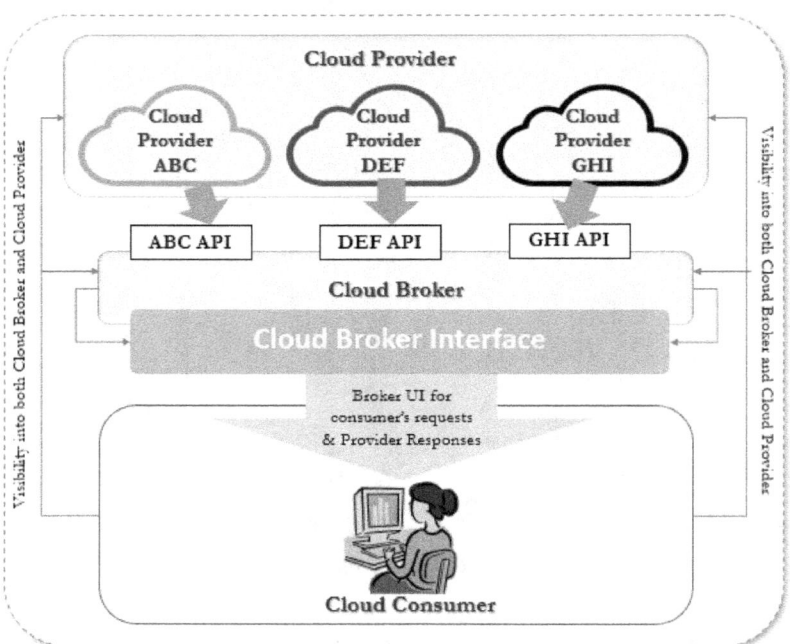

Figure 26 - Example of Cloud Broker Interactions

Cloud Integrators

For better performance and lower business risk, integrators automate workflows with a single orchestration across hybrid environments. After the migration has been completed, the integrator can offer continuing assistance to the business as required. Based on data attributes and service requirements, this broker can select services from a variety of Providers.

Cloud Customisers

Customisation, as its name implies, entails adjusting preexisting cloud services to suit a certain business's requirements better. The broker may create new cloud-based services if necessary for the business. To construct a fully functional cloud with enhanced visibility, compliance, and integration of essential IT operations, this role is indispensable.

There are many benefits of Cloud Service Brokerage. The most significant advantage is getting relevant and professional cloud expertise, for which there is always a challenge.

Another significant advantage is that the broker can negotiate with the provider on behalf of the customer or get better prices for significant consumption, which they can share with the customer giving them cost advantages.

They can simplify operations, optimise resource utilisation, and provide monitoring, reporting and other service-level management commitments.

The responsiveness of IT to the operational demands of an organisation can be enhanced with the help of a cloud service broker because of the unified cloud strategy they provide. Afterwards, IT can move away from reactive assistance and toward proactive solutions. It can lessen concerns about moving security services to the cloud by screening potential service providers to ensure they meet stringent safety requirements. A secure system is crucial in any industry, but it is especially important in highly regulated sectors like healthcare and finance.

Cloud Service Providers (CSP)

In the "Cloud Computing Fundamentals" chapter, I introduced different Cloud Service Models such as IaaS, PaaS and SaaS; this chapter will look into the suppliers who provide them. Services and resources provided by a cloud computing provider and made available to users on demand over the internet are known as "cloud services". "IT services refer to the application of business and technical expertise to enable organisations in the creation, management and optimisation of or access to information and business processes. The IT services market can be segmented by the skills employed to deliver the service (design, build, run). There are also different categories of service: business process services, application services and infrastructure services." – as defined by Gartner[22]. The same IT services when the Cloud Computing provider's server provides them become a "cloud-based" Service.

There are many key players in the Cloud Computing market. Infrastructure As a Service (IaaS), Amazon Web Services (AWS), Microsoft Azure, and Google Cloud Platform dominate. There is also increasing dominance of Software As a Service (SaaS) providers. In the hybrid shift, players such as IBM are making a big move forward.

Cloud providers can increase revenue by promoting technologies like artificial intelligence, the Internet of Things, and analytics. All three major cloud providers—Microsoft Azure, Amazon Web Services, and Google Cloud Platform—use similar tactics to attract new clients and keep them as paying ones by offering basic services like computation, cloud storage, and serverless activities and then gradually upselling them to.

Below are descriptions of different Cloud Service Providers and their features from the respective websites. For the most updated data, you might like to go to their websites:

Amazon Web Services (AWS)

AWS provides services for a broad range of applications, including computing, storage, databases, networking, analytics, machine learning and artificial intelligence (AI), Internet of Things (IoT), security, application development, deployment, and management.

Microsoft Azure

For analytics, virtual computing, storage, networking, and more, Azure is a public Cloud Computing platform with solutions including Infrastructure as a Service (IaaS), Platform as a Service (PaaS), and Software as a Service (SaaS).

Google Cloud Platform

As a collection of Cloud Computing services, Google offers what it calls its "Google Cloud Platform" to the general public. Hosted services for computation, storage, and application development are all part of the platform and operate on Google's servers.

Alibaba

Alibaba Cloud is a division of the Alibaba Group that specialises in cloud computing. E-commerce, big data, Database, the Internet of Things, Object storage (OOS), Kubernetes, and data customisation are only some of the services offered by Alibaba Cloud, which may be administered via the Alibaba website or the aliyun command-line tool.

IBM

IBM Cloud provides a full-stack, public cloud platform with various offerings in the catalogue, including compute, storage, and networking options, end-to-end developer solutions for app development, testing and deployment, security management services, traditional and open-source databases etc.

Oracle

Through its global network of Oracle-managed data centres, Oracle Cloud offers users access to various hosted servers, storage, networks, apps, and services. The business facilitates the Internet-based provisioning of these services on demand.

Salesforce

Salesforce offers applications for all aspects of business, including CRM, sales, ERP, customer service, marketing automation, business analytics, mobile application building, and much more. And it all works on the same, connected platform, drawing from the same customer data.

SAP

SAP Cloud Platform is an enterprise platform-as-a-service (enterprise PaaS) that provides comprehensive application development services and capabilities, which lets you build, extend, and integrate business applications in the cloud. The SAP cloud platform is SAP's innovative cloud development and deployment platform.

Workday

The workday cloud platform allows our customers and partners to confidently build, test, deploy, and manage full-stack applications. These extensions and applications use the same services that power all Workday products to help accommodate unique business needs and create streamlined workflows.

Several others are making it to this list, which I am mentioning below:

- Kamatera
- DigtialOcean
- Rackspace

- Navisite
- OpenNebula
- Pivotal

- MassiveGrid
- LiquidWeb
- VMware
- ServiceNow
- Verizon Cloud

- CloudSigma
- Dell Cloud
- LimeStone
- Quadranet

"Winners never quit and quitters never win."
- Vince Lombardi

Managed Cloud Services (MCS)

The term "Managed Cloud Services" (MCS) refers to outsourcing one's company's day-to-day IT management for cloud-based services and technical support to streamline and improve business operations. An organisation's IT team may lack the expertise necessary to monitor and operate a cloud system adequately. In these cases, businesses will employ a cloud-managed services provider to handle all aspects of their cloud infrastructure, including but not limited to security, computing, storage, network operations, application stacks, suppliers, and more. Cloud MCSs can also manage monitoring and reporting, performance testing, backup and recovery, and other tasks as required by an IT organisation. The monthly cost of using a managed cloud service provider is typically lower than the cost of employing a full-time staff member.

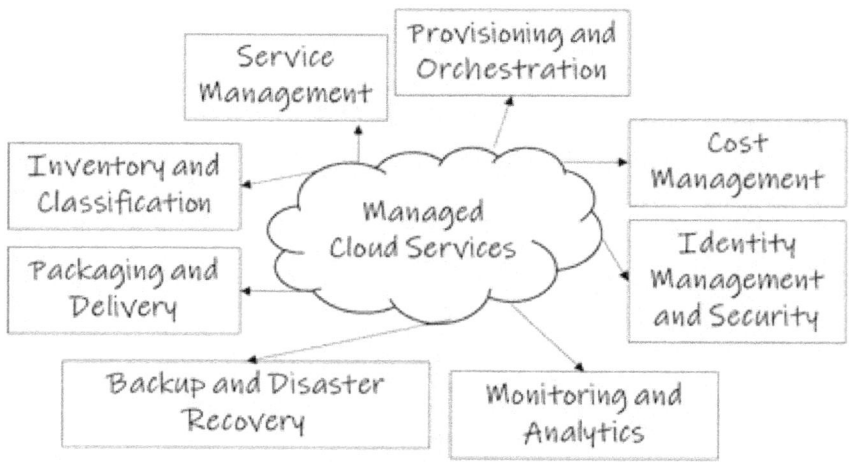

Figure 27 - Managed Cloud Services

An ecosystem of professional and managed service providers (MSPs) has arisen to provide services on top of public cloud (including IaaS and

PaaS) offerings. According to Gartner: "By 2024, more than 50% of cloud service deals will include both application development services and cloud infrastructure professional and managed services, up from 10% in 2019." They also imply that while deploying and maintaining systems on AWS, Azure, GCP, GAC, IBM Cloud, or Oracle Cloud, enterprise architects and leaders in technological innovation can benefit from working with a high-quality professional and managed services provider.

"You began your DevOps journey, the day, the infrastructure,
the operations team will stop saying, oh no, you can't
deploy the application until you show me everything
is perfect and starts saying how
can I help you to use your application faster."
- Enamul Haque

Benefits of Managed Cloud Services

Outsourcing Cloud Services to a professional Managed Cloud Service Provider has many benefits. According to Cybersecurity expert Sean Spicer, the top ten benefits of Managed Cloud Services are described below:[23]

Cost Saving

As we observed in earlier chapters, outsourcing the management of the entire business cloud platform service can lead to significant cost savings. You can save tens of thousands of dollars annually by using a managed service provider that focuses on the cloud, such as Agile IT.

Predictive Budgeting

You may set your own budget for IT services with the reassurance of a predictable monthly fee by using cloud-managed services. Managed service providers' data analytics can help with IT spending management.

Future-proofed Technology

We discussed this in the cloud benefits chapter. This is also valid here as the service provider will ensure all technology is at the top with qualified professionals.

Custom and Integrated Service

Managed service providers in the cloud offer adaptability. Payment plans and pay-per-service models are available from some vendors; these will free up capital for expansion. Additional savings can be realised using a convergent solution offered by some cloud-managed service providers. Security, network monitoring, and introducing a new service area are just some of the many possible applications of these convergent solutions.

Robust Infrastructure

Managed cloud service providers to ensure the infrastructure was always up and running. Furthermore, they can incorporate preexisting business procedures and policies into network management in order to better align your infrastructure with the objectives of your organisation.

Centralised Operations

The Managed Cloud Service Providers ensure you have a centralised operation; you don't need to run into several stakeholders for firefighting; it also reduces escalation and finger-pointing behaviours.

Service Level Coverage

Control over service quality, performance, and upkeep are enhanced when using a cloud service provider. Service continuity is achieved for your company with a complete SLA.

Disaster Recovery

Like CSP's, Managed Cloud Service Provider ensures cross-region replication and the ability to restore to points in time for comprehensive, reliable disaster recovery.

DevOps

They can deliver new features quickly through automation and enable a DevOps and Agile approach to provide services in the cloud.

Innovation Driven

Managed Cloud Service Providers can create new cloud-native workloads in public or private clouds. They can help to expand product/service features while improving ease of use. Rapidly prototype, develop and deploy new products and services and maintain gaining entry to a new industry or market.

Managed Cloud Services Providers (MCSP)

Individuals or businesses who supply Managed Cloud Services are known as Managed Cloud Service Providers. Professional and Managed Services for Public Cloud Infrastructure is another name for them. It is the most up-to-date iteration of the traditional MSP (MSP). MSPs have been compelled to provide cloud services, manage hybrid cloud setups, or resell additional cloud capabilities as clients' IT infrastructure components move to the cloud. In a nutshell, MSPs have embarked on a path to develop into MCPs (MCSP). MCSPs provide businesses with access to more significant economies of expertise. In addition to managing their customers' hardware, software, and operating systems, they also provide cloud service management and governance and take care of the complex tools and application stacks that run on top of that infrastructure.

Today's businesses are looking to their managed service providers for assistance with their cloud migration. Half or more of the businesses surveyed in recent research by CompTIA (The Computing Technology Industry Association) have used an MCSP for cloud-based services within the previous 12 months. There will be a rise in that figure. Only MCSPs who can offer unique value through cloud services will thrive in this new market.

The Managed Cloud Services Provider can benefit any organisation from managing cloud adoption to continuous innovation in a strategic partnership.

Below are a few fundamental areas that would help companies understand the importance of approaching an MCSP and benefitting. They will provide the following:

Better Control

Managed Services Providers allow companies to take better control of the environment and the services their people can provision from a centralised provisioning platform. They can offer a unique integrated experience with customised solution application and infrastructure with advanced integration into your business.

Business Agility

By providing SLAs that match the solution to the business, MCSP are responding to changing market conditions and allowing the ability to adapt, scale and contract solutions based on business needs

Cost Management

They can help to replace CAPEX with OPEX and significantly reduce operation costs. They can help right sizing to meet actual demand and also shut down resources when not in use.

Reliability and Privacy

Highly available, resilient, redundant infrastructure provides secure Virtual Private Cloud data encryption. 24/7 operations monitoring and management, plus the robust security and protection mentioned in previous chapters.

Speed to Value

Managed Services providers can offer a catalogue of ready-to-go blueprints. It can help dramatically reduce procurement lead times and resource bottlenecks by rapidly delivering the project with the ability to automate and orchestrate provisioning tasks.

Security

This has always been the primary obstacle to cloud adoption for many concerned organisations regarding how to ensure a secure public cloud. Managed Cloud Service Providers have been heavily investing in cloud security.

Global Managed Cloud Service Providers

Some of the global players in providing managed cloud service are presented below. This list is in alphabetical order, and the descriptions of their cloud service-providing capabilities are directly taken from the respective websites. All sources are mentioned accordingly in the same description.

Figure 28 - Different Managed Cloud Service Providers

2nd Watch

In the public cloud, 2nd Watch offers both professional and managed services for business-critical workloads. For over five years,

Amazon Web Services has recognised us as a Premier Partner and audited and authorised us as a Managed Service Provider due to the quality of our customer service, the breadth and depth of our product offerings, and our capacity to grow to meet the needs of our customers. In addition to being a Microsoft Gold Azure Partner, we also have the Microsoft Workload Competency. 2nd Watch is the largest cloud-native service provider, managing over 200,000 instances monthly across 14 global regions and providing support to customers in 196 countries.-2ndwatch.com

Accenture

Accenture writes about their MCS capabilities "Research shows that nearly two-thirds of companies have not achieved the benefits they expected out of cloud initiatives. Our singular focus is helping clients design intelligent cloud solutions – whether public, private or hybrid – that maximise business value and drive innovation. With deep industry understanding and more than 30,000 cloud projects under our belt, we can expertly navigate the many paths to realising the value of cloud. Let us be your guide". - accenture.com/gb-en/services/cloud-index

Atos

On their website, Atos says on their cloud-managed services, "Atos Cloud Foundry is a trusted cloud application platform supported by experienced global DevOps teams across both public and private clouds". - atos.net/en/solutions/multi-cloud-application-platform

Bespin Global

About their MCS capabilities, Bespin Global says on their website: "We at Bespin Global believe that we can "Awaken the Possibilities of Your Cloud." Strategic consulting, managed services, and Cloud-based solutions drive digital innovation for many of our customers. Bespin Global is building trust with more than 400 global customers in its first three years of establishment. Bespin Global is the only MSP in North-East Asia Recognized by Gartner Magic Quadrant of Public Cloud MSPs for Two Consecutive Years". - en.bespinglobal.com/about/

Capgemini

Capgemini says about their managed cloud service capabilities, "Capgemini Cloud Platform brings together the right technology, processes and culture to help organisations of every size leverage the efficiency and agility of the cloud. It is a portfolio of cloud services and accelerators in a single cloud management platform. Ready-to-go cloud platform: A ready-built, tried, tested, and proven platform." - https://www.capgemini.com/gb-en/service/cloud-services/capgemini-cloud-platform/

Capgemini Cloud Platform provides services such as:

- *Ready-to-go cloud platform*: A ready-built, tried, tested, and proven platform
- *Advanced user portal*: A single, integrated solution with a full suite of cloud business services to deploy new services faster
- *Automation*: Replacing manual, repetitive processes with automated tasks
- *Billing and consumption transparency*: Consumption dashboard and daily updates give you full control over spending and cost optimisation recommendations
- *Cloud accelerators*: Support for rapid development of new innovative services through auto-provisioning, containerisation, microservices, integration, and other accelerators
- *Cloud target operating model*: A culture that supports a cloud business and takes full advantage of cloud capabilities

Capgemini Cloud Platform has a very comprehensive brochure on their offering, which could be downloaded from here:

https://www.capgemini.com/gb-en/resources/capgemini-cloud-plat-form-brochure/

Cloudreach

Cloudreach says, "Cloud Strategy and Adoption - Develop a business-aligned cloud strategy, a comprehensive plan to move to the cloud and the foundations to help accelerate initial adoption. Cloud Management - Fully manage your customer's cloud environment so they can focus their limited time and resources on innovating rather than maintaining. Cloud Innovation - Modernize your legacy applications using cloud-native technologies and deliver predictive and prescriptive insights via machine learning and AI" - cloudreach.com/en/home/

Cognizant

As described in their website: "At Cognizant, we help companies deploy cloud within their digital transformation journeys to meet their business objectives and drive growth. Our experts employ a tailored, risk-mitigated cloud strategy that considers all possible deployment models, with minimal downtime. We provide a seamless, modern, secure and agile journey from in-house IT to cloud infrastructure". - cognizant.com/cognizant-digital-systems-technology/cloud-enable-ment-services

Deloitte

The Deloitte website describes that "Cloud is more than a place, a journey, or technology. To us, the cloud is an advantage, innovation, and opportunity—it's where your possible becomes more than a plan. It becomes actual and scalable. At Deloitte, we combine business acumen, integrated business and technology services, and a creative, people-first approach to enable enterprise transformation through innovative cloud applications. We offer a full spectrum of capabilities to support you throughout your journey to the cloud and beyond." -

deloitte.com/us/en/pages/consulting/solutions/cloud-consulting-services.html

DXC Technology

On cloud-managed services DXC Technology describes: "Our proven services and solutions help you securely move the right workload to the cloud and rapidly modernise and integrate applications. Explore our services for multi-cloud, data centre, storage and compute services". - dxc.technology/cloud/offerings/140037-solutions

HCL Technologies

HCL, in their website, writes: "HCL's framework and best practices-driven Cloud Consulting services allow enterprises to crystallise broad cloud objectives into real execution roadmaps, based on individual, department-specific, or enterprise-wide requirements, and a guided assessment of the current state". - hcltech.com/cloud

Infosys

Explaining their service offering, Infosys writes: "Expanding the business, making operations more efficient while keeping customers satisfied are some of the top priorities of enterprises today. Modern enterprises are turning to digital transformation with cloud-driven, clear business-focused drivers in their quest to create more business value. With its comprehensive portfolio of offerings, the Infosys cloud practice focuses on helping enterprises realise strategic business outcomes from their digital transformation initiatives. We are the partner of choice to help you navigate your digital transformation on the cloud". - infosys.com/services/cloud.html

Logicworks

They say on their website how Logicworks can help companies for their cloud transformation: "Logicworks helps customers achieve operational excellence and compliance on the cloud. Our innovative platform dedicated, certified engineers and decades of traditional IT experience combine to enable our customer's success across every stage of the cloud journey. Companies in regulated industries across healthcare, financial service, and SaaS rely on our compliance expertise and unique combination of maturity and innovation to help them scale securely, automate compliance, and gain efficiencies in private and public clouds". - logicworks.com/

Nordcloud

Nordcloud says on their cloud-managed services on their website, "Our position as an independent cloud services provider means that we work with the leading public cloud platforms. We are proud to be an AWS Premier Consulting Partner, a Google Cloud Premier Partner and a Microsoft Gold Cloud Partner. We are also Managed Services Provider to AWS, Google and Microsoft". - nordcloud.com/

Rackspace

Rackspace explains its service offer – "As a Leader in Professional and Managed Services for public cloud infrastructure, here at Rackspace, we deliver unbiased guidance on best-fit managed cloud solutions to organisations around the globe. We go beyond simple migration assistance and cloud infrastructure management with multi-cloud managed services, professional services and managed application services to enable true digital transformation" – Rackspace.com

Samsung SDS

Samsung SDB says on their cloud-managed services on their website: "Backed by extensive expertise across industries and capabilities acquired from managing Samsung IT systems for 30 years, Samsung SDS has successfully converted traditional data centre infrastructure to a cloud environment to fit the business objectives and policies of our customers. Choose the right cloud for your business with Samsung SDS for customised services that fulfil your needs". - sam-sungsds.com/global/en/solutions/bns/cloud/cloud.html

Smartronix

On their website, Smartronix writes, "Smartronix Cloud Assured Managed Services - deliver the flexibility customers need and demand from today's cloud-managed service providers. We offer the ability to select services across our Core, Security, and Add-on Services, which enables and assures a managed services solution that meets unique customer needs. Free IT operators from the daily "run it" activities that do not add business value and allow them to focus on growth. Our CAMS are audited, certified, and here to assure your operations stay available 24x7x365". - smartronix.com/services/Cloud-Computing/Pages/Managed-Services.html

Tata Consultancy Services (TCS)

TCS writes on its website: "TCS Enterprise Cloud provides a broad range of flexible cloud infrastructure options to support dynamic cloud services. The hybrid cloud platform is powered by OpenStack software, integrated with SDx capability, enabling automation at all levels. It is enriched with a strong layer of the platform as a service (PaaS) and robust container services from Docker, Kubernetes, and Cloud Foundry. With an open architecture-based backbone, the offering enables cloud portability, eliminating vendor lock-in and boosting cloud ROI. Moreover, we offer data services built on a proven open-source stack - Spark, Mesos, Akka, Cassandra, Kafka (SMACK) - supporting big data, analytics, IoT, and streaming data workload requirements for global digital enterprises, while optimising TCO". - https://www.tcs.com/tcs-enterprise-cloud

Unisys

Unisys says on their cloud-managed services on their website, "Unisys offers a full suite of cloud managed services and data centre management capabilities for some of the most demanding and complex businesses and governments in the world". - unisys.com/offer-ings/cloud-and-infrastructure-services/cloud-and-data-center-managed-services

Wipro

In their website, they explained their Cloud Computing solution capabilities: "Wipro empowers enterprises in their continuous transformation journey by providing full-stack cloud services - Edge to Cloud - across domains delivered through Cloud Studios. Wipro's unique 'Business First' strategy and industrialised solutions approach supported by strong industry domain and partner ecosystem positions us uniquely to help the enterprises of tomorrow to drive business acceleration, customer experience and connected insights" - wipro.com/cloud/

MCSP Capabilities

The Managed Service Providers take away all the hassle from the organisations who want to move to the cloud. They offer many services, some are mentioned below:

Cloud Target Operating Model: The model will introduce a culture which supports a cloud business to take full advantage of the capabilities of the cloud.

Cloud and Digital Accelerators: This feature supports the rapid development of new innovative services.

Billing and Consumption Transparency: A consumption dashboard is provided with daily updates giving complete control over business spending.

Automation and DevOps - Automating repetitive processes takes companies towards DevOps.

Ready-to-go Cloud Platform: A ready-built, tried and tested platform.

Fully Managed Cloud and Digital Services: Fully managed means companies can focus on their business strengths and outcomes.

Self-Service Catalog: A catalogue of tools to enable the business to deploy new services faster.

Anti-lock-in: MCSPs being cloud-agnostic and vendor-neutral means companies can evolve their cloud strategy over time.

Centralised User Portal: A single-integrated solution with a full suite of cloud services.

Cloud Workload Migration: MCSPs assess, prepare and execute the right migration strategy for your business

Selecting the MCSP

For a successful digital transformation journey or just for simple cloud migration, selecting the right MCSP has become critical for long-term success. While there are so many essential aspects to be considered, depending on volume and organisational structure, a few important ones are mentioned below (as recommended by Cloudjournee[24]), which shouldn't be forgotten:

End-to-end capabilities – it's essential to ensure the selected MCSP can support you through your entire cloud journey—from planning and adoption to monitoring, management and optimisation.

In-depth domain knowledge and experience - The provider should be able to align with your business objectives, understand what you are looking to do and match it up with their technical expertise.

Pricing - Though calculating the costs in advance for managing a cloud environment can be extremely difficult. Still, it is advisable to select a vendor who has its pricing plans in place.

Security practices - MCSP's data backup and retention policies and procedures should be in place and can help you prevent and counter any security threat. The provider should have a business continuity plan and established risk management policies to safeguard sensitive data.

Performance-based SLAs - The provider should be able to define and provide you with the necessary levels of SLAs as per your business needs.

Automated Approach – The MCSP should have a suite of tools, digital capabilities, and collaboration models to reduce human intervention and improve quality and productivity.

Customer Support - The MCSP should be able to specify the level of support they could provide as part of their SLA.

MCSP Operations Framework

The MCSP market is very competitive; hence the services provided are mostly advanced, with possibilities for organisations to operate, grow and be innovative with their cloud strategy.

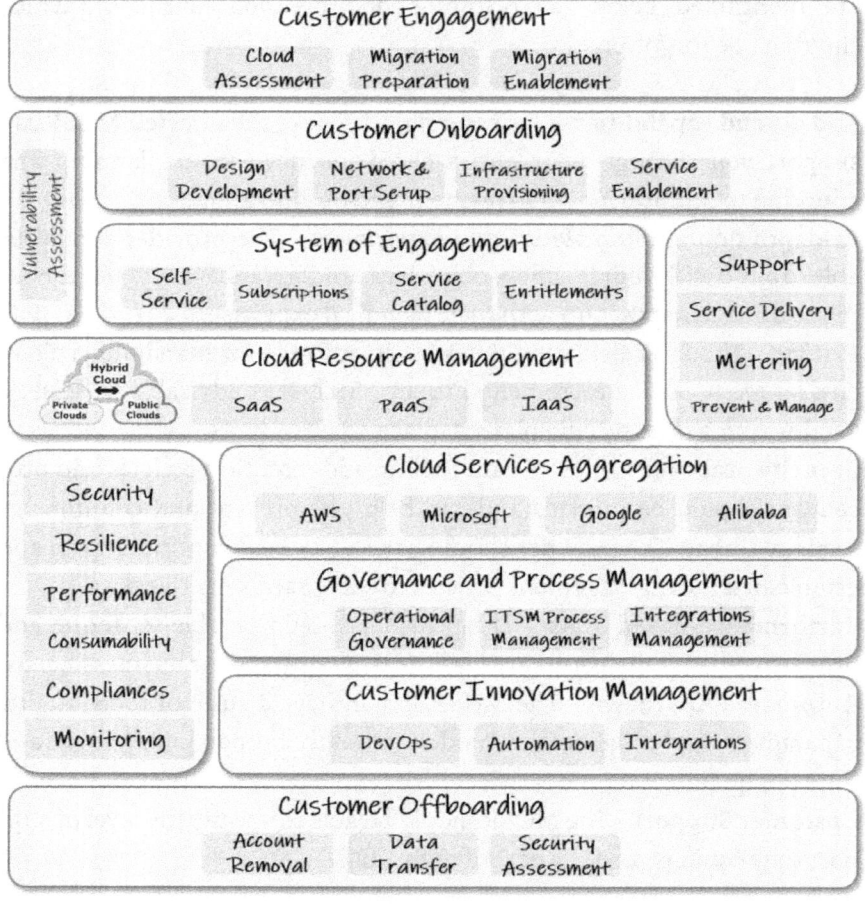

Figure 29 - MCSP Operations Framework

MCSP can bring the technology, processes, and culture to leverage the cloud in all use cases, from traditional data centre migrations to innovative cloud-native solutions driving our client's digital transformation.

Customer Engagement

At the Customer Engagement stage, MCSP will agree on the migration approaches based on the recommendations from cloud assessment. The assessment can help visualise the state of organisational current IT landscape using solutions that would rate IT performance against the peers and help elevate cloud strategy and measure digital readiness. It can also include designing the "as is" operating model if it's not already in place. Preparing for migration would consist of documentation, change management planning, e.g., all required groundwork and finally, the migration. As I have dedicated chapters on assessment, migration, etc., I will not discuss too many details here.

Customer Onboarding

Onboarding customers on MCSP's platform will include setting up network, ports, toolchain integrations, support queue and resolver group setup, setting up the customer to cloud management portal etc. It is the service enablement part.

Vulnerability Assessment

Vulnerabilities are defined, found, categorised, and prioritised during the assessment process. This strategy is highly suggested.

System of Engagement

This is where the running part starts. Users can engage with the Cloud Management Platform and are able to access the consumable services. This includes the service catalogue, shopping cart, and entitlements. Users can manage their subscriptions, report incidents, or even monitor their service usage.

Cloud Resource Management

MCSP will provide cloud resources from the chosen cloud service model or models based on the deployment model designed in the original cloud reference architecture created from the assessment findings. Provisioning services across public and private clouds or setting up a multi-cloud environment.

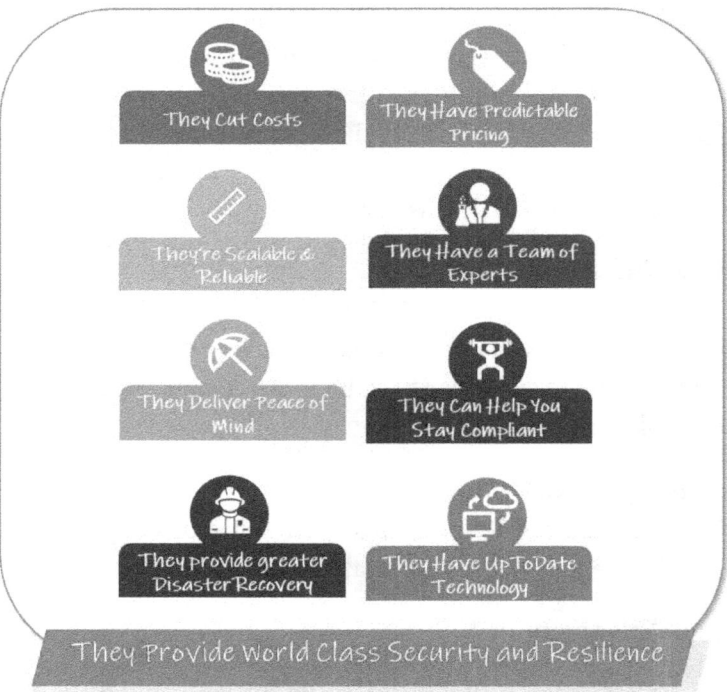

Figure 30 - Top Advantages of Cloud Managed Services

Cloud Service Aggregation

MCSP will package and integrate multiple Cloud Computing services into one or more composite services. This integration can include services from various cloud providers or an organisation's private environment.

Support, Service Delivery, Metering, Prevent and Manage

These are the combined services provided for business continuity; we will see more on these areas in the chapter on Cloud Service Management. Managing workloads consistently, bringing together virtual machines, containers, and functions to work in harmony with SaaS and on-premises IT, for example, and ensuring patching, upgrading and support of the operating system, application server and application containers within the VM or docker container.

Governance and Process Management

Cloud Service Governance will include taking care of cloud service lifecycle policies, data governance, reporting etc. we will look more at governance in the cloud governance chapter.

Customer Innovation Management:

One of the best features that MCSP can do for taking full advantage of digital transformation for any organisation is by increasing business velocity and improving speed-to-market using ready-to-go cloud services and accelerators that deliver digital, cloud, regulation, and cyber use cases. Enable the release of new features into production on a regular and controlled basis. Deliver new features quickly through automation and enable a DevOps and Agile approach to provide services in the cloud.

Security, Resilience, Performance, Consumability, Compliances and Monitoring:

These are the subsets of crucial activities that make the MCSP operational excellent. Identity and Access Management, Security governance, data governance for compliance purposes, resilience policy management, ease of consumption, and monitoring/analysis are a few activities MCSP in support of the customer business.

Customer Offboarding

This is an essential task that MCSP performs with much attention as it might lead to data compliance violation issues if failure happens. Data governance is critical in how an offboarded customer can take the data away. Account removal, virtual environment ramp-down and many other activities are conducted to ensure a secured customer offboarding.

"The Internet of Things is not a concept; it is a network, the true technology-enabled Network of all networks."
- Edewede Oriwoh, IoT researcher

CHAPTER 4:
Cloud Transformation Acceleration

"The sustainable success of digital transformation comes from a carefully planned organisational change management process that meets two key objectives, one being the company culture, and the other one is empowering its employees."

- Enamul Haque

Cloud Adoption

Cloud adoption is how businesses implement digital transformation. As we saw in the chapter about digital transformation, the number one technological move for companies to survive is Cloud Computing; without it, digital transformation would not be possible. Cloud adoption is the centre of this book and the foundation of cloud transformation. It's the embryo of digitalisation.

Figure 31 - Cloud Adoption for Digitalisation

The heart of the wide-ranging transformation is the use of technology to digitise complex services. Growing and established businesses need digitalisation to lead in the competition and for their continuous growth. Faced with a competitive business environment and shrinking budgets, the focus of IT organisations is on "keeping the lights on in an optimised manner". All services firms view IT Optimisation as a high-priority initiative to cut costs, improve agility, and boost efficiency.

According to Luke Harrigan, the Global Vice President of Capgemini Cloud Platform, "The cloud natives have arrived, and they've fired the starting gun on the race to cloud automation. Participation isn't a choice for businesses that rely on legacy systems, and it's critical if they hope to keep pace with their younger, more flexible rivals."

With cloud transformation, the simplification of IT is not only a need, but it is mission-critical to improve agility, focus on core business activities, reduce TCO of applications and infrastructure, reduce operational costs, improve organisation image, reduce capital expenditure and many more. These make moving to the cloud mandatory for many companies. Cloud-native leaders develop and deploy applications faster than their competitors and are further ahead in monetising their application programming interfaces. Cloud-right is a compelling concept: build exciting new offers, get to market more quickly, and save money.

IT architectures have progressed from mainframe to client-server to web to cloud to meet the needs of the modern workplace. The ancient is, in a sense, the new: The capacity to connect remotely is one way modern cloud-computing technology is similar to mainframe design from the user's perspective. However, the cloud is far more widely distributed, scalable, and durable.

Regarding size, scope, and availability, modern Cloud Computing is unmatched by whatever the pioneers of computing had in mind. Among others, Amazon, Microsoft, and Google have made significant investments to deliver elastic, pay-as-you-go cloud services. These services have displaced on-premises systems and even private data centres. The cloud is no longer a playground for IT experimentation but increasingly an operational mandate for organisations of all sizes.

Key Objectives of Cloud Adoption

Generally speaking, the objectives for cloud adoption are very much linked to the purposes of digital transformation; this is where they get materialised. Here are a few very closely matched to cloud adoption.

Automation to Drive Efficiencies

Think this is an essential subject in digital adoption. It's a complicated subject from a technology aspect, such as selecting tooling and using cloud-native vs specialist 3rd party tools. But the way it can help streamline headcount and bring OpEx reductions in support and service management, but it also speeds up responsiveness and agility. We will see this more closely in the Cognitive Service Management chapter.

Scale Business Transformation

Drive revenue, innovation, growth, and resilience by streamlining operations and managing risk.

Experiment to Drive Digital Innovation

Boost profits, new developments, expansion, and stability for your company by streamlining operations and controlling risks.

Move Beyond Migration

Instead of just starting an IT transition, develop a business strategy to maximise cloud opportunities.

Challenges of Cloud Adoption

Too many choices

Many choices are available for application, infrastructure or network transformation and decisions in selecting a Managed Cloud Service Provider. Which new services should I use, what happens when the ones I use are deprecated and many more such questions that I hear from various organisations.

Figure 32 - Challenges of Cloud Adoption

Operational Complexities

Cloud adoption is complicated; there is a fear of disrupting something intricates that "already works".

Security Requirements

Strict compliance and industry standards must be met to avoid penalties. Data and information security in the cloud are usually at the optimum levels and generally reliable and proficient.

Legacy Technology

Legacy technology slows cloud adoption unless a new approach is taken.

Skill Shortages

Cloud skill requirements are constantly changing; skilling a workforce is a challenge.

Shadow IT

Duplication of services created through partial cloud adoption.

Service quality

Service Level Agreements (SLAs) by the providers are not stringent and adequate to assure that the services will run with the desired level of availability, performance, and reliability.

Legal Implications

The companies must ensure that the cloud providers have adopted reasonable technical, physical, and administrative measures to protect agencies data from loss, misuse or alteration.

Cloud Adoption Principles

Principles for cloud adoption form a basis of conduct. Companies should adopt the cloud considering the cloud-first strategy. The cloud-first approach reduces. IT costs by leveraging the benefits of using shared infrastructure and services. The companies will only pay for the resources consumed.

Enablement

Companies should plan for Cloud Computing as a strategic enabler rather than as an outsourcing arrangement or technical platform

Cost/Benefit

They should evaluate the benefits of cloud adoption based on a full understanding of the costs of the cloud compared with the costs of other technology platform business solutions

Enterprise Risk

Companies should take an Enterprise Risk Management (ERM) perspective to manage the adoption and use of cloud

Capability

Adopting the cloud should integrate the full extent of capabilities that cloud providers offer with internal resources to provide comprehensive technical support and delivery solution

Accountability

Companies should manage liabilities by clearly defining internal and provider responsibilities

Trust

Companies should make trust an essential part of cloud solutions and build confidence in all business processes that depend on Cloud Computing.

Stages of Cloud Transformation

There is no doubt that cloud transformation enables innovation by reducing costs and improving business by standardising applications, service processes and infrastructure. It helps businesses to operate with improved flexibility and scalability. It allows companies to work smarter and take advantage of the increased digital, networked world in new ways. There are three stages to the enterprise cloud transformation journey: Application, Network, and Security.

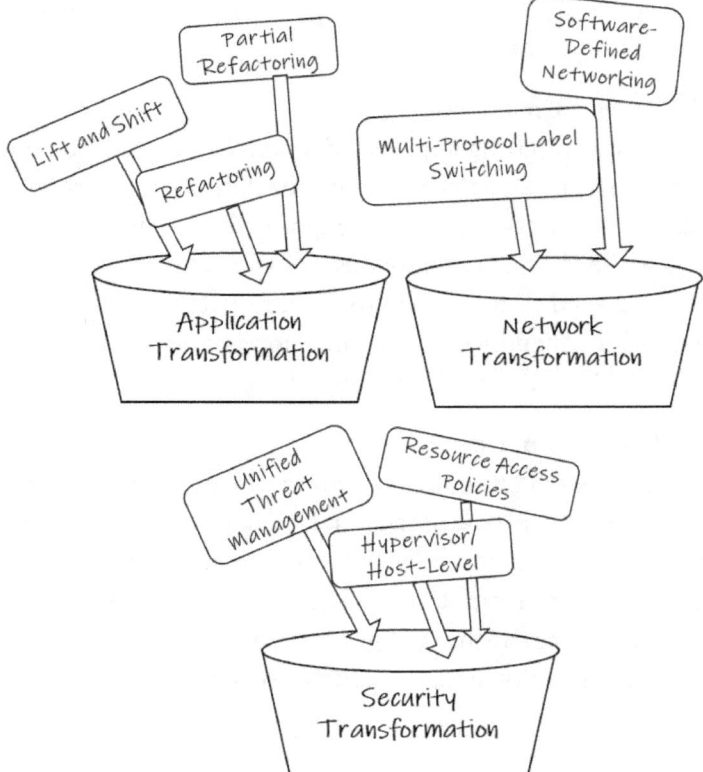

Figure 33 - Stages of Cloud Transformation

Application Transformation

Cloud transformation provides companies with an ideal opportunity to manage corporate applications better. Application transformation could be done in three parts:

1. **Lift and Shift:** It takes all internal web-enabled applications and hosts them in the cloud.

2. **Partial Refactoring:** Relocate parts of an application to the cloud, typically the user interface. Put all your trust in the company's data centre for handling old records (for now).

3. **Refactoring:** Re-writing applications for the cloud. Host the entirety of the application, e.g., front-end, middleware, and database, in the cloud.

Network Transformation

The cloud computing approach dismantles the traditional network architecture. The potential for network revolution lies in users' ability to access cloud resources directly through local internet breakouts. The method is backed by SDN capabilities that can determine where a packet is headed and send it there or on to the internet. And the cost of maintaining that broadband internet connection is much lower than that of leased MPLS (Multi-Protocol Label Switching) lines.

Security Transformation

The cloud-based inline security check post uses a granular policy engine to ensure that only authorised users are granted access to all of an organization's applications. All users gain something from the danger intelligence gathered from the traffic. Like a UTM (Unified Threat Management) device, traffic is filtered numerous times, however, the architecture here is multi-tenant and highly scalable.

Guidelines for Cloud Readiness and Adoption

Adopting the cloud is a radical shift from the way technology is being used and will require support and readiness from the highest level of stakeholders to be informed, create a business case and find a sponsor.

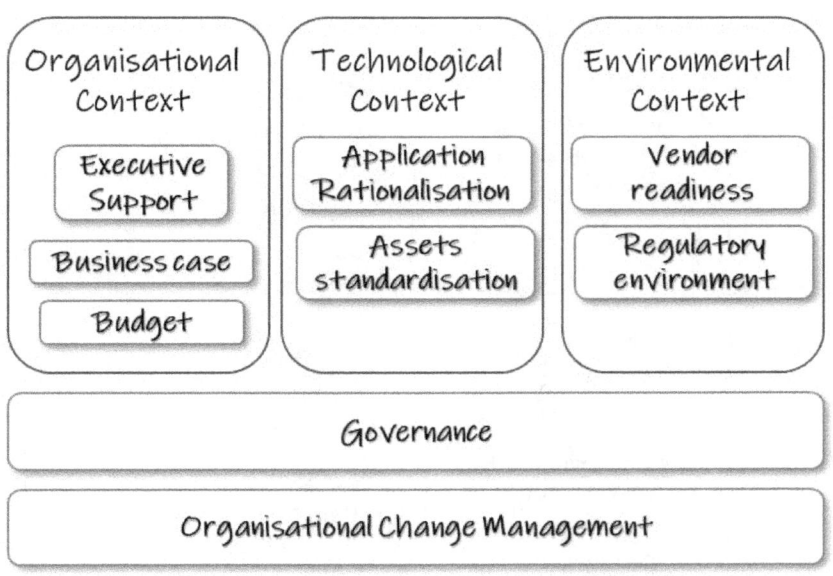

Figure 34 - Cloud Readiness and Adoption Framework

The critical elements of readiness at different stages of adoption are mentioned below:

Organisational Context

For the successful adoption of the cloud, organisations will need deep involvement in business functions and overhaul of the existing technology landscape. This would necessitate executive support at various levels within and between the agencies to create program objectives, keep up with the adoption plan, and provide oversight at a sustained level.

Depending upon the size of the organisation – a large organisation usually will go through an RFP process to articulate its objectives and requirements for external partners and identify organisations to provide consulting on the cloud, implementation, and sustenance in the cloud. The RFP process will be a learning opportunity for both the external partners and the agency. It will help define the service level definitions and overall expectations from the cloud adoption program.

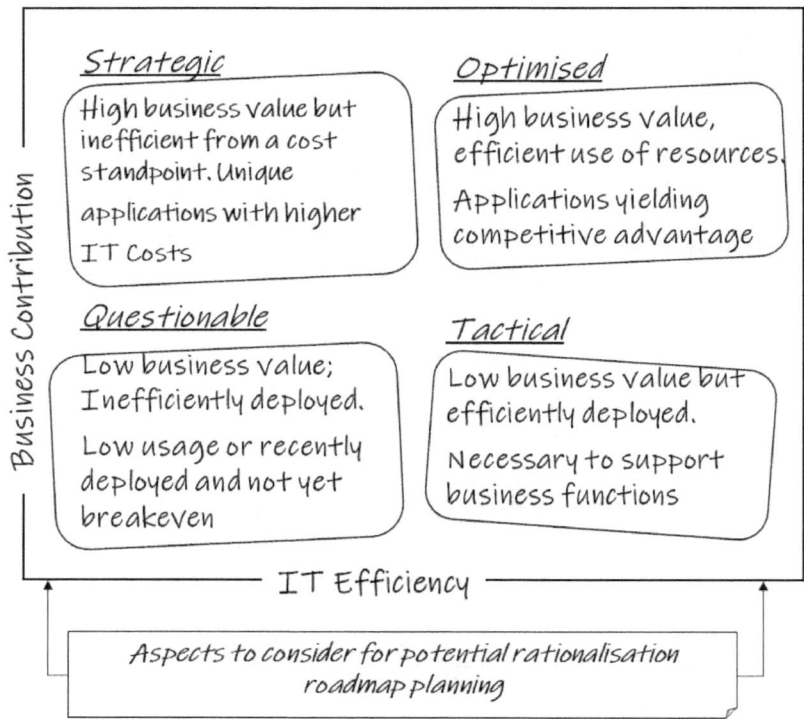

Figure 35 - Application Rationalisation – Evaluation Attributes

Technological Context

Organisations will need to focus on the market's internal and available cloud technologies and solutions. Internally, adopting the cloud will rely on competent employees who can manage an appropriate technical infrastructure and have e-business know-how.

Application Rationalisation and Modernisation: For organisations, a move to the cloud would allow them to evaluate their application landscape, understand the usefulness of the applications and perform a clean-up. Application portfolio modernisation is essential to moving to the cloud as it will help rationalise the portfolio and avoid having two environments – the cloud and the legacy environment. Maintaining these two environments will prove costly. For any organisation, the modernisation and move to the cloud should be as per the expected organisational standards.

Hardware and Software Standardisation: For any organisation to adopt cloud computing, the first step would be to consolidate its infrastructure, platforms, and software. For the adoption of the cloud, every organisation would need standards driven by architecture group initiatives that would transform the cloud adoption journey. Until standardisation is not overdone, every organisation can encourage flexibility and agility. Hardware and software standardisation would be a critical driver for most cloud benefits, and every organisation would require a balance between today's priorities and future aspirations.

Environmental Context

The environmental context includes the readiness of the vendor to offer cloud services, the cloud competitors in the market, the macroeconomic framework, and the regulatory environment.

Vendor readiness will affect cloud adoption to a great extent when switching cloud providers. Any organisation that wants to adopt a cloud model will have to consider vendors' readiness, which may or may not be part of their historical consideration. The organisation will also need to find solutions which are open-source standards.

Cloud Adoption Framework

The Cloud Adoption Framework defines the fundamentals and perspectives important to consider for successful cloud adoption. It converts the aspirational goals of a cloud adoption strategy into an actionable plan. Gartner recommends that organisations continue to mature their cloud-first strategy — where the cloud is primary, prioritised and promoted. "If you have not developed a cloud-first strategy yet, you are likely falling behind your competitors," says Elias Khnaser, VP Analyst at Gartner[25]. Cloud adoption framework is factored into five different stages, and they are described below:

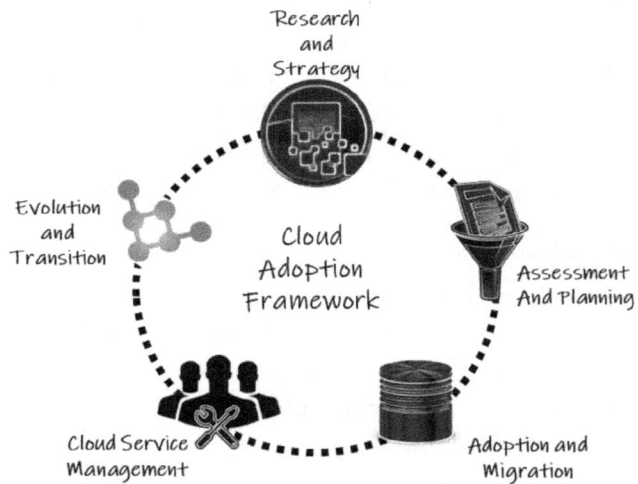

Figure 36 - Cloud Adoption Framework

Research and Strategy

The first phase will involve understanding cloud services from the business perspective and the impact of adopting the cloud on existing IT having a clear business strategy based on the current position, and thinking about where to go. It should consider all the aspects described in previous chapters on digital transformation needs, the need for Cloud Computing transformation, and key business drivers to stay modern and competitive. It should also include cloud team planning, selecting a strategic partner for the cloud journey from Cloud Service Provers or selecting a Managed Services Provider for the cloud transformation. Overall, having a clear roadmap for business transformation with the cloud.

Assessment and Planning

The second focus will be assessing the existing IT environment with an understanding of the business processes and current application landscape and planning for the destination with a sense of migration scenarios, required staff and resources, support from service providers and so on to create a business case for adoption. Workload assessment, and the suitable cloud model, also need to be looked upon.

Adoption and Migration

The adoption and migration stage will involve defining the IT and data governance architectures and policies with solution architectures and interpreting and understanding the security in the cloud. This should also consider architectural aspects, risk mitigation plans, and secure cloud implementations, which should be designed for continuity. Migration should result in the orchestration of cloud workloads, provisioning, and automation of cloud services.

Cloud Service Management

Cloud service management is where the companies should work with the provider to manage the assured SLAs; we covered this in the Cloud Service Management chapter.

Evolution and Transition

Cloud as a service has evolved over the years, and the companies should work with the provider to understand how the provider cloud has and will grow for processes and technologies per the business's requirements and compliances.

Cloud Assessment

Cloud Assessment helps companies to check their readiness and the level of preparedness required for a smooth transition to the cloud. Cloud Assessment is a cloud-agnostic, vendor-aware methodology focusing on low-risk, high-return business transformation. The cloud assessment is generally done with pre-built accelerators like automated discovery templates and tools, cloud technology compatibility checkers, portfolio analysers, and ROI calculators. It can be used to analyse an application or hundreds of applications. The assessment is per the customer's intent, IT landscape, and application characteristics.

A cloud assessment can give companies a structured cloud strategy based on the findings, and it can help to create the business, and financial value adds to making decisions for moving to the cloud. A cloud assessment can deliver a deployment roadmap with high-level clustering of applications and mapping them in terms of business value and implementation effort, resulting in a preliminary roadmap. For example, for some Cloud Service Providers, AWS offers an online cloud readiness assessment tool detailed roadmap for cloud migration. Microsoft Azure also provides online cloud assessment and migration planning tools. Google Cloud Physics also allows conducting such an evaluation. Some of the inspirational outcomes of cloud assessment are described below:

Defining the Cloud Strategy

Cloud assessment findings can help determine cloud strategy, architecture, and operating model.

Establishing an Application Portfolio

The assessment can create a clear view of the application landscape. It can find which are cloudable, and which are not. It can deliver a high-level vision and a statement per application of a specific migration path, including a prefilled Business Case to aid the decision process.

Modernising the Legacy Applications

The assessment can create new business values for the existing application portfolio by modernising the underlying technology. It can drive cost, scalability, stability, and other operational benefits through application portfolio analysis.

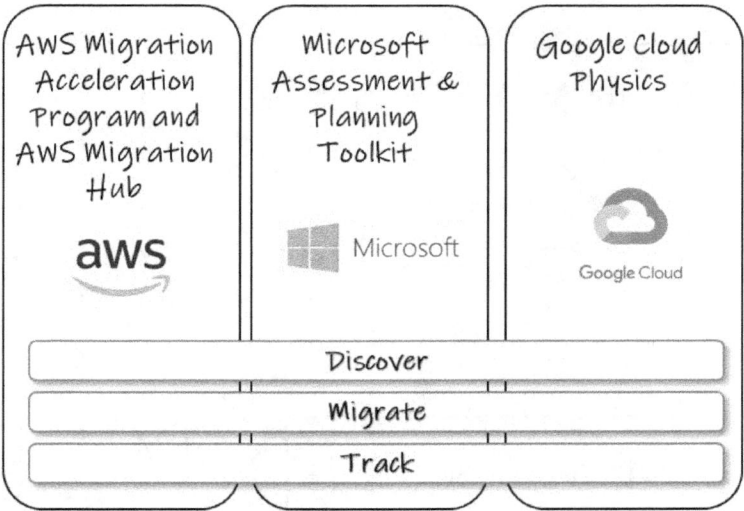

Figure 37 - Online Cloud Assessment Planning Capabilities

Defining the Landing Platform

With gap analysis, it can provide platform recommendations. Most applicable cloud service model to be adopted, technology, integration needs etc. If an organisation already has some cloud platform, the assessment can provide insights to transform the current platform into the best foundation for migration.

Creation of Operating Model

One of the critical deliverables of cloud assessment is the target operating model. It can help define guidelines for environment provisioning and environment management to drive optimum usage of the cloud.

Cloud Assessment Process

The cloud assessment is conducted in five different phases, and they are described below:

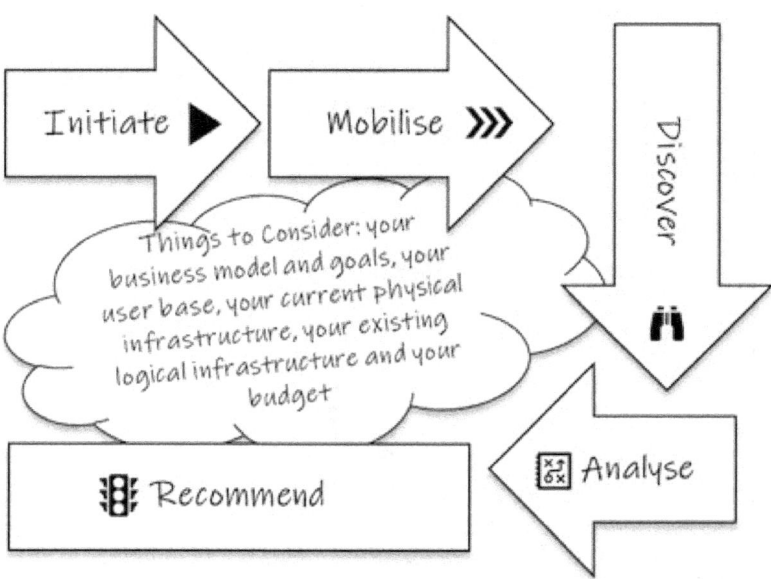

Figure 38 - Cloud Assessment Process

Initiate

This initial phase is where the first contact is made for setting expectations and understanding key drivers.

Mobilise

At this stage, collating and managing applications and applications will start. If there are tools to be used for assessment, installation of such tools will be considered.

Discover

This is the most prolonged phase, where a detailed assessment is conducted.

Analyse

The report on applications/ infrastructure readiness for cloud migrations is prepared in this phase.

Recommend

This final stage is where recommendations are produced and delivered to the customer.

It is also essential to understand that cloud readiness assessment tools stop at application and network evaluation. Today, almost any type of application can be moved to the cloud. However, evaluating your business model and goals, your user base, your current physical infrastructure, your existing logical infrastructure and your budget is essential.

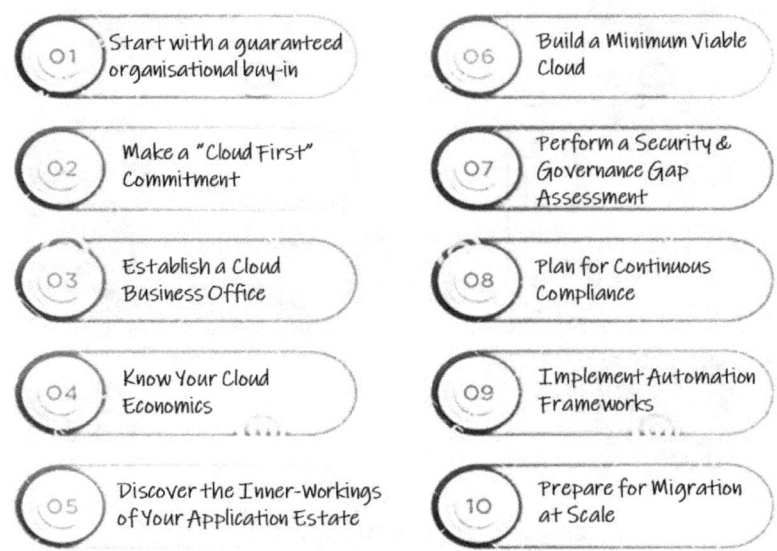

Figure 39 – Cloud Adoption - Best Practices for Success

Cloud Assessment Methodology

Cloud assessment methodology describes the tool and methods undertaken for a detailed assessment of applications to confirm cloud suitability.

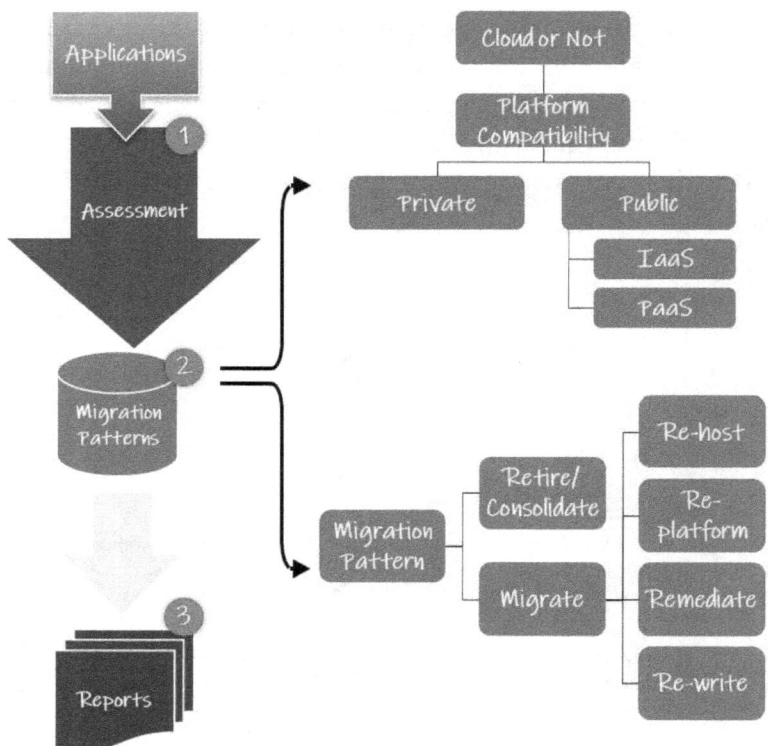

Figure 40 - Cloud Assessment Methodology

Cloud Suitability Assessment

Proving the viability of public cloud. Determining if an application is compatible with public IaaS and PaaS platforms. Determining if IaaS or PaaS patterns are suitable options.

Migration Pattern Assessment

Identifying applications that can be retired and consolidated. Determining the appropriate migration pattern. Estimating the rough level of the migration effort.

Reports

Assessment reports publication, with high-level Cloud Platform Architecture with Proof-of-Concept (POC) planning and justification.

Cloud Assessment Tools

There are different tools available for conducting a cloud assessment. Using data gathered from the organisational network, these tools produce visual representations of the organisation's needs, along with details about what steps need to be taken for the migration to go smoothly in the cloud. Individual tools may have dependencies or may require a specific environment and certain processes within particular industries. They might have unique protocols that must be followed concerning data management or security. Selecting the right tools based on the overall goals, existing framework, and the future environment is the first step toward having a smooth migration.

Popular tools such as Cloudamize and RISC are used for discovery and planning. For applications and server migration, CloudEndure, ATADATA, Racemi etc. For application profiling and operations, Appdynamics, Dynatrace, New Recli, and so on.

"If you want to be a viable cloud vendor selling products, you have no choice – your product must be multitenant in order to survive in the cloud world."
- Alok Misra, Cofounder & Principal – Navatar Group.

Cloud Migration

As the name suggests, cloud migration is migrating applications, moving data or other business elements to a Cloud Computing environment. The essential part of any cloud migration is making sure the movement gets your company where it needs to be, and this must consider long-term success.

The migration process could involve multiple clouds. Both public clouds, where services are made available to anybody with an internet connection, and private clouds, wherein only authorised users have access to the cloud's protected underlying architecture, exist. Hybrid cloud environments, which combine public and private clouds with on-premises resources, are increasingly popular among businesses.

The advantages would be the same as those stated in digital transformation, cloud transformation, etc., equating to scalability, cost-effectiveness, security, and rapid adoption for businesses eager to take advantage of emerging technologies. Some key drivers would make cloud migration mandatory, such as application transformation, speed required for releases, automation, and optimisation are necessary for modern IT operations. The most critical part of cloud migration is to ensure a transparent end-user experience without any business interruption.

Cloud Migration Principles

Many considerations, including the pros and downsides, as well as the cloud service model and kind most suited to your company's needs, should go into your first cloud migration. In this article, we'll look at the high-level elements that you should consider as you contemplate a move to the cloud and here are some principles for outlining your migration strategy:

- Improve productivity
- Increase resilience
- Business agility
- Right-size infrastructure

- Lead global expansion
- Change of leadership
- Improve security
- Reduce CAPEX and OPEX
- Manage cost avoidance
- Grow the business
- Alleviate the lack of IT resources
- Assure strategic re-alignment
- Resolve overwhelming technical debt
- Increase innovation
- Improve service availability
- Out-pace disruptors
- Re-align the role of IT
- Foster compliance requirements
- Empower new market entries

Cloud Migration Strategy

The key to a smooth transition to the cloud is having a well-thought-out strategy in place that details your migration's objectives, timing, potential obstacles, and criteria for success.

Decisions about which workloads to migrate to the cloud, which to maintain on-premises, and which new capabilities and applications to implement once in the cloud are all part of a comprehensive migration strategy. Software development initiatives, data backup and recovery programmes, and productivity and collaboration programmes are all examples of enterprise apps that fall within this category. Your migration plan should address use cases for the workloads being moved. Using case definition helps you establish a sound plan and lays the groundwork for a well-executed migration.

Whether a public or private cloud will be used to house the workloads in question is also often considered and planned for in migration strategies. Corporations are increasingly adopting a multi-cloud strategy, which results in a hybrid cloud system with the potential to become highly intricate. Management of the situation should be addressed consistently and simplified by migration tactics.

Cloud Migration Plan

Next, you'll move on to the migration planning stages once your approach has been finalised. Each workload and its intended cloud destination should be factored into the migration strategy. Migration success is more likely if your team of implementers can pick up new skills as they go. When beginning a migration, implementers will often select a single task to initially move over in order to test the procedure and evaluate the results. Because of this, modifications can be made as needed.

Organisational executives, implementers, cloud providers, and—where applicable—all stakeholders should be kept apprised of the migration plan's progress at regular intervals. This includes updates to the plan's roadmap, schedule, project metrics, migration tools, and services. Users who the migration will impact are included in the latter group.

Within the migration plan, also consider whether your applications fall under the lift-and-shift category, where you need to move them as they are or if you need to make modifications to the data or requests to get the best out of cloud platforms.

Choose the Cloud Deployment Model

Choosing the cloud deployment model is one of the most crucial processes of cloud migration. You can opt for either a single-cloud environment or a multi-cloud environment.

Choose Your Service Model

In this step, you need to finalise the type of service model required for different operations. These service models are Platform-as-a-Service, Software-as-a-Service, and Infrastructure-as-a-Service.

Set the KPIs

These are the metrics you need to understand for your cloud service's operation. These KPIs typically include user experience, app performance, and infrastructure parameters.

Once you have finalised all the steps necessary to make the cloud migration, you can make the shift to the cloud. After a previously set deadline passes, make sure to check whether all the requirements are getting fulfilled with the help of KPIs.

Cloud Migration Success KPIs

Key performance indicators (KPIs) provide senior management with useful pointers to the health and progress of a business. And when used and interpreted in the right way, they can offer a valuable guide to the performance of your cloud migration. The KPIs could include:

- Comparing upfront costs.
- Customer-facing metrics like order fulfilment times
- Customer churn rate
- Cart abandonment rate
- The average revenue per customer etc.
- User satisfaction metrics like time to response, first contact resolution rate etc.
- Time to market
- Time is taken for daily use
- Monitor data governance
- Measure ability to innovate
- Calculate the ability to solve user problems
- Find mean time to complete tasks

Cloud Migration Models

There are many models available for cloud migration, depending on your organisation, and there are choices to be made based on a defined strategy and where you want to be.[26]

Lift and Shift

Lift and shift give you access to the same applications used by your business at the data centre but in the cloud. This is the least disruptive and quickest approach to moving apps to the cloud. Cloud applications require no training period because they are functionally equivalent to their predecessors.

Shift to SaaS

To switch to SaaS, you must find a cloud services provider specialising in managing the specific applications you plan to use. Businesses migrate only the applications that are essential to their operations. Static programmes are fine to keep in-house. By adopting SaaS, companies can free up their staff to concentrate on what they do best and what sets them apart from competitors. When you go to a SaaS model, you can reduce the number of licences for software used in your company. In order for the move to SaaS to be successful, however, the correct service must be chosen.

Application Refactoring

App modernisation is the strategy of choice for businesses with cloud-optimised software. This strategy prioritises programmes that run better in a cloud environment. Refactoring allows businesses to move their existing applications to the cloud without changing any of the code. In addition to the minimal risk, the immediate benefits of agility and speed to market are realised because legacy applications can continue to function in tandem with the development of new applications.

Cloud Migration Strategy

Gartner created a concept of five "Rs" for application migration strategy. Gartner states, "When moving application workloads to cloud platforms, organisations must choose among five distinct strategies: rehost, revise, rearchitect, rebuild and replace. This research helps technical professionals weigh the trade-offs of each and select the right one for their goals and priorities."[27] We believe that IT professionals seem to stick to slightly different R's, for instance, Retire, Replace, Retain/wrap/expand, Rehost and Re-envision.

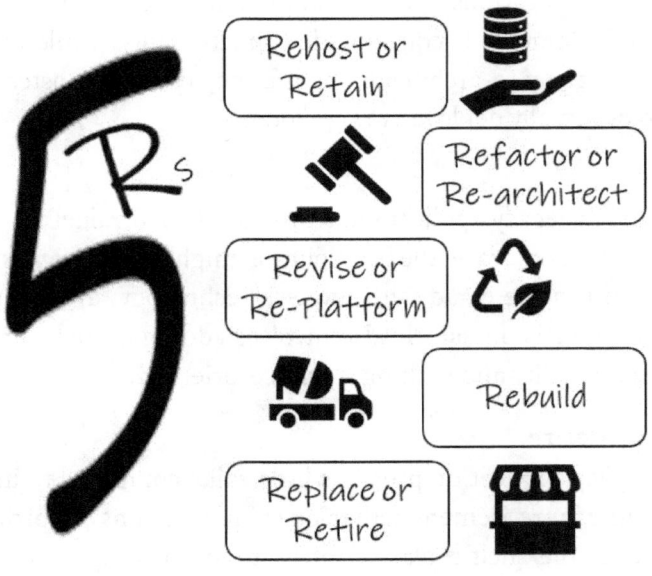

Figure 41 – The Rs of Application Migration Strategy

Rehost or Retain

Retain, wrapping and expanding might be the strategy for legacy applications providing excellent value with an acceptable total cost of ownership (TCO). A modern wrap-around can gain additional value and benefits. Examples are adding external application functionality through APIs or extending the legacy application with third-party tools. Through this, you can obtain a hybrid cloud solution.

Refactor or Re-architect

In order to take advantage of cloud-native services and functionalities in already-existing applications, refactoring is a useful tool. The most cost-effective use of the cloud platform would need refactoring, which is also the most expensive choice. Business justification is likely to be necessary when migrating an existing application to the cloud.

Revise or Re-Platform

Certain applications must be modified more extensively to migrate to the cloud. Some will require added functionality, while others may need to be entirely re-architected before they can be rehosted or refactored and eventually deployed to the cloud.

Rebuild

Suppose a legacy application is providing good value but cannot be easily moved. In that case, the best solution might be to re-envision it and build it again in the cloud with modern technology, architecture, and practices. Re-envision usually also involves adding more business value to core functionality and making it service-oriented.

Replace or Retire

If a legacy application provides little value compared to its costs, it might be time for retirement. Other legacy applications can provide some value, but off-the-shelf replacements with lower total ownership costs are available. Many legacy applications were built initially because there was no alternative at the time. A modern, readily available application – which may be a cost-effective SaaS – could replace the old one sufficiently and even replace multiple legacy systems.

Cloud Migration Tools

Preventing frequent mistakes during the migration of data and apps to the cloud calls for a specific set of technologies. Many legacy applications on an organisation's network are not optimised for the cloud. Therefore, they must be prepped for the move with tools created expressly for the task. Many different tools are available now, each specialising in a different component of the migration process.

SaaS (software as a service)

SaaS tools are cloud-based apps that link on-premise data and destination clouds and enable a secure data flow. Cloud-based tools are often the most straightforward and automated.

Open-source

Typically, open-source tools are either free or inexpensive and provide extensive customisation options. Experience in their use is necessary so that they can be adapted to each project.

Batch Processing

Initially employed in mainframe environments, tools for batch processing are built to transport massive amounts of data. As a rule, they are scheduled to operate at off-peak times to reduce network congestion during peak usage.

AWS Migration Services	Azure Migration Tools	Carbonite Migrate
Corent SurPaaS	Google Migration Services/Velostrata	Micro Focus PlateSpin Migration Factory
Turbonomic	VMware/CloudHealth Technologies	Cloudscape
ScienceLogic	AppDynamics	Dynatrace

Table 2 – Cloud Migration Tools

Cloud Migration Services

Migration to the cloud is a service offered by many CSPs, some of which specialise in management. Organisations can get the tools, automation, and know-how they need to safely move their data to the cloud with the help of migration services. The organization's needs determine whether the service is configured to transfer individual workloads or in batches.

When choosing a migration service provider, a few critical areas to consider will include:

- Certifications and Standards of the Service Provider
- Technologies and Service Roadmap
- Data Security, Data Governance and Business policies
- Data Assurance and Legal Protections
- Service Dependencies & Partnerships
- Service Delivery and Business Terms
- Contracts, Commercials & SLAs
- Reliability & Performance
- Migration Support, Vendor Lock-in & Exit Planning
- Business Health & Company Profile
- Understanding their Success Stories/use cases

Figure 42 - Things to Consider when choosing a Cloud Migration Partner

Cloud Migration Methodology

Cloud Migration Methodology outlines the methods followed in cloud migration, and they are described below:

Design – In this stage, due diligence is conducted with a detailed plan wherever it is necessary.

Rewrite – If required, rewrite or refactor the application.

Build – Establishing build details and creating build artefacts

Orchestrate – Orchestrating the build and testing the cloud environment

Test – Testing of application and cloud infrastructure. This includes smoke test, security, performance and UAT.

Migrate to Production – Build and test the production environment with automation, production data migration, operational hand-over and cut-over.

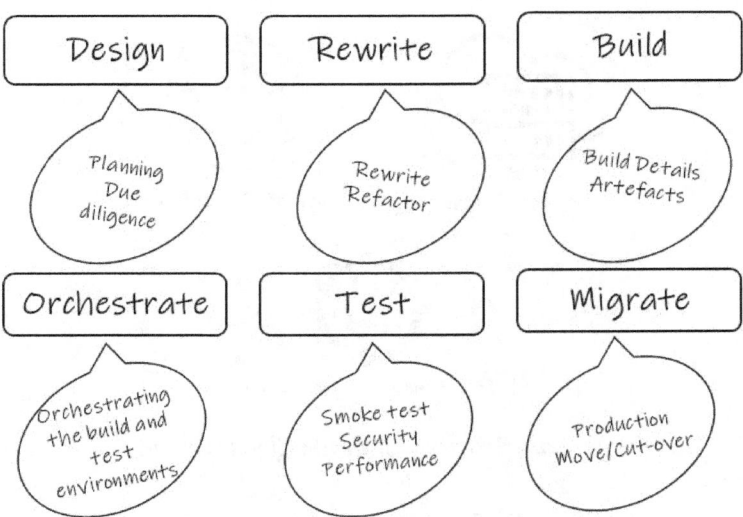

Figure 43 - Cloud Migration Methodology

Cloud Migration for Environmental Sustainability

Cloud migration can offer several benefits for environmental sustainability, including:

Energy efficiency: Cloud providers often invest in energy-efficient data centres and infrastructure, resulting in lower energy consumption and a smaller carbon footprint than on-premises IT systems.

Reduces energy use

Decreases greenhouse gas emissions

Dematerialisation

Datacentre efficiency

Shift to renewable energy sources

Figure 44 - Greener World with Cloud Computing

Resource pooling: Cloud computing allows resources, such as computing power and storage, to be shared among a large number of users, which can lead to more efficient use of resources and reduced waste.

Virtualisation: Cloud platforms make it easy to use virtual machines, which can be more energy efficient than physical servers, as they allow multiple applications to run on the same hardware.

Reduced e-waste: Migrating to the cloud can help reduce e-waste by allowing organisations to decommission outdated or underutilised hardware, as the cloud provider can provide these resources.

Carbon offset programs: Some cloud providers offer carbon offset programs, which allow organisations to offset their carbon emissions by investing in projects that reduce or remove carbon from the atmosphere.

Overall, cloud migration has the potential to significantly reduce an organisation's carbon footprint and contribute to greater environmental sustainability.

CHAPTER 5
Cloud Operational Excellence

"The cloud services companies of all sizes...The cloud is for everyone. The cloud is a democracy."
- Marc Benioff

Cloud Target Operating Model (TOM)

Defining a Cloud Target Operating Model (TOM) at the commencement of the cloud adoption and migration journey is a must. Many digital transformation projects would start with this. The TOM should include Cloud Operating Model (COM), Cloud Service Management (CSM) and Cloud Governance Framework (CGF). Cloud TOM is the enablement model for utilising cloud services within an organisation. It encompasses all the elements enabling the use of the cloud from project inception to the end of the lifecycle. It is the blueprint of the organisational vision of cloud transformation.

The primary purpose of the cloud TOM is to enable the management of the full lifecycle of cloud services, ensuring control, visibility, and delivery of business value such as cost savings and agility or responsiveness involving people, processes and technology.

Decision-making processes, criteria, and rules for designing, building, deploying, operating, and managing a Cloud Computing capability are all part of the Cloud Target Operating Model that the Cloud Center of Excellence (CCoE) team develops and keeps up to date.TOM should support an IT value framework, which should have the following visions:

Enablement: The exploitation of emerging and existing technologies to enable new business models and strategies.

Alignment: The synchronisation of goals between corporate and IT Strategy such that IT spending is "value-add" to the business.

Delivery: The Synchronisation of Cloud Service Delivery with IT Strategy to provide the business with efficient and consistent cloud solutions.

TOM Structure

TOM is always an excellent starting point to define the "To-be" status for any transformation. It should be organised as a composition of six separate topics, as shown below. This would provide a fitting abstraction for grouping or categorising the elements that constitute a working framework. The topics are:

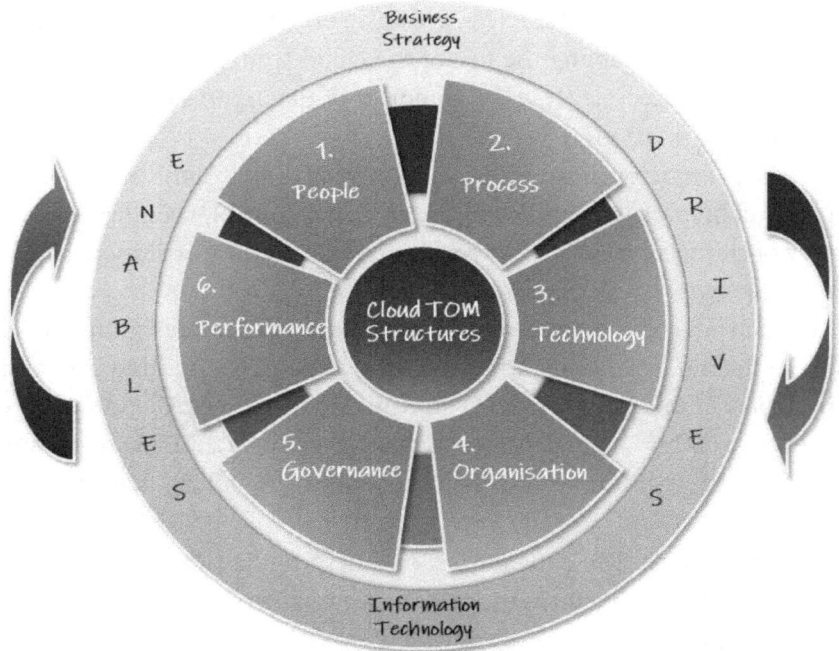

Figure 45 - Structures Of Cloud Target Operating Model

People

This includes the stakeholder roles and responsibilities for managing and supporting cloud services. It provides architecture approvals, the centre of excellence (CoE), application management, business ownership and application development (projects).

Cloud adoption is a strategic change that requires involvement from both business decision-makers and end-users. People strategy is one of the essential aspects of cloud adoption. Where appropriate terms of reference skills are required, including a full RACI (Responsible, Accountable, Consulted, and Informed) matrix.

Process

The best practice-driven methods that organisations should adopt to deliver an effective and efficient framework model. It will include a RACI matrix defining the functional roles and areas of responsibility.

Technology

Management of tools used specifies the supported environments, cloud architecture and the management and use for which they are designed.

Organisation

The organisation would need to transit and transform. It will include governance of culture and style, risk management, the shift of focus from operational to managerial competencies, relationship Management to internal and external stakeholders, learning and development, and a total preparation for this new world.

Governance

Governance structures that implement and direct business development and architectural changes. Describing the ways of working includes principles, approval mechanisms, security governance, service management/SLAs, and cloud services catalogue.

Performance Management

This is the effectiveness of measurement practices. After all, what can't be measured can't be managed.

TOM Framework

Cloud TOM framework consists of the following critical components linked together to deliver the optimum cloud experience for users while providing visibility and control to the business.

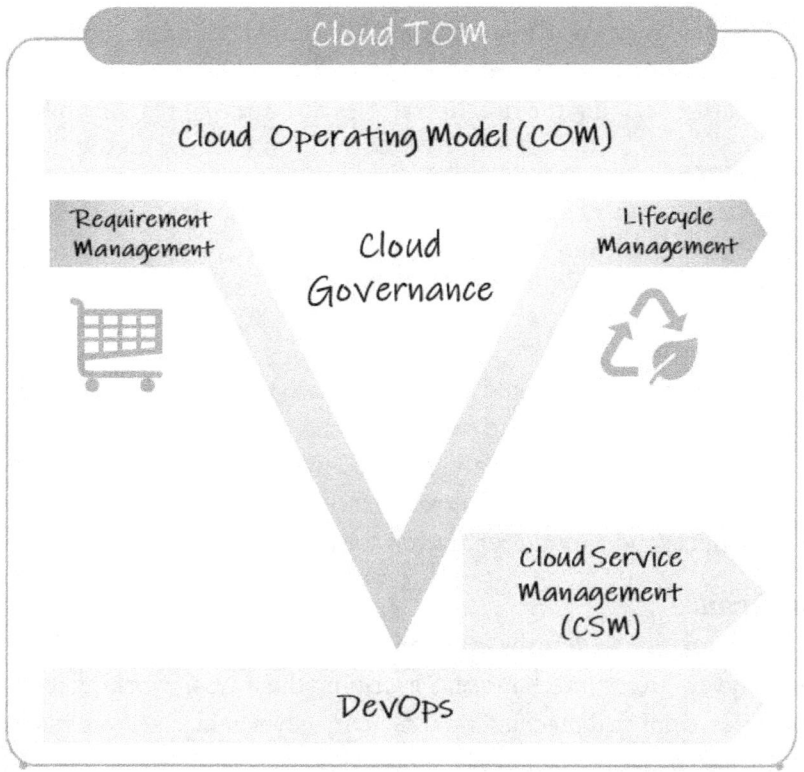

Figure 46 - Cloud Target Operating Model (TOM) Framework

The system design "V" approach could fit in designing the TOM framework. Two stages are covered within the Cloud Operating Model. On the left side is requirement management which captures business requirements, including technical specifications and high-level and detailed design. Then the design definition converts to a service catalogue item. Then it will go on the right side for delivering, testing, deployment, and release to in life service, which will be part of Cloud Service Management. Centralised governance will cover critical element to ensure secure and cost-effective cloud adoption and ongoing use. The CSM function commences with the acceptance of the design definition blueprint for deployment. CSM focuses on the in-life support aspects of both the platform and the services/workloads running on top of it. Critical parts of the TOM framework:

- **COM** – Cloud Operating Model – This is where business requirements get converted to a working solution for cloud services.
- **CSM** – Cloud Service Management – the ITSM process for configuring, administration, monitoring, and supporting deployed workloads onto the cloud platform.
- **CGF** - Cloud Governance Framework – provides a framework of controls and processes for ensuring cloud services are fit for purpose, controlled and secure.
- **DevOps** - DevOps - is the culture that promotes close collaboration between development and operations. DevOps aims to release software more rapidly, more frequently, and more reliably. Klaus Schwab of the World Economic Forum once said, "In the new world, it is not the big fish that eats the small fish; it's the fast fish which eats the slow fish".

"The most powerful tool we have as developers is automation."
- Scott Hanselman

TOM Scope

The unprecedented disruption created by the emergence of cloud technology obliges organisations to adopt a modern IT operating model; hence, the target operating model should outline the "to be" aspects of the fundamentals mentioned in the TOM structure. Each of those would need to be factored in a while creating the TOM and ensuring that a clear synergy between them is established. To develop and target Operating Model and to guide the configuration and the operation of the technology function, organisations must consider the following areas:

- Products Over Projects
- Adaptive Business Engagement
- Agile, DevOps and Continuous Delivery
- Customer-Centric Design
- Application Building Blocks
- Cloud-Based Scalable Infrastructure
- Strategy Over Governance, Management Over Operations
- Data Strategy and Ownership
- Adaptive Skills and Mind-Sets

*The Book on **Cloud Service Management and Governance** by Enamul Haque has a more in-depth analysis of Cloud Service Management and Governance. All Cloud Service Management Processes are detailed, with process workflows described using IT4IT, ITIL 4, DevOps, Lean, Agile, Digital Service Management and other popular service management methodologies. The end chapter of this book has more details on this.*

TOM Shifts

In this TOM section, I value that we also look into the scenarios that would help us to understand the required conversion for such digital transformation. Suppose we see carefully the traditional IT operating model illustrated below. In that case, there is a gap in some of the essential value adds for digital TOM, such as speed, innovation and talent.

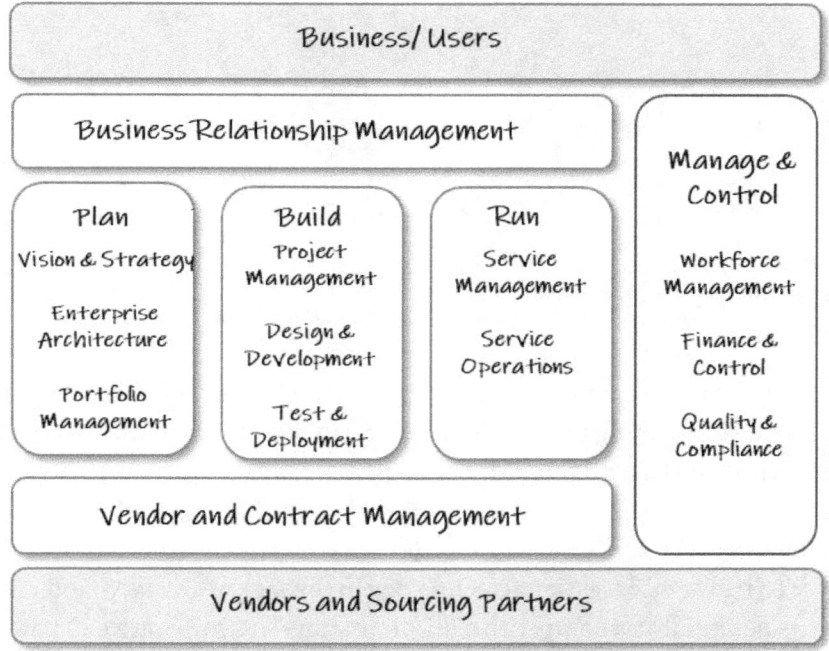

Figure 47 - A Traditional IT Operating Model

With a lack of speed, organisations cannot respond quickly to market opportunities. The lack of change is a significant threat in today's competitive digital marketplace. Companies cannot experiment with new digital technologies to create digital solutions, and, as a result, any innovative efforts are focused on incrementally improving existing situations instead of creating new innovative solutions for customers.

Organisations cannot attract and retain the talent they need to drive digital innovation.

So, the digital shift impacts how we work, the resources we use, and the nature of technology itself. In the traditional model, innovation is happening; however, it will be done in a siloed manner compared to a new model where the innovation ecosystem is more integrated.

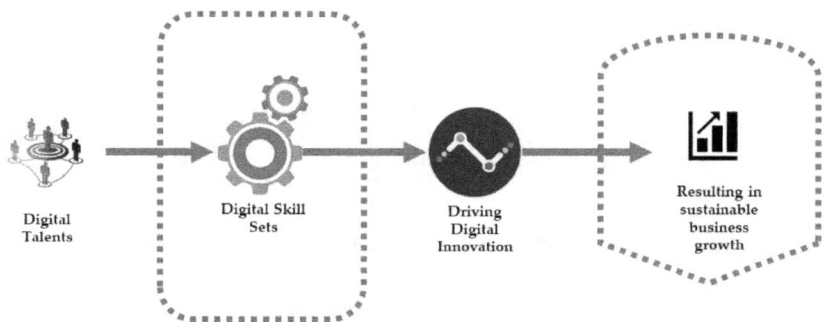

Figure 48 - Digital Talents Driving Digital Innovations

Applications and infrastructures are loosely coupled. A modern integrated IT operating model will focus on driving stakeholder experience, help with fact-based speedy decision-making, drive process efficiencies and improve scalability and performance. I have illustrated this in detail in the below figure:

To truly embrace digital technology in the face of change—and realise its potential as a competitive differentiator—it's imperative to have a plan, however, since there is a fundamental mismatch between how companies operate today and what model of operation digital transformation will bring, it is paramount to understand the shifts required to materialise organisational goals and objectives.

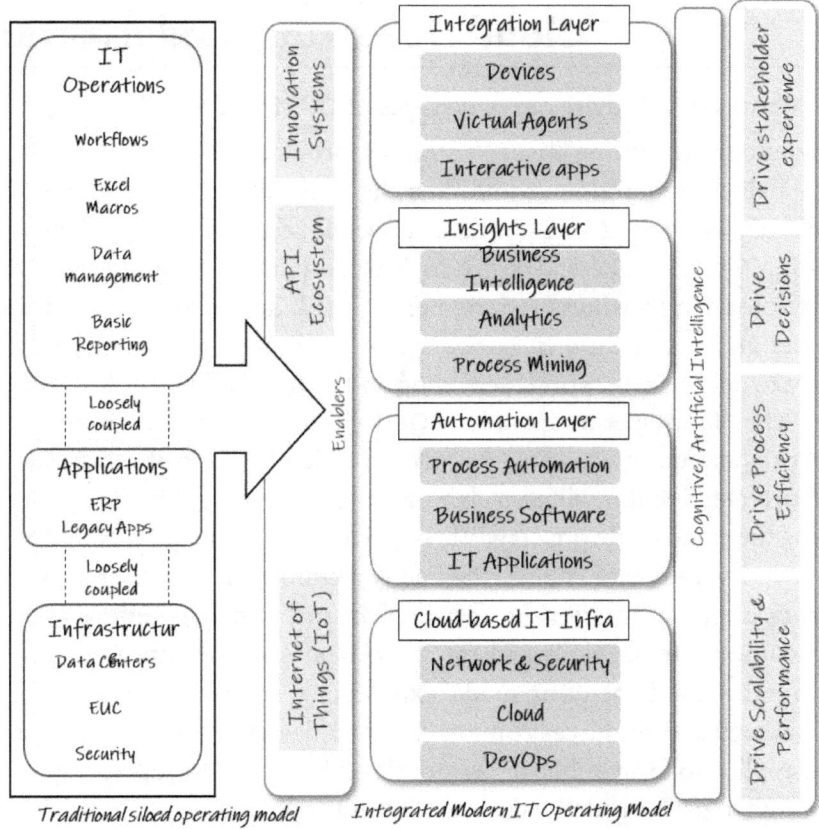

Figure 49 - IT Operating Model Shifting Explained

Cloud Operating Model (COM)

As we discussed, there are two stages of COM, and the first stage will look into transforming business strategy into a tangible form, by capturing business requirements and then the next phase will be service lifecycle management. As we saw in the previous section on TOM, Cloud Operating Model will be one of the critical components forming the TOM. After obtaining business requirements, it will define technical requirements and specifications, create a high-level design, and move from there to delivering, testing, deploying and in-life service.

The Cloud Operating Model (COM) will not only ensure new technology runs smoothly, ensuring the correct implementation of new business requirements, but it will also elaborate the ways of working for projects using the cloud platforms. It will bring together all stakeholders who have an invested interest in delivering and consuming the cloud services, ensuring a shared mission by focusing on soft and hard elements and structure, systems, skills and shared values. A set of critical processes within the cloud operating model explain how an organisation's people, technology and resources come together to design, develop, deploy and run applications on public or private cloud-based platforms.

When properly defined, a cloud operating model as a critical driver for cloud operations management can:

- Improve efficiency and minimise the risk of disruption;
- Help identify changes to existing processes within day-to-day operations through a consolidated and agreed set of policies and procedures;
- Provide the quickness and quality that customers require;
- Save money on providing cloud services and defend your spending decisions;
- Ensure cloud service management is taken care of for operational efficiencies;
- Ensure the coherent control of lifecycle changes – whether bug fixes, software patches, application releases or system upgrades;

- Establish the governance, standards and RACI that enforces how the cloud services will operate.

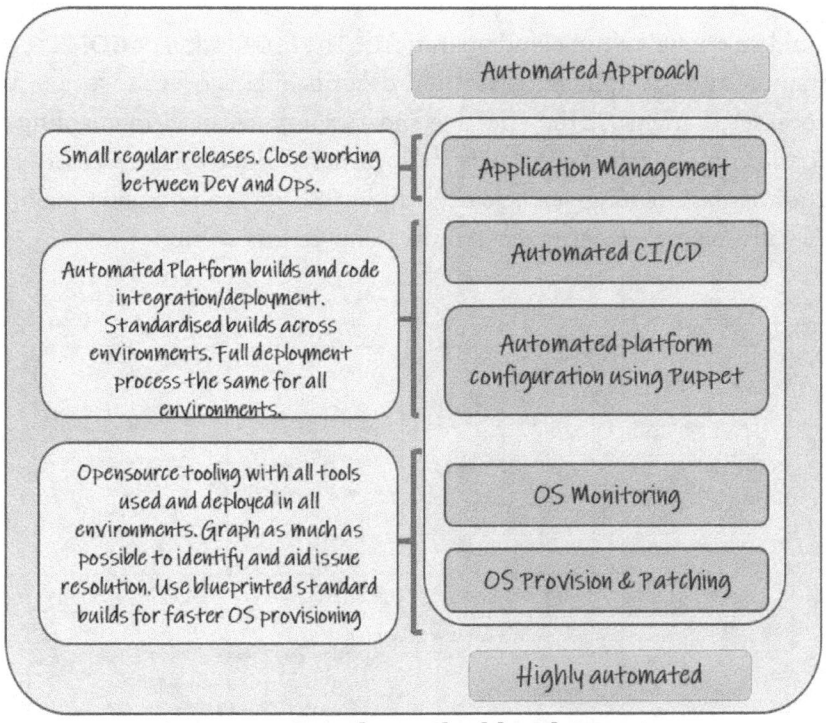

Figure 50 - Approaches to Cloud-based Operations

"Never tell people how to do things. Tell them what to do, and they will surprise you with their ingenuity. "
- George S. Patton

COM Structure

I have created the below COM structure focusing on different layers that would be crucial to run cloud operations. The foundation of COM is governance and compliance. Gartner describes IT governance as "the processes that ensure the effective and efficient use of IT in enabling an organisation to achieve its goals"[28], governance encompasses an organisation's mission, long-term goals, responsibilities, and decision making. We will look into governance in more detail in this section.

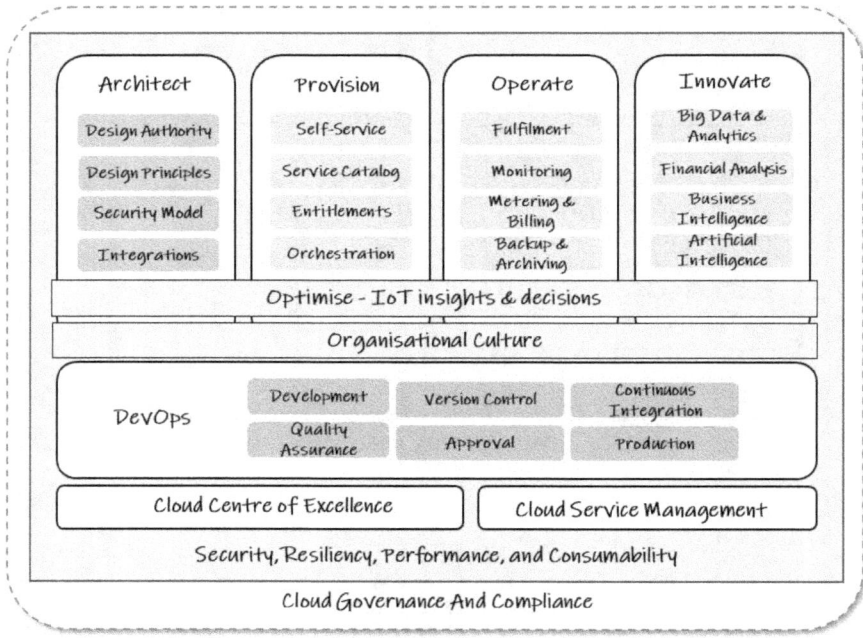

Figure 51 - Cloud Operating Model Structure

Security, Resiliency, Performance, and Consumability would be the platform of a sophisticated cloud operating model. Security covers identity and access management principles and protection governance by securing infrastructure against threats and vulnerabilities. It will be an essential part of the discovery process for data integrity and protecting data and information assets. Resiliency monitoring and analysis, resiliency policy management, continuity management and data resiliency will need to work hand in hand with security by ensuring the seamless performance of the cloud platform. Consumability is about ease of business, positive first experience, rapid adaptation, rapid integration etc.

An essential part of the cloud operating model is establishing a Cloud Centre of Excellence (CCoE). It will provide leadership in defining and deploying the cloud strategy, design, architecture, technical and operational standards, best practices and training. We will park this topic here for more details in the governance chapter. Like CCoE, the cloud service management part is covered mainly in its section. They both need to be present in the COM. DevOps create the ability for continuous software delivery that enables organisations to seize market opportunities and reduce time to customer feedback, within COM, DevOps is an essential part. The lack of continuous delivery impacts the entire business enterprise in the new reality of systems of interaction.

With cloud adoption, managing organisational culture becomes the heart of a successful cloud operating model. We looked into this subject quite many times before in this book. It's a continuous process. Cloud should drive innovation; insights should create new business opportunities. Continuous operating model optimisation can be achieved by making informed decisions from analytics and business intelligence.

All the horizontal components in this COM structure should provide an overall foundation for the pillars mentioned in the vertical. Let's understand them:

Architect

Cloud computing architecture denotes the components and subcomponents required for Cloud Computing. The Architecture team captures the business needs and evaluates and ensures the project mandates before it moves for project implementation. Cloud solution design, security model development, and integrations are critical in this pillar.

Provision

It's the service consumption part by the end-user. The Self-Service enables users to select services based on entitlements or subscriptions from a service catalogue. It can also provide service request management facilities with integration to IT service management systems, could also have reporting dashboard etc.

Operate

The operational part will manage and deliver cloud services and infrastructure. This involves ensuring peak performance and maintaining availability to satisfy the needs and expectations of customers and meet service level agreement standards.

Innovate

As mentioned earlier, the essence of cloud adoption is to become innovative in improving the business. "Cloud Computing represents one of the most misunderstood, yet valuable, innovations in current IT and business strategies," said Daryl Plummer, vice president and Gartner fellow.

Cloud Centre of Excellence (CCoE)

A Centre of Excellence (CoE) is a team of executives who lead the introduction of new capabilities into an organisation—typically through new skills, technology, working practices or services. They champion the transformation process, providing guidance, support, and training to employees throughout the transition, ensuring everyone is committed and pulling in the same direction. It will be responsible for introducing new structures or frameworks, standardising processes, managing disruption, and overcoming barriers to cloud adoption.

"A Cloud Centre of Excellence (CCoE) is a cross-functional team responsible for developing and managing the cloud strategy, governance, and best practices that the rest of the organisation can leverage to transform the business using the cloud. The CCoE leads the organisation as a whole in cloud adoption, migration, and operations. It may also be called a Cloud Competency Centre, Cloud Capability Centre, or Cloud Knowledge Centre." — Cloud Management Report 2017

The CCoE team transitioned the newly built cloud infrastructure and developed operating standards and best practices for the Cloud Operations team to run and operate. The Cloud Operations team is responsible for the daily operations and support of the cloud infrastructure to ensure timely and reliable delivery and fulfilment of IT services.

Microsoft defines CCoE as "A cloud centre of excellence (CCoE) is a function that creates a balance between speed and stability." the CCoE should ideally include members who already have cloud experience. People with a broad set of related skills are precious in these roles owing to the multi-disciplinary nature of the cloud, which sits at the centre of a range of emerging IT technologies.

The best way to create a winning CCoE is to start forming the team. The team needs to be highly engaged. It should be composed of engineers with strong technical skills and diverse backgrounds — the next essential step in delivering quick wins and gaining leadership support. Once the team gets experience, it should start building a reference architecture to standardise patterns.

CCoE Mode of Operations

CCoE mode of operations will include helping the organisation to materialise the business requirements through agile approaches with the compositions sub-teams of below capabilities:

Solution Design Authority

This team assures business process and information-related changes before them being approved by the IT Management team.

Architecture Governance Board

This board assures that all cloud solutions and investment decisions comply with organisational architecture strategies, standards, and guidelines to achieve the best outcome for them by maximising value and minimising risk.

Architecture Assurance Board

This board will approve all enterprise architecture strategies, standards, guidelines, and other position documents.

Cloud Security and Cyber Threat Management

This team is responsible for people, processes, policies, and technology that protect data and applications that operate in the cloud.

Metering, Billing and Accounting team

The team is responsible for supporting capacity planning, billing, metering, etc.

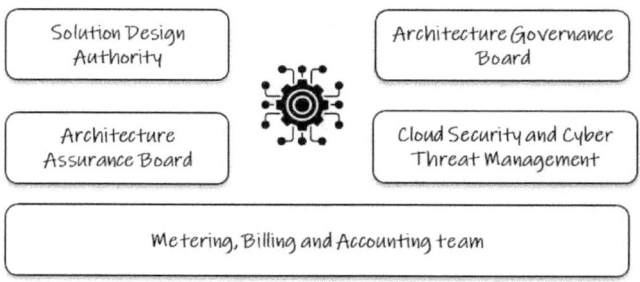

Figure 52 - CCoE Capabilities

CCoE Core Responsibilities

The CCoE will provide the cloud services' best practices, standards, and technical oversight. It will be the guiding force behind the following critical steps in a successful cloud transformation.

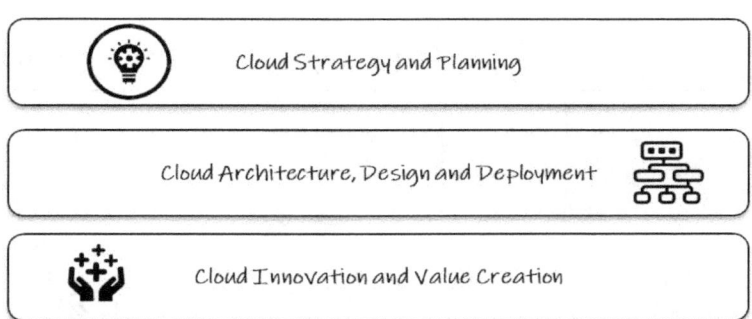

Figure 53 - CCoE Value Creation

Cloud Strategy and Planning

Considering business scope, managing stakeholders, creating policies, and decision-making processes. This could also include cloud acquisition, vendor selection and contract negotiation, cloud contingency, provider and migration planning, failover architecture, and recovery planning. Cloud awareness, training, cost optimisation and allocation should also be considered.

Cloud Architecture, Design and Deployment

Considering cloud architecture with an approval mechanism, an essential part of this would be the approval board administrations for solution architecture, security review, integrations etc. This includes agile project management methodologies and DevOps with asset and change management capabilities.

Cloud Innovation and Value Creation

Considering the added value that the cloud brings to the organisation with innovation for business acceleration. Taking transformation initiatives and continually improving them.

CCoE Structure

Amazon Web Services (AWS) describe that a CCoE should be structured based on three core operational entities; they are described below: [29]

Figure 54 - CCoE Operational Entities

Functional

A Functional CCoE creates a hands-on team that acts as a delivery catalyst, engaging with project teams to drive cloud initiatives.

Advisory

The Advisory CCoE comprises consultative team members who give advice and guidance on best practices. They establish and drive standards for new policies which are suited well for more substantial, high-energy organisations with multiple projects in flight.

Prescriptive

Prescriptive CCoE creates a policy board that provides leadership and blueprints to teams on how cloud projects should be constituted and executed within the organisation. They lead by defining policies and standards covering everything from application deployment and automation standards, identity, and access management to security and audit standards. They typically fit large enterprises or regulated industries where governance is critical.

CCoE Team Members and Responsibilities

The roles in a CCoE will vary based on the organisation's maturity in the cloud and its specific needs. Small organisations might have several people sharing particular tasks (for example, security and networking), but large organisations are likely to separate functions by individuals. The intent is to create a team with the ability to move at the pace necessary to achieve the organisation's strategic goals. The following roles are recommended for a typical CCoE:[30]

Roles	Responsibilities
Cloud COE Lead	He oversees the Cloud COE. Responsible for working with the executive team on cross-team collaboration, next steps, sponsorship, and overall management of the Cloud COE
Developer Operations and Infrastructure Lead	Responsible for the team's project management and execution. Also, aligns developers to best practices and essential standards. Consults on edge cases and unique needs. Builds the applications and tools needed for app deployment and management.
Software Engineer/ Cloud Architect	Specialises in working on Cloud Computing systems. Develops the next-generation products and applications on cloud technologies. Helps determine how the system should operate and guides the programmers who support write the application code, aligning developers to best practices and essential standards. May design new systems or upgrade existing systems.

Site Reliability Engineer	Ensures that services — both internally critical and externally visible systems — have reliability and uptime appropriate to users' needs and a fast rate of improvement while keeping an eye on capacity and performance. Responsible for availability, latency, performance, efficiency, change management, monitoring, emergency response, and capacity planning.
Cloud Engineering Lead	Responsible for the team's project management and execution. Oversees the cloud architecture, network engineering, security, and software engineers, cloud engineers, and developers in the team.
Network Engineer	Responsible for external-facing network infrastructure (public-facing IPs, firewalls, cloud DNS, cloud interconnect, NAT/egress control), including connectivity to provide private networking to other infrastructure. Helps to develop and ensure that the design and feature enhancements keep systems running smoothly.
Security Engineer	Responsible for the security of applications and infrastructure in the cloud. Helps to ensure that software and services are designed and implemented to the highest security standards. Performs security audits, risk analysis, application-level vulnerability testing, and security code reviews for various products. Works closely with other software engineers to enhance the overall security posture.
Cloud Developer	Guides the process of configuring and deploying the cloud infrastructure, consisting of

Operations and Infrastructure Engineer	identity and access management, network architecture, application security, logging, monitoring, billing, and more. Consults with various teams across the organisation on how to design their cloud applications for optimal scaling, including CDN design, load balancer setup, caching, compute optimisations, continuous integration and delivery pipeline, and more. Additionally, works closely with Product Management and Product Engineering to build and drive excellence across products.
Technical Solutions Engineer	Work closely with engineering, site reliability, and deployment teams to improve the critical tools and support processes that enable cloud support engineers and internal customers to succeed. Applies in-depth technical experience to develop a deep understanding of, and drive enhancements for, cloud tooling architecture. Builds and implements a global service and tooling platform to ensure stability, reusability, testing, compliance, and overall reliability. Acts as the first line of defence, in regular contact with cloud site reliability engineers, network engineers, and security engineers.
Data Scientist Lead	Leads the team of data scientists. Responsible for the team's project management and execution. Oversees data analytics and machine learning initiatives within an organisation. Enables data-driven decision-making by collecting, transforming, and visualising data.

	Designs, builds, maintains and troubleshoots data processing systems with an emphasis on the security, reliability, fault-tolerance, scalability, fidelity, and efficiency of such systems.
Data Scientist	Evaluates and improve the organisation's products. Collaborates with a multi-disciplinary team of engineers and analysts on a wide range of problems. Brings scientific rigour and statistical methods to the challenges of creating, developing, and improving products with an appreciation for the behaviours of the end-user. Works with engineers to analyse data and plan/design experiments, develops metrics and methodologies to support strategic decisions, builds statistical models, integrates new methods into existing systems, and communicates findings to engineers and others, both verbally and in writing.
Data Analyst	Supports initiatives related to systems, processes, and data transformation. Dives deeply into the data and understands the business processes supported, applying statistics and data modelling to gain actionable business insights and drive recommendations. Interacts with multiple stakeholders across the business, product, and engineering teams, while working closely with the data team to support reporting and business metrics.

Organisational Change and Communication Specialist	Assesses the impacts of cloud adoption on the organisation as a whole, as well as on individual teams and lines of business. Helps align change initiatives with business value and strategic cloud goals. Develops and leads strategies to communicate key efforts and successes across the enterprise.

Table 3 - CCoE Team Members and Responsibilities

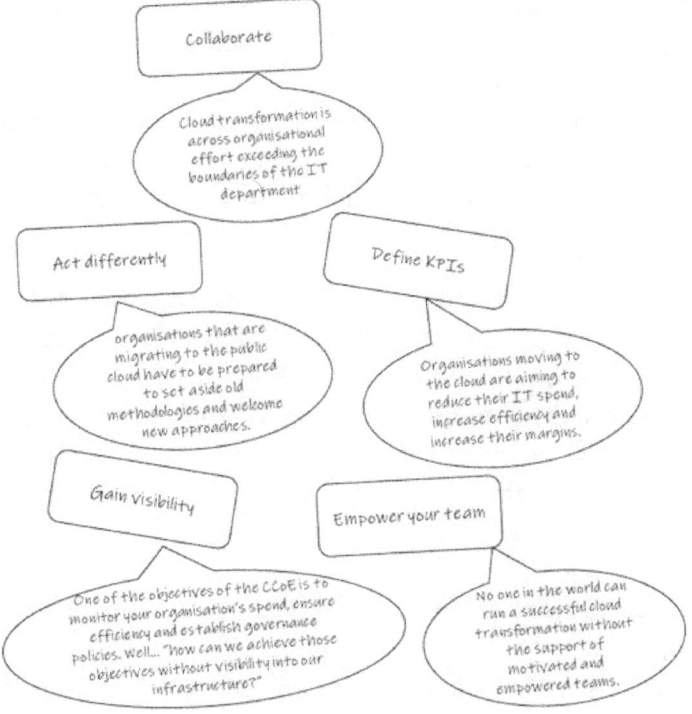

Figure 55 - 5 Best Practices for Forming A Cloud Center Of Excellence

Cloud Service Management (CSM)

Cloud service management refers to the management of any services coming from the cloud. And because the new business model drives organisations to re-evaluate their current processes and re-structure for process standardisation and governance control, cloud service management focuses on aligning Cloud Computing and service management practices introducing good cloud management practices among customer, consumer, and supplier organisations. As a result, the management of cloud services would encompass all activities associated with the provision, maintenance, and improvement of services requested by or presented to cloud users.

The administration of services in the cloud can be characterised from the vantage points of business support, provisioning, and configuration, as well as the need for portability and interoperability.

Business Support

The term "business assistance" refers to a wide variety of services that help businesses interact with their customers and carry out their daily tasks. It consists of the parts of a firm that interact directly with customers. Account administration, including opening, closing, and terminating client accounts; user profile management; relationship management via establishing points of contact and resolving customer concerns and complaints; etc.

- **Contract Management**: Oversee service agreements' beginning, middle, and end.
- **Inventory Management**: Develop and control service catalogues and similar structures.
- **Accounting and Billing**: Take care of the money side by keeping track of invoices and billing information, sending out statements, accepting payments, etc.
- **Reporting and Auditing**: View user activity, compile reports, etc.
- **Pricing and Rating**: Assess cloud offerings, set rates, manage

discounts and other pricing tiers according to customer profiles, and more.

Provisioning and Configuration

This would include the following:

- **Rapid Provisioning**: Cloud-based infrastructure is deployed mechanically in response to a user's request for a certain service, set of resources, or set of capabilities.
- **Resource Changing**: Repairs, upgrades, and adding additional nodes to the cloud all necessitate redistributing configuration and resources.
- **Monitoring and Reporting**: Finding and tracking cloud services, keeping tabs on activities in the cloud, and churning out performance stats.
- **Metering**: Depending on the nature of the service, a metering capability at an appropriate level of abstraction must be provided (e.g., storage, processing, band-width, and active user accounts).
- **SLA Management**: The SLA lifecycle includes defining the SLA contract (the underlying schema with the QoS parameters), monitoring the SLA, and enforcing the SLA based on predetermined policies.

Portability and Interoperability

The widespread adoption of cloud computing is expected to reduce IT maintenance costs and shorten the time it takes to release new versions of software. Prospective customers care about data and application portability if they can easily, cheaply, and with little downtime migrate them between different cloud environments. Users worry about the capacity to communicate across or among different clouds, which is an issue of interoperability.

ITIL 4 in Cloud Service Management

ITIL has changed beyond the delivery of services to providing end-to-end value delivery. In February 2019, ITIL released an updated framework called ITIL 4. The name reflected the role of IT as an integral part of supporting individuals and organisations to navigate into the Fourth Industrial Revolution. ITIL 4 evolved to provide an end-to-end IT/Digital Operating Model, covering the full delivery (and sustaining) of technology-enabled products and services, guiding how IT interfaces with and even leads the broader business strategy.

The updated framework focused on facilitating value cocreation via a Service Value System (SVS). The SVS represents how different components and activities can work together in any organisation to enable value creation through IT-enabled services. It brings ITSM practices in the context of customer experience, value streams, and digital transformation, as well as embracing new ways of working, such as Lean, Agile, and DevOps. The guidance provided by ITIL publications can be adopted and adapted for all organisations and services, including cloud-based services.

The Service Value Systems (SVS)

SVS provides seamless integrations and coordination activities across the organisation, which are value-based, durable, and cohesive. The core component of SVS is the ITIL service value chain, ITIL practices, ITIL guiding principles, governance and continual improvements. This value creation is the primary aim of any business entity. When creating value for the customer can help to sell products, creating value for stakeholders will mean more investment opportunities similarly, when IT creates value, it helps business to generate revenue or return on investment. ITIL 4 service value systems would help in value co-creation through active collaboration between cloud service providers, cloud service consumers and cloud management service providers.

The Four Dimensions of ITIL 4

The four dimensions are the factors that ITIL 4 introduces to ensure a holistic approach to service management. These are organised and people, information and technology, partners and suppliers, and value streams and processes.

Six Activities in Service Value Chain

The heart of Service Value Systems is the "Service Value Chain (SVC)". It is a set of consistent activities that the organisation performs to deliver a valuable product or service to its consumers and to enable value realisation. The service value chain can be adapted to multiple approaches, including DevOps and centralised IT, to address the need for multimodal service management. The adaptability of the value chain enables the organisation to respond to the changing demands of its stakeholders effectively and efficiently.

1. ***Plan:*** Plan within ITIL 4 takes care of activities such as aligning the cloud planning in response to the business strategy. Part of cloud strategy and planning will include defining the architecture and standards, cloud migration planning, integration, security model, policy management, risk issues etc.

2. ***Design and Transition:*** Design and transition ensure that the product and services it creates have synergy with its stakeholders' expectations meeting the required quality with cost efficiency and at the correct time for the market. It will consist of activities such as solution design, the decision of public cloud, private cloud or hybrid cloud deployment model selection etc.

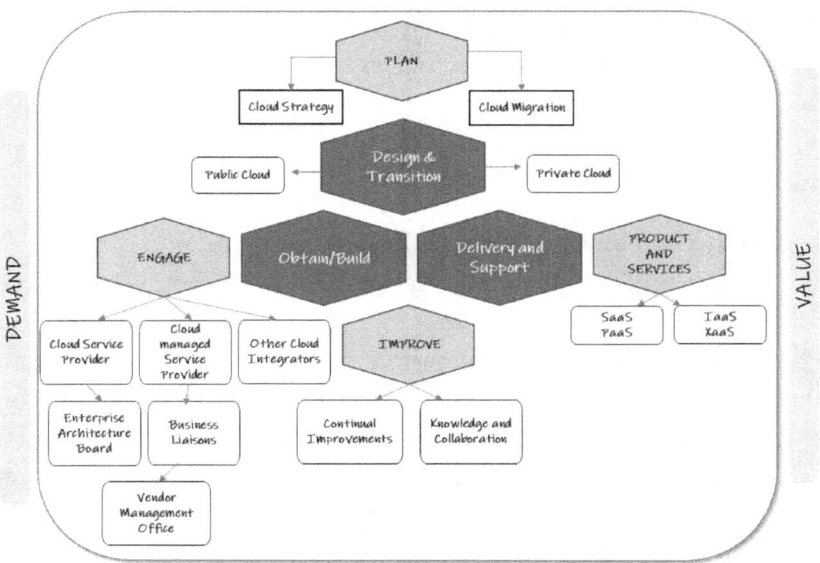

Figure 56 - ITIL 4 Service Value Chain in CSM Context

3. **Engage:** An essential part of cloud implementation is the engagement required with all relevant stakeholders to foster the relationship and open-minded communication across all respective parties. This can translate to improved cloud acquisition, better vendor selection and profitable contract negotiation. Engagement is also essential with vital internal sponsors such as the enterprise architecture team and vendor management office.

4. **Obtain and Build:** This ensures all service components are available when required for a timely response. The build needs to be focused on automation with continuous integration (CI) and continuous deployment (CD). Obtaining required coordination from enterprise architecture board, security team, project management office is significant.

5. **Deliver and Support:** Delivery of the service and its support to fulfil user expectations is the goal of delivery and support. This would include the fulfilment of requests, event management, incident, problem management, change control, cloud optimisation and capacity planning, subscription usage and

chargeback, and other processes discussed in the next chapters.

6. ***Improve***: Continuous improvements of cloud services is essential to ensure its value creation to the organisation through automation, cost efficiencies, and innovation for competitiveness and business agility.

"In moving to the cloud, the organisation is outsourcing certain elements, tasks and responsibilities to the cloud service provider. This means the organisation, and the IT function as the internal IT service provider, shift away from managing some of the technical components involved in delivering that service. After all, the cloud is a form of outsourcing. This shift changes the approach the organisation and the IT function will need to take regarding areas such as IT process management, risk management, financial management, IT architecture, interoperability of systems, security and IT service management in general.

It is worth remembering that the proliferation of cloud-based services does not change the fundamentals of what frameworks such as ITIL, or a movement such as IT service management, aim at. They want to achieve quality products and services which are fit for purpose, fit for use and aligned to the strategic goals and needs of the organization.

Cloud was born out of disruption and has caused much disruption itself to established norms. The latest developments in cloud and digital technologies are allowing organizations to develop new business models, thus pressurising existing tried-and-tested businesses. However, the latest developments in cloud and digital technologies are also requiring organisations, IT professionals and the wider workforce to upskill, change, adapt and innovate like never before."

- Mark O'Loughlin - Managing Director,
Cloud Credential Council
06 March 2019

IT4IT in Cloud Service Management

The IT4IT[31] is the Reference Architecture[32] approach for the IT Value Chain and is anchored by four pillars – the Service Model, the Information Model, the Functional Model, and the Integration Model. When captured and modelled correctly, these areas remain constant regardless of process, technology, or capabilities changes. The operating model serves better the digital enterprise as well as more traditional approaches:

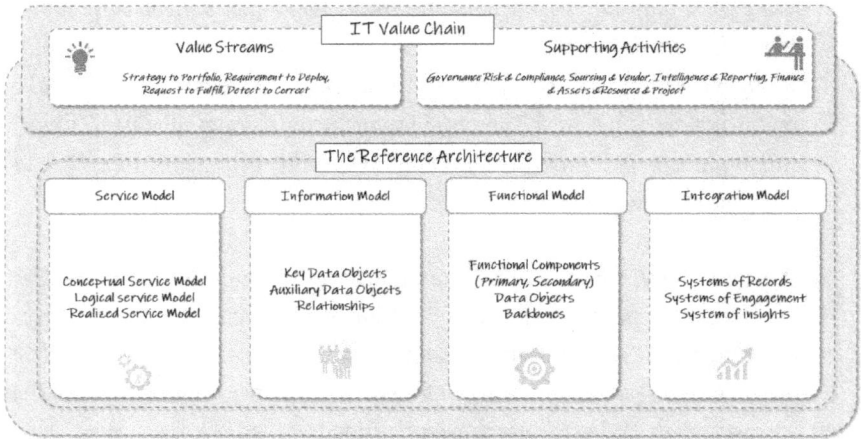

Figure 57 - IT4IT High-Level Structure

These value chains can also be mapped to the conventional ways of representing such as plan, build, deliver and run – you can say phases of the lifecycle

The value Streams, according to IT4IT, produces benefits to IT organisation; however, other supporting activities do not directly deliver value but contribute to creating value as part of an IT organisation. They contribute substantially. Keeping only doesn't mean that an IT organisation can leave without them, so they are:

- Finance and assets
- Sourcing and vendors
- Intelligence and Reporting

- Resource and project
- Governance, risk and compliance

According to IT4IT, choosing this value chain approach makes it very common in the industry, and it's not something that the Open Group invented, this concept comes through business management and was first described by Michael Porter in his 1985 best-seller, *Competitive Advantage: Creating and Sustaining Superior Performance*.

Therefore, using this value chain approach should instead improve IT to align more effectively with business as the business runs on it, and people in the industry understand it better because the core idea is to bring business and IT closer and allow us to speak the same language. This also ensures that IT is seen as nothing but a business – it's like running IT like other businesses.

IT Value Chain is divided into two parts: - Value Streams and Supporting Activities. The value chain in IT4IT consist of four Streams:

- PLAN - Strategy to Portfolio (S2P)
- BUILD - Requirements to Deploy (R2S)
- FULFIL - Request to Fulfil (R2F)
- RUN- Detect to Correct (R2D)

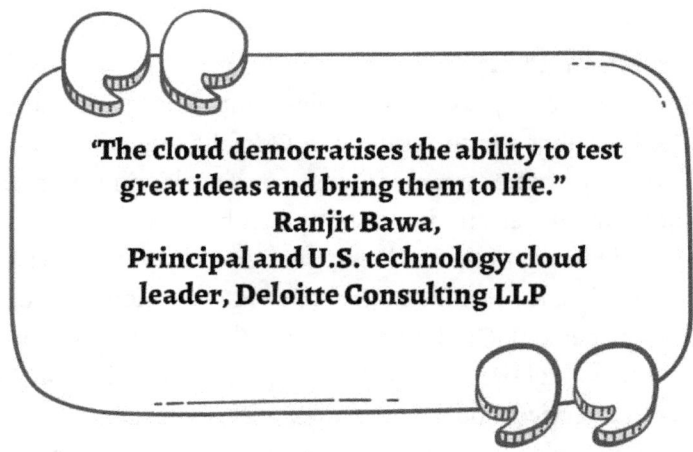

'The cloud democratises the ability to test great ideas and bring them to life."
Ranjit Bawa,
Principal and U.S. technology cloud leader, Deloitte Consulting LLP

CSM Value Streams

The Cloud Service Management value streams are aligned with the IT4IT framework, and this chapter describes the details of process activities and key deliverables.

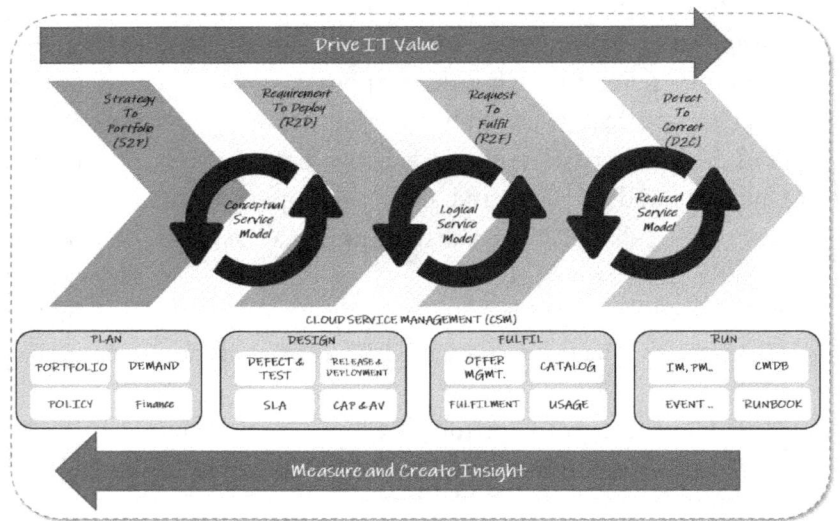

Figure 58 - IT4IT Value Chains Mapped to Cloud Service Management

Value Stream – 1: Plan

This is the conceptual service blueprint. The plan value stream within CSM is aligned with Strategy to Portfolio (S2P) reference model within IT4IT. This value stream is focused on the planning activities of IT and the subsequent selection of investments by IT in each period to respond to the demands of the business. The S2P Value Stream within CSM will be responsible for looking after: Policy Management, Cloud Service Portfolio Management (CPM) and Demand Management. As a part of the Service to the Portfolio (S2P) value stream, the IT organisation produces the conceptual service model, which means IT organisation understands what the service will be, how it would look like, it is not something which is released, but this is the positioning, which then goes to the requirement to deploy (R2D).

Value Stream – 2: Design

CSM's design value stream aligns with the Requirement to Deploy (R2D) reference model within IT4IT. This value stream is focused on building or sourcing the required components and capabilities identified in the S2P Value Stream and turning the investment decisions from S2P into services. This includes planning the work, designing, or developing the service, testing the service and releasing the service. R2D receives the Conceptual Service Blueprint data object and uses it as a foundation to design and develop the Logical Service Model. It takes care of Service Design, Service Level Management, Cloud Availability and Capacity Management, and Test and Defect Management to Build.

So basically, here, the service is being created, released and ready for deployment as the name of the value stream says. Because of this value stream, we have a logical service model, a kind of blueprint of the service but already quite specific as we have released, and as part of the request fulfilment, this release has been deployed, and all the users have been granted access rights to use the service, all the subscriptions have been created.

Value Stream – 3: Fulfil

Fulfil value stream within CSM is aligned with the Request to Fulfil (R2F) reference model within IT4IT. Here we have the realised service model, which becomes an integral part of CMDB, which then goes to detect to correct, basically "Operate".

As you see, it is a very generic and widespread cycle of service –we drive IT value from left to right by being more and more specific with our service, providing more value by having features and so on and going back, there is a feedback loop that we have to measure and create insights that could be used in other services.

Demand for Satisfaction (R2F) The focus of Value Stream is on streamlining the process through which the services outlined in R2D are made available to customers. This motivates IT to interact with its customers by means of a catalogue of services. After the Logical Service Blueprint has been through the creation, testing, and release approval phases, it is delivered to R2F. The R2F Value Stream is in charge of the activities necessary to bring a service that is used frequently into production and make it usable by the company. This entails making a Service Catalogue Entry that can be used with a centralised provisioning portal. It also incorporates Charge Back and Show Back and Usage, Cloud Catalog Management and the Execution of Fulfillment.

Value Stream – 4: Run

The IT4IT Detect to Correct (D2C) Value Stream is in sync with the CSM Run-Value Stream. Production service uptime is the primary concern. This exercise aims to find problems and fix them before they affect users. D2C provides a framework for combining the various operational facets of both completed and unfinished services, such as monitoring, management, and remediation. In addition, the article gives a thorough summary of the IT operations industry and the services provided by IT departments. This entails Asset and Configuration Management, Problem Management, Knowledge Management, Collaboration, and Runbook Automation, in addition to Service Monitoring (Event Management), Cloud Incident Management, Cloud Change Management (Change Control), and more.

CSM Processes

Apart from the typical service management processes, some processes are required for CSM to run optimally. We will look into those here:

Policy Management

Policy Management is the management of guidelines for organisations to operate their cloud services. They are usually implemented to preserve company-owned information's integrity and privacy. Policy Management consists of the following components:

- Regulatory Policy
- Security Policy
- Compliance Policy
- Organisational Standard Policy
- Pricing and costing policy

Policy Management activates the Cloud Service Portfolio Management process. The first stage in establishing the practice of Cloud Portfolio Management is creating and maintaining a portfolio of cloud service portfolios.

Cloud Service Portfolio Management (CPM)

Organisations may benefit from the plethora of cloud technologies, which is the goal of Cloud Portfolio Management (CPM). Adopting the cloud involves several strategies, one of which is a formal framework for Cloud Portfolio Management. Cloud portfolio management provides a way through which an organisation may regulate and govern existing services, new services, and the cloud providers and their connection with them. CPM manages portfolio services in the planning, production, and retirement stages. It is fed numbers from IT cost models, and IT cost budgeting, IT benchmarking, and IT pricing models. This also guarantees the Conceptual Service Blueprint is developed with high-level business process specifics and touchpoints as its result.

Cloud Availability Management

Cloud Providers utilise numerous technologies such as auto-scaling and bursting, redundancy, failover, disaster recovery, data replication, and multiple datacentres to ensure system availability. The technologies used in a modern datacentre and cloud facilitate failing-overactive servers, VMs, and applications to secondary systems to accommodate maintenance and upgrades. The expectation is that a cloud provider should never intentionally or accidentally have all systems offline and unavailable to its customers. Inclusion of availability statistics should be included in the cloud management portal for customer visibility.[33]

Cloud Capacity Management

Constant monitoring of the cloud computing servers and storage systems is required. Because ordering and provisioning are done automatically, 24-7, it is easy for the system to run out of available physical servers or storage, thus causing a failure in future provisioning of new orders. The lead time is required to purchase, install, configure, and certify any new equipment, so monitoring and establishing alert thresholds is critical; the cloud provider needs sufficient time to add capacity. The cloud provider could purchase too much capacity that remains idle until utilised, but this costs money to procure, power, and cool, costs which are eventually passed on to customers. It is far preferable to have a reasonable amount of extra capacity but also put into place rapid replenishment plans.[34]

Consumption Management

The consumption portal is an interactive online application that helps users order, manage, monitor, and optimise consumption-based IT services for private and public clouds. It assists enterprise IT in building, deploying, and controlling access to multiple private and public clouds for effective hybrid cloud orchestration. An offer consumption portal includes:

- Self Service Support
- Crowd Sources Knowledge

- Cognitive Assistance
- User profile entitlement and
- Shopping cart

Service consumers can use this portal based on subscriptions; it provides billing details, billing frequency and status to chargeback and showback process. It is tightly connected to the Catalog Management process to enable adding, modifying and deleting any catalogue item.

Cloud Catalog Management

- The service catalogue is a fundamental part of Cloud Computing's overall design. The creation, upkeep, and dissemination of the service catalogue are all the purviews of Cloud Catalog Management. Services that can be found in the cloud catalogue:
- Include a collection of cloud services that a client can request (through the Consumption Portal).
- Provides cloud service pricing and SLAs to end customers through an online buying system. The terms and conditions for service delivery are included.
- In addition to ensuring conformity with governance and standards through default configurations and service options, it can also be used as a demand management tool, steering customers toward desired services or service configurations and away from legacy or dwindling ones.
- Has the feel and appearance of a self-service system; users can browse the cloud service catalogue and create service requests to have instances of the services they find interesting provisioned.
- Aids in the design of workable cloud-based solutions opens the door to other IT and commercial services, which in turn generates value propositions for investment in cloud architectures.
- includes qualities and attributes
- Provides access to preconfigured (and ideally priced based on a "cloud chargeback" mechanism) services that are automatically fulfilled by a cloud orchestration subsystem.

Chargeback and Showback

By revealing the actual cost of IT services to their end users, the chargeback is a common method for reining in rising IT expenditures. With pay-as-you-go pricing structures, elastic scaling of resources, and the use of shared virtualized infrastructure, the cloud fundamentally changes the economics of IT, but it may improve decision-making, match behaviour with organisational goals, and lead to more effective use of IT. When an organisation provides cloud services to its employees, the cost of such services must be covered, and chargeback is the method through which that cost is distributed back to the departments that actually use the cloud services.

In an IT showback, the value of the IT services used by the firm is calculated but not charged. Showback was developed to increase confidence in IT's value creation without actively pressuring businesses to decrease costs or outsource.

Service Monitoring (Event Management)

An event is any observable occurrence that warrants attention for the purposes of IT infrastructure management, IT service delivery, and the assessment of the potential consequences of any deviations in these areas (Source: ITIL v3). When an incident occurs, it's important to be able to identify it, figure out what it means, and take the necessary steps to fix it. When an IT service or Configuration Item fails, the Monitoring Tool will typically send out an alert, or "event" (CI).

An IT asset or infrastructure hosted in the cloud can be monitored through a process of evaluating, monitoring, and managing its operational workflow and processes. It's the process of keeping an eye on and managing a cloud platform or infrastructure, either manually or automatically. Once the Event Management system notices an outlier, one event's occurrence may cause another.

Cloud Incident Management

The lifecycle of every issue is the domain of incident management. In order to keep tabs on what's going on, tool-chains are installed in the virtual machines as part of cloud service administration. The incident management procedure and any necessary reaction activities to mitigate an incident will be triggered if these tools detect an event that meets the criteria for an incident. This is a more proactive approach.

The Incident Management Process aims to get services back to normal as soon as possible while limiting any damage to business activities. This will keep services at their highest quality and availability. Here, "normal service operation" means Service Operations within the parameters set by the Service Level Agreement.

It can initiate a request for change (RFC) whenever an event occurs, which is then processed through the organization's established change management procedures.

Cloud Change Management (Change Control)

ITIL change management refers to a set of standards and methods for managing changes in IT services. The rules allow firms to make changes without hurting the customer's experience. Within Cloud Service Management, change control needs to address automation, auto-provisioning and decommissioning of services. Cloud-based solutions that may conduct configuration modifications and track management approval procedures can be customised to approve or deny additional configuration or subscription changes. By adopting pre-approved change tasks for Cloud Computing scenarios (e.g., Autoscaling, DNS update), an organisation can minimise the wait in approval processes while keeping flexibility in the change process.

Asset Management

The need for Asset management is to track the lifecycle of an asset from request to disposal. This may include ordering, shipping, receiving, tagging, deployment, decommissioning, retirement, and disposal. Track procured, issued, and installed licenses for industry-standard software. Manage and maintain the Asset Management database (AMDB) to ensure that asset lifecycle tracking information is readily available at any given time.

Within the cloud service management process, the asset management is driven by a set of toolchains capable of managing licences of

DevOps tools, asset locations, relevant information of virtual machines for a federated CMDB and helps to manage life-cycle expectations to help you predict costs and control spending.

Configuration Management

Federated CMDB, in existing in-house CMDB expanded to collect and consolidate information on cloud resources from the Cloud Provider via standard or custom APIs. There is a requirement to Introduce automation to capture dynamic changes in the cloud environment for CMDB to reflect current architecture via toolchains.

Problem Management

Problem management is an area of ITSM aimed at resolving incidents and problems caused by end-user errors or IT infrastructure issues and preventing the recurrence of such events. Within the Cloud Service Management process, problem management, it just adds an extra analytics step that will help with preventive actions.

Knowledge Management and Collaboration

The Knowledge Management process aims to improve the warranty (fit for use), and utility (fit for purpose) of IT services by enabling everyone in the service delivery chain, including end-users, to use standardised, correct, and authorised solutions and methods to solve their problems. Knowledge Management ensures that accurate and relevant information is made available to users promptly to enable informed decision-making and reduce the risks of wrong actions.

Knowledge collaboration within Cloud Service Management is a necessary process which is to ensure knowledge across different teams, and cloud service providers are shared proactively via a centralised knowledge management system.

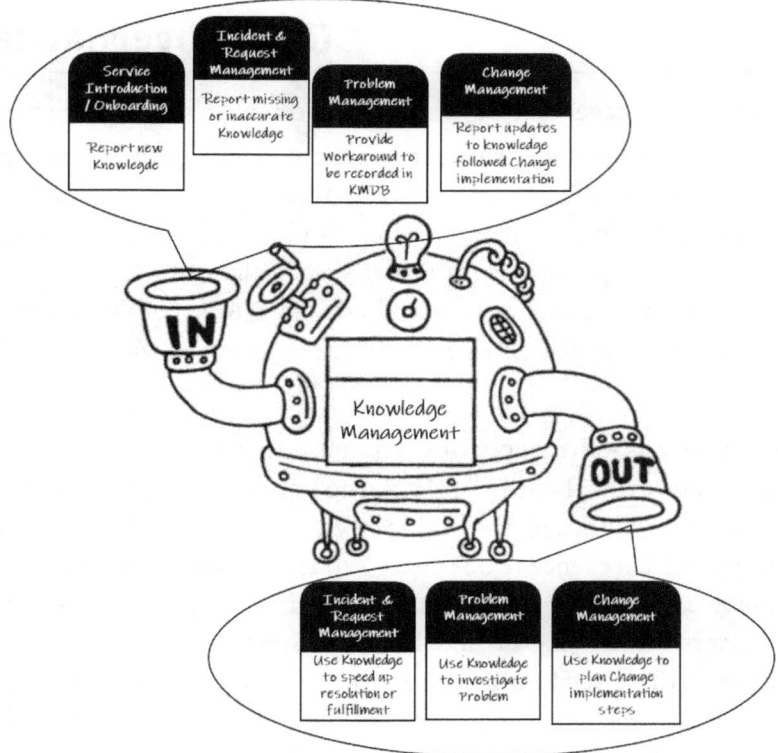

Figure 59 - Knowledge Management inputs and Outputs

Waste Management

Waste management is part of cloud cost management; it is around managing stale resources and optimising the usage of resources. Foundational functionality can be found in native products such as Trusted Advisor for AWS. Trusted Advisor inspects your AWS environment and recommends saving money, improving system performance, or closing security gaps.

CSM Governance

Cloud Service Management Governance will establish and enforce how the organisational cloud service management will work, both from a day-to-day cloud service delivery perspective and for new business initiatives (projects and programmes) that wish to host new functions on the platform. Additionally, governance provides the mechanisms that enforce how the public and private cloud suppliers and DevOps toolchains will work to deliver a unified service ensuring the cloud services are run seamlessly.

Executive Boards – Strategic Governance

Executive Review Board should be the governance layer involving the CIO of the organisation, the business relationship managers and the Cloud Centre of Excellence (CCoE) teams to enable review of the overall Cloud Service Delivery and Performance, inclusive of all the Cloud Service providers, underlying IT and Business Services. This review will focus more on the agreed Business Service Levels (BSLs), rather than the vendor SLAs. The role of this review board will be to provide the management and overall visibility into the CSM performance and enable them to make informed decisions regarding Strategy, future roadmap, investments, etc. This will also act as a forum to capture the demand from businesses along with the plans on expansion, change in strategic directions/ business drivers or expansions.

This review may include some statistics/ scorecards on suppliers, but the key objective will only be to present the overall performance of the IT organisation in the context of the services being delivered.

End-to-End Governance Review Board (Tactical Governance)

End to End governance will handle operational level escalations, and it will review End to End Service levels and Key performance indicators. Discuss Service Target breaches and assign actions owners for Service Performance Improvement. Discuss Service Improvement plans.

Operations Review Board

The Operational Review Board should be the meeting place between the CSM Process Managers, Vendor's Operations Managers/ Delivery Executives, and the Point of contact (POC) from the Technology Towers. These reviews will ensure fast and smooth resolution of daily operational issues regarding cloud service and collaboration between teams for collective service delivery responsibility. The expectation will be to discuss challenges/ issues between groups, or between individual resources during day-to-day operations, handshake and hand-off procedure and any related problem, regular technical team reviews, critical/ high priority incidents (if any), resolution methodology, lessons learnt, upcoming changes, etc. The Process Manager will drive and coordinate these meetings, and the CSM Team will facilitate the reports to be discussed/ presented in this forum. These are expected to be high in frequency, some occurring more than once daily.

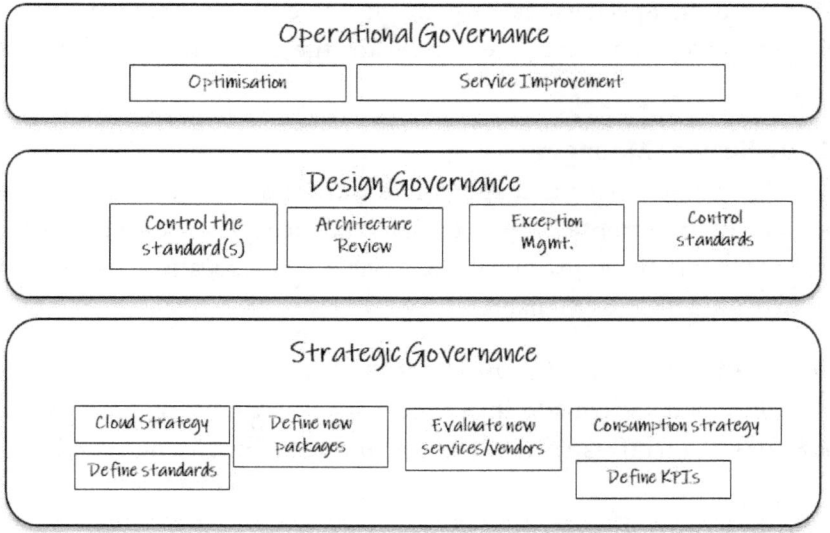

Figure 60 - Cloud Service Governance

CSM Roles

Many new roles have emerged because of digital transformation and cloud adoption in different organisations. We looked into this in the CCoE chapter as well. Here are some recommended roles as proposed to start organising your cloud team:

Cloud Service Architect

This role is fundamental in determining how a private cloud supports the goals established for the investment. This is a professional responsible for overseeing organisational Cloud Computing strategy.

Cloud Orchestration Specialist

Cloud orchestration is typically used to provision, deploy, or start servers; acquire and assign storage capacity; manage networking; create VMs, and gain access to specific software on cloud services. The Cloud Orchestration Specialist is responsible for defining and maintaining high-level workflows that are needed for the automation of cloud services.

Cloud Service Manager

The cloud service manager will ensure the cloud service management is "fit for purpose". It will look after service levels, policies and rules associated with each private cloud service. Some organisations will call this a "Cloud Success Manager".

Cloud Infrastructure Administrator

The cloud system administrator will provide daily operational support for several infrastructure components that form a cloud service.

Modern Service Management (MSM)

Modern Service Management is an approach that Microsoft has adopted to make ITSM relevant in the cloud world. Cloud Services Foundation Reference Model (CSFRM)[35], published in 2013 by Microsoft, forms the foundation of the framework for managing Private and Hybrid cloud scenarios.

Modern Service Management (MSM) for the cloud modifies existing CSFRM processes and capabilities and introduces new processes and capabilities. According to Microsoft, these changes are required for IT organisations to evolve their service management practices (people, process, technology) for today's rapidly changing mobile-first, cloud-first businesses. I have decided to publish here a few critical cloud service management processes with their comparisons between the traditional and modern ways of working from the Microsoft website.

Process Name: Capacity Management	
Traditional way	*Modern way*
Traditionally characterised by what the current IT infrastructure is capable of scaling to support the business demand, which requires forecasting for short/long term with manual activities to support the process.	Focused on business demand forecasting and utilising the elasticity of cloud resources to grow and shrink to meet the business demand, this is incurred with charges as demand increases. Proactively monitoring current resources in the cloud to help make sure that allocated cloud resources are right-sized to control costs.
Process Name: Change Management	

Traditional way	Modern way
Substantial changes are managed and approved through a Change Management process with Change Advisory Boards, managing the risk of change to the production environment. Change Management processes are often skipped and unenforced due to bureaucracy that results from poorly implemented change management	Smaller changes driven by Release Pipeline, where change schedules are known, mitigation and risk controls (e.g. no standing rights in the target environment, automated deployments, automate the mandatory testing, mandatory approvals) are engineered into the change operations, and support is provided by the same team involved in engineering the change.

Process Name: Incident Management

Traditional way	Modern way
The traditional approach to Incident Management is to handle incidents as tickets. The user feels the impact and takes action to contact support. Depending on the issue, the appropriate level of help desk agent engages the end-user to work the problem. Some customers move towards a Tier 0 approach to help desk where end-users can run automation for common issues.	Focused on business demand forecasting and utilising the elasticity of cloud resources to grow and shrink to meet the business demand, this is incurred with charges as demand increases. Proactively monitoring current resources in the cloud to help make sure that allocated cloud resources are right-sized to control costs.

Process Name: Problem Management

Traditional way	Modern way
Problem Management is often either not implemented or implemented as an additional support tier and is often under-staffed and under-appreciated for its value in removing defects. When applied, Problem Management most often focuses on incidents and may not incorporate application development teams or events from monitoring.	Modern Problem Management takes a collaborative approach involving multiple teams responsible for operations, infrastructure, applications and the business. These teams work together to identify primary issues from a service, collect and measure data to drive relevance and analysis and propose team-recommended changes to improve overall service applicability and quality. This is an untapped area where Machine Learning and predictive analytics can augment and automate this process.

Process Name: Service Level Management	
Traditional way	Modern way
The service provider and service consumer determine the conditions and service levels while creating a contract for an IT service. These service levels are in line with the service consumer's requirements and represent the essence of the	SLA's become XLA's (experience level agreements) aligned to what business users' value (the experience), traditional SLA metrics clarify/underpin the business user knowledge of the delivered service.

service in concrete metrics. Financial penalties can back the agreed parameters if the service provider fails to deliver. Once the service is provided, the service provider will monitor and report these metrics to the service consumer as part of the overall service.	

Table 4 - Modern Service Management Processes

The hybrid cloud environment disrupts IT with undefined roles, responsibilities, and activities. IT teams are challenged to adopt and realise rapid value from the cloud. Organisations must move to modern service management practices, including Agile and DevOps, and accelerate digital transformation. Microsoft Modern Service Management takes a value-based approach to service management that helps organisations maximise their Microsoft Cloud investment.

Microsoft Modern Service Management is not a new framework, a set of books, or intellectual property. It's an evolved perspective that can be stated as: "A lens, intended to focus ITSM experts around the globe on the most important outcomes that evolve our customers from earlier, traditional IT models, toward easier, more efficient, cost-effective, and agile service structures."

- Modern Service Management for Azure
Published: 21/12/2016

Cognitive Service Management

Cognitive Service Management is next-generation service management enabled by digital automation, AI, and machine learning that drives new levels of agility, productivity, and efficiency.[36] The speed that comes with cloud adoption is very aggressive, which means that operation sees more complexity and changes come out more quickly than ever before. Organisations need cognitive solutions to automatically recognise the kind of thing that will help them improve their environment so that they can help run their system effectively, efficiently, and reliably. Today organisations need agile solutions, and things are changing fast, not just because applications are rolling out quickly but because the underline infrastructure is much more dynamic, and changes are coming unexpectedly.

One of the things that organisations want is that they want solutions; they want capabilities that anticipate emerging issues. They want IT systems to become more proactive, so when you become cognitive, you can become more dynamic instead of constantly reacting to problems that have occurred. So, when you are cognitive, you can have flashing lights, you are wise, and you are anticipating your early warnings, so you can work on problems before they become threatening.

Cognitive tools learn from your monitoring data how your environment is supposed to behave, efficient management where there is a lack of resources, and to do more with less. Their capabilities, like virtual agents/chatbots, can assist IT and businesses 24/7 to complete tasks faster and improve productivity. This enhances service delivery experiences. Also automates repetitive and rule-based task with cognitive automation without human intervention and drive value and cost savings for the business.

It differs from traditional service management because it is more reactive, and Cognitive Service Management is somewhat proactive. Like, in the conventional method, if you need to raise an incident, diagnose it and resolve it. You need to raise a service request, approve and fulfil it. You need to create a problem ticket and identify the root cause. With machine learning, extreme automation, self-healing, and continuous delivery, these are now done proactively and even without human intervention.

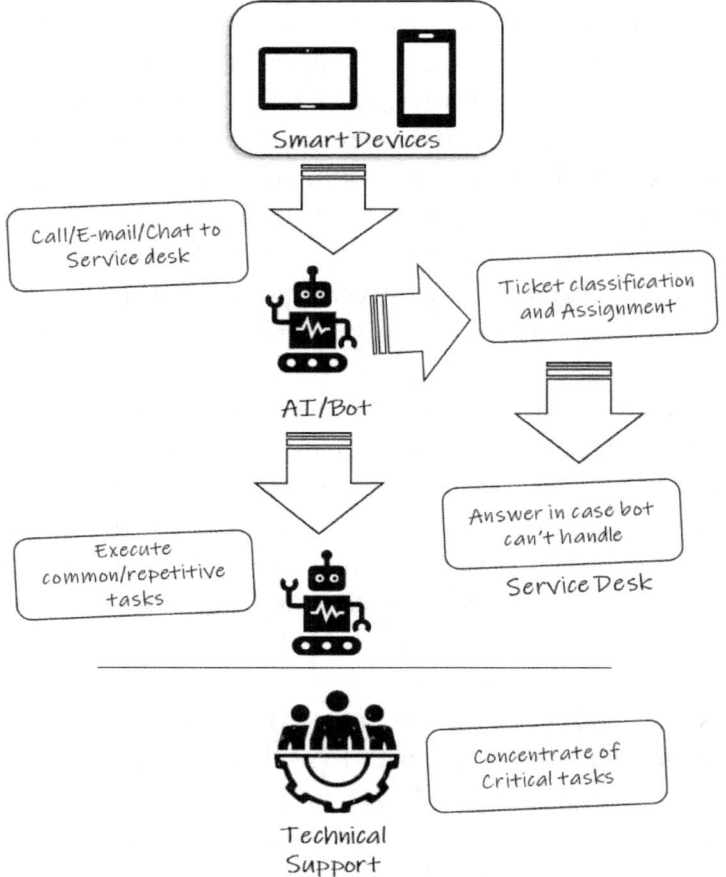

Figure 61 - Transforming Enterprise Service Management with Cognitive Technologies

With the move to the cloud, when you purchase a SaaS, you no longer care about the supplier's infrastructure, and only track the services so move to a Service Composition database (SCDB). For change management, as an example, if you need to add a node to a cluster or shift from one host to another, in the ITIL framework, you need to raise an RFC and get it approved before implementation; this now happens dynamically when using virtualisation technologies like VMware. Conversely, CMDB, in a typical enterprise, would be expected to capture all the infrastructure and application components, and they are related to each other.

Cognitive Service Management has extended service management beyond managing and supporting the technology that has traditionally been the domain of the IT organisation. This has transformed how service management is done, resulting in new ways and new models for service management, and like digital transformation for the business, however, traditional service management and cognitive service management are going to coexist for a long time still.

Advantages of Cognitive Service Management:

- It uses Natural Language Processing (NLP) to identify questions and to provide answers, and it is supported by analytics to improve self-help or system auto-healing.
- It uses advanced Natural Language Processing (NLP) algorithms and recognises the intent of a user and answers based on the context using reasoning, and can handle a conversation with the user
- Machine Learning methods are used to improve quality and precision.
- It enables integration and orchestration of actions of various API integration types and links with sensors, the Internet of Things (IoT), etc.

Every organisation must have a different level of ITSM maturity, from a basic help desk to service management powered by intelligent automation. Organisations mostly fall into three main buckets on their journey to digital transformation:

1. Normal Helpdesk or Service Desk
2. Service desk with multi-cloud and multi-channel digital enterprise (Digital Service Management — DSM)

3. Service desk automation with latest Cognitive technologies like Artificial intelligence, Machine learning and chatbots (Cognitive Service Management)

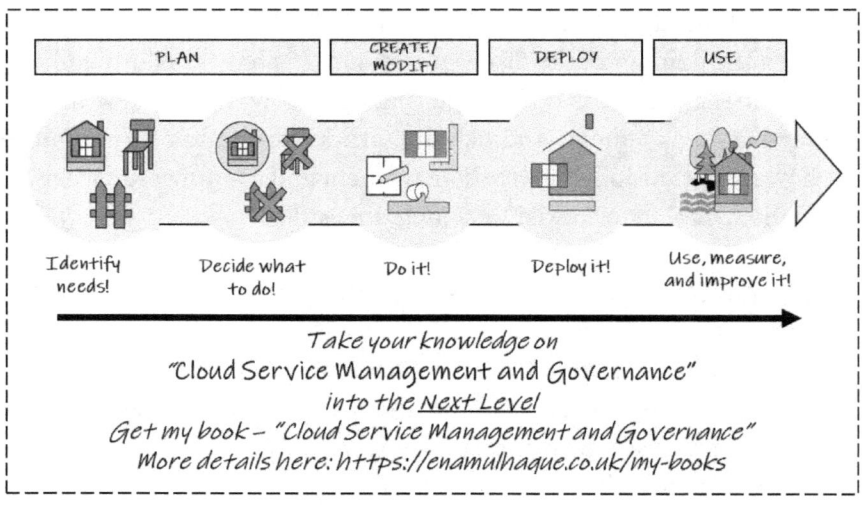

Cognitive Service Management in Digital Workplace

Using Cognitive technology effectively in your organisation increases customer and employee productivity, and we previously saw how digital transformation could empower employees. CIOs and business leaders can decide to adopt digital technologies like Cognitive Service Management and create engaging employee experiences and increase employee retention. Their time can be utilised more productively. Enabling cognitive capabilities in the existing environment revolutionises people-centric future experiences. This is, at present, known as the "Digital Workplace".

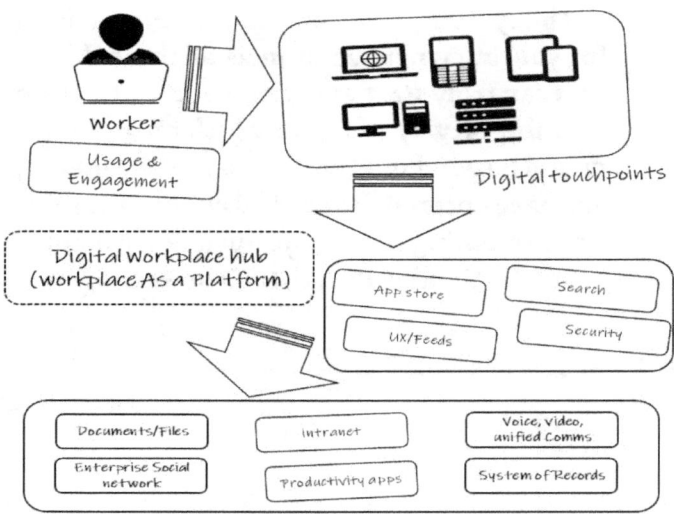

Figure 62 - Digital Workplace hub

Digital Workplace is the use of cognitive computing, analytics, and automation to build employee engagement and collaboration. Their capabilities, such as speech recognition, Natural Language Processing (NLP), analytics and the other advantages mentioned before, can be mixed in different combinations to create a cognitive solution to engage and improve collaboration. Gathering insights can help optimise operations, improve customer satisfaction and reduce complaints, and enhance employee productivity and operational efficiency.

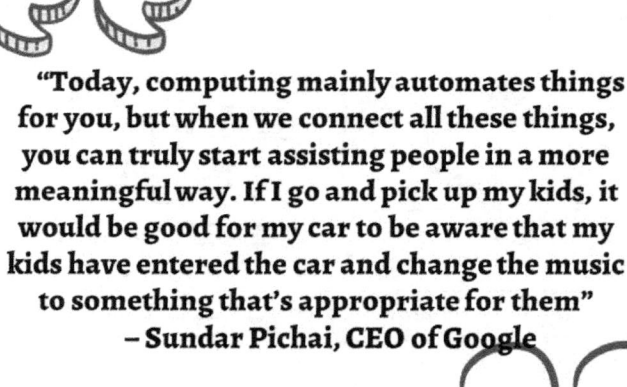

"Today, computing mainly automates things for you, but when we connect all these things, you can truly start assisting people in a more meaningful way. If I go and pick up my kids, it would be good for my car to be aware that my kids have entered the car and change the music to something that's appropriate for them"
– Sundar Pichai, CEO of Google

Digital Service Management (DSM)

The term Digital Service Management (DSM) has become a buzzword recently, and it arose in alignment with the latest trends like cloud technologies, IoT, BYOD, DevOps, digital workplace, etc. Digital Service Management is based on a straightforward platform with two orthogonal dimensions. The vertical dimension and the horizontal one. The verticals will include the customer-facing products, owning the end-to-end value chain and lifecycle, and the horizontal size will have conventional capabilities, processes, architecture, tooling, standards, policies etc.

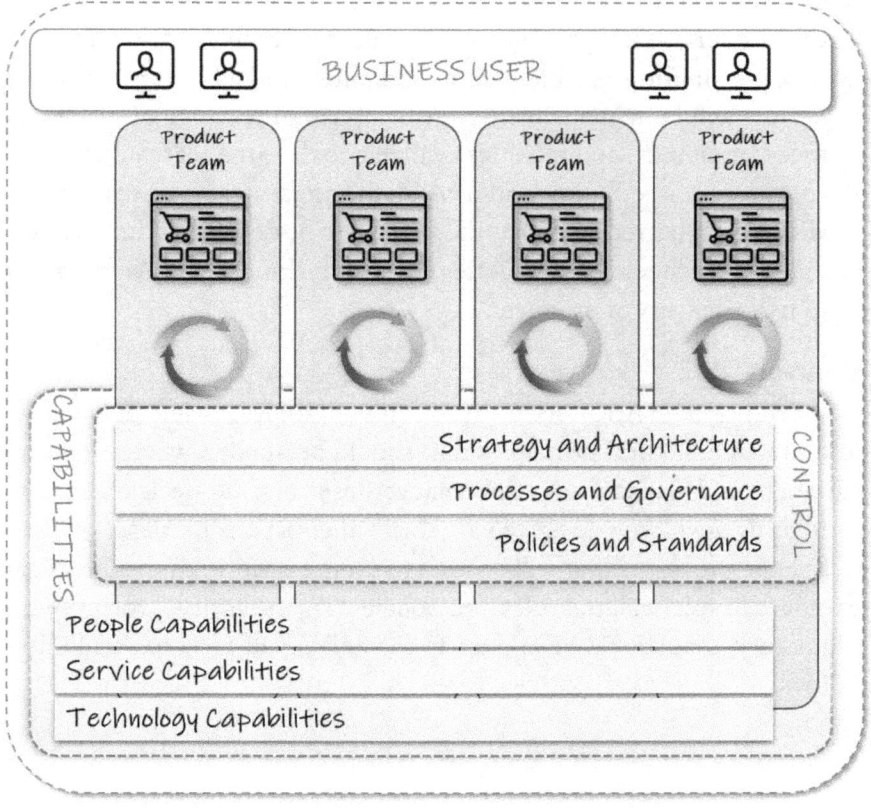

Figure 63 - Digital Service Management Framework

Product Teams

Product ownership is adopted across all customer-facing services, not just the digital areas. They will be customer focussed, prioritising delivery to the needs of the business. A great community with a high culture to deliver changes frequently and iteratively. Feel motivated and enthusiastic, with a real passion for achieving success and a sense of owning the end-to-end solution from within the team

Capabilities

People capabilities to provide the professional resource pools and governance for the aspects of delivery (Programme and Project Management, Application Development CoE etc.) and Service Capabilities to enable the service integration and management required to operate and control distribution reliably. These capabilities should be created for reuse. They will be responsible for ensuring that the range of processes, services, resources, and facilities available to the product team are all fit for purpose, cost-effective and have all the attributes, features, and accreditations required such that they can be to be deployed painlessly and seamlessly. Technology capabilities form the technical platforms that underpin the delivery of products.

Controls

Strategy and Architecture set out the high-level vision and strategy and the architectural principles that should be applied when delivering Products and Capabilities. Governance describes the decision-making structures, including delegated authority and responsibilities. Processes define the processes that will be used to progress work. And policies and standards explain all the rules and policies (e.g., security, procurement, regulatory) that should be applied to the delivery of products and Capabilities.

Cloud SIAM
(Service Integration and Management)

Service Integration and Management (SIAM), also known as MSI (Multi-Supplier Integrations) – is an approach to managing multiple suppliers of information technology services and integrating them to provide a single business-facing IT organisation. SIAM brings together separately contracted and supplied IT services to ensure they consistently work together to deliver business benefits. Emerging cloud models demand a new approach to complement SIAM's traditional ITIL-based method that supports new-age services such as cloud and converged infrastructure, DevOps and Agile.

With the new ways of working, organisations already running SIAM would require changing their operational framework. Working across a wide range of the cloud service supply chain is needed to drive flexibility, efficiency, and service quality. New roles in cloud brokerage, cloud service providers, and managed cloud services providers would need to be adjusted in the governance model. A new IT Operating Model is required to span the end-to-end chain of services, providing a consistent process and performance measurement to create accountability across the supply chain and establish strong and unified governance with a strict security framework.

SIAM transition and transformation planning for cloud service management should include integration within the new or existing SIAM operating model. Aggregating cloud services providers into a tower structure, using workflows within a service management platform. The service management platform will require modernisation to accommodate cloud providers, and integrations will need cloud management platforms and related toolchains. Existing KPIs and performance management frameworks will require to be re-looked.

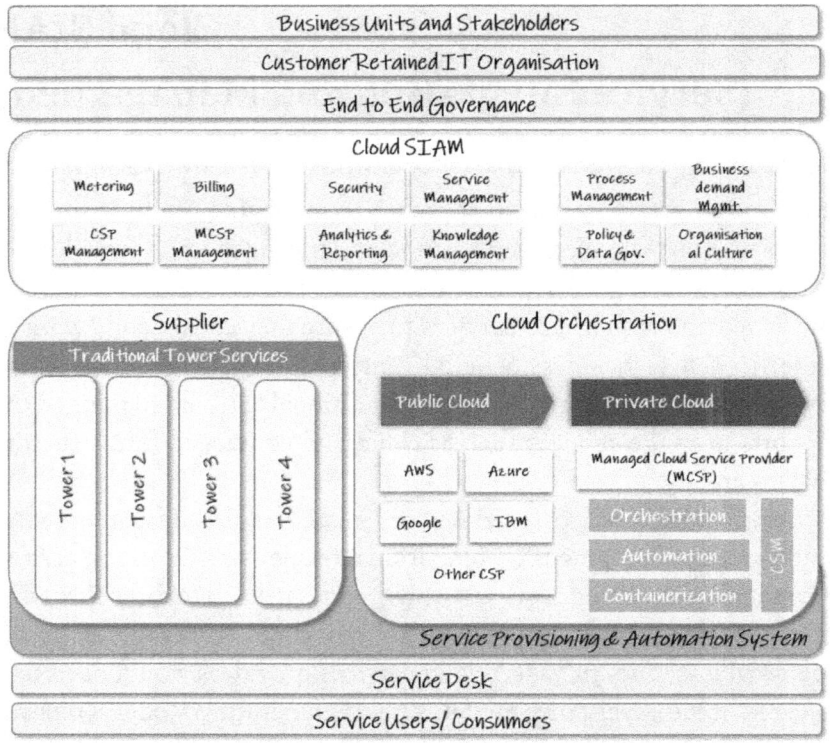

Figure 64 - A Cloud SIAM Functional Model

The cloud SIAM governance will require the addition of cloud-specific governance streams, and this could include:

Policy Governance

This will consist of tasks such as defining catalogue access policy, setting usage limits, data residency guidelines and approval process. Cloud hosting plans based on guiding principles and data classification, and alignment of cloud security, compliance policies with IT security and compliance guidelines.

Cloud Financial Governance

Governance of account and subscription strategy, tagging, billing strategy, as well as chargeback and show-back approach.

Cloud Incident and Problem Management Governance

Aligning with the cloud service provider's incident management process to ensure accountability and manage all incidents' lifecycles across the boundaries.

Subscription, Usage and Chargeback Governance

Track the actual usage of subscribed IT services. Automated Process and break down usage information for each cloud subscription, its consumers, and providers. Collect internally and externally sourced cloud service usage metrics etc.

Facts about SIAM:[37]

- *Organisations have been using services delivered by multiple service providers for many years. They have recognised the need for service integration across service providers and used different approaches to try and achieve end-to-end service management.*
- *In most cases, these service providers also delivered significant systems integration capabilities, but with no clear separation from service integration. These organisations were typically called Systems Integrators (SI) or IT Outsource (ITO) providers.*
- *The UK public sector, which also gave birth to other best practice methodologies like ITIL, is credited with creating the name "Service Integration and Management," or SIAM, and the concept of SIAM as a management approach in around 2005.*
- *This approach was originally conceived for the United Kingdom's Department of Work and Pensions to improve the efficiency and effectiveness of the department's procurement of services from a variety of service providers and, more specifically, of decoupling service integration capabilities from systems integration and IT service provision. There was less work done twice by different service providers.*
- *In 2010, the UK Government published a new Information and Communications Technology (ICT) strategy. This included moving away from large prime supplier contracts to a more flexible approach using multiple service providers and cloud-based solutions.*

Cloud Governance Framework

When talking about the creation and upkeep of a Cloud Computing capacity, the design, architecture, acquisition, deployment, operation, and management of which are all referred to as "Cloud Governance," the Cloud COE team is responsible. It provides a standard set of guidelines as related to the cloud paradigm across all the pertinent Business and IT areas in the extended company.

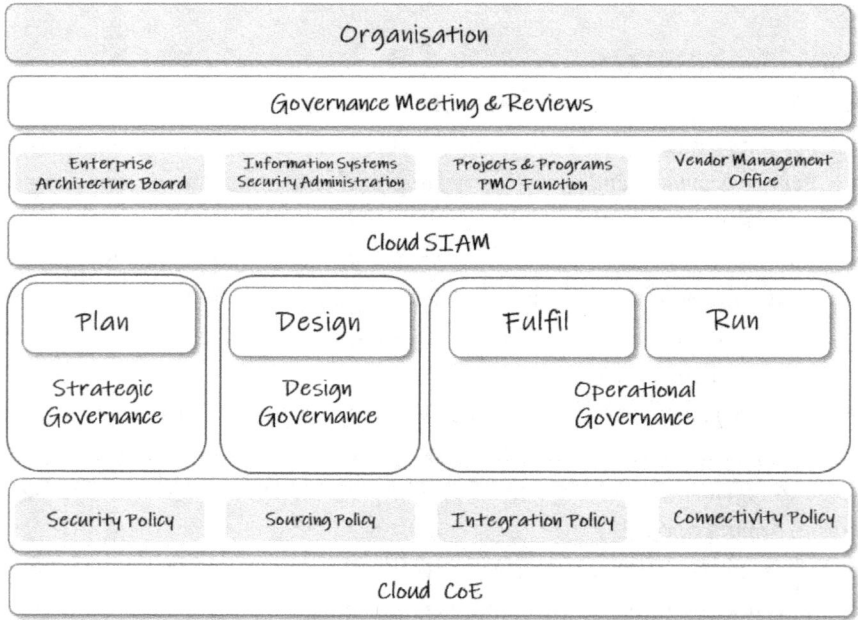

Figure 65 - Cloud Governance Framework

Governance and Review Boards

Cloud governance is divided into three different review boards moderated by the Cloud Centre of Excellence (CCoE).

Strategic Cloud Governance – Plan

Strategic Governance provides input on how best to align cloud services with the needs within the organisation, and it should provide policy definitions and guidelines. It covers the following key areas:

- Cloud Strategy
- Portfolio / Catalogue Management
- Policy Management
- Contract Management
- Demand Management
- Financial Management

Cloud Design Governance – Design

Design Governance focuses on transforming business requirements into a logical service model to convert to a wholly realised service model. It takes care of:

- Requirement Management
- Design and Risk Management
- Testing and Validation Plan
- Release Management Plan

Cloud Operational Governance – Fulfilment and Run

Operational governance includes fulfilment and run, and this is the service consumption and assurance of warranty of a realised service model.

Fulfilment

- Design handover to build teams
- Fulfilment of the request
- Deployment Testing
- Release Management
- Handover to Operations

Run

- Event Management
- Incident / Problem Management
- Cloud optimisation and Capacity Planning
- Change Control
- Configuration Management
- Subscription usage and Chargeback

Cloud Policy Framework

There are a few fundamental areas to be considered for cloud implementation, and one of them is cloud policy management. We talked about this process in the CSM chapter. We will try to elaborate on this more in this section. A cloud risk assessment must be completed for all projects that may use one or more Cloud Computing services. Hosting cloud solutions that will store personally identifiable data in a public cloud facility must be in line with GDPR and other countries/region-specific policies. If data stored with a cloud service provider is to be encrypted, this should be done using cryptographic keys owned and managed by the relevant security groups of the organisation. A detailed CSIA (Cyber Security Impact Assessment) is also recommended. Integrating the vendor's cloud solution with other services/data sets/solutions should follow approved/endorsed interoperability standards. The policy framework must be defined for:

- Authentication and Access Control Policies
- Cloud Assets and Data Classification Policies
- Metrics and Logs Polices
- Encryption and key management Policies
- Logical segmentation Policies
- Cost optimisation Policies
- Network Security Cloud Policies
- Proactive Automation Policies for Operations

Data Governance

To support business outcomes, organisations need to plan how they use data so that it's handled consistently throughout the business. The Data Governance Institute (DGI) describes it as a "realistic and actionable approach" that can be used by businesses of any size to understand better and address the information demands of their various data stakeholders.

A company's success is increasingly dependent on its data, which is becoming its most valuable asset. Organizations can only make use of their data assets and successfully undergo a digital transformation if they have a solid handle on data governance. As a result, it is crucial to implement a data governance framework that works for the company and its long-term goals and strategies. For this journey to be successful, your organisation needs a framework to govern the data standards that will be used and to assign appropriate duties both internally and externally, in the context of the broader business ecosystem.

Different data protection standards could also impact an organisation in terms of how they use data from external sources such as the internet or data obtained from 3rd parties. Suppose the data privacy terms and conditions are not respected. In that case, it can breach data protection law, be subject to severe consequences such as penalties, and influence its reputation and brand value.

Rigorous data governance considerations should be included in all contracts with cloud service providers. Things to include:

- A Non-Disclosure Agreement (recommended before provisioning any service)
- Data ownership – organisations should retain exclusive ownership of all data held in a cloud provider's solution, entered by their staff, systems, or affiliates in all media forms, e.g., online, backup and archive, etc.
- Any other standard intellectual property clauses (as are relevant to the service)
- Data location (the countries where the data can be held should be explicitly stated in contracts – this should be based on the

outcome of the cloud risk assessment and any associated privacy impact assessment)

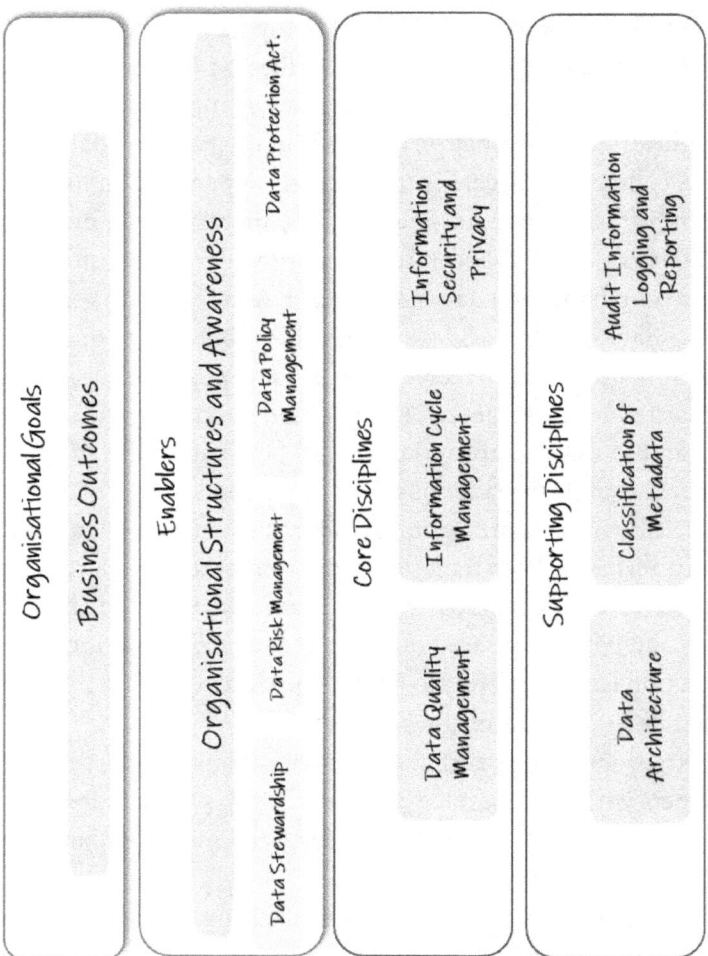

Figure 66 - Data Governance Framework

- Privacy legislation compliance
- The application of appropriate retention policies to stored data based on its classification means the cloud service provider's solution must not hinder following any records act such as GDPR.

- A transparent process is documenting the responsibilities of each party concerning extracting and destroying data at the end of the contract, as we discussed on MCSPs offboarding part.
- Provision for a cloud service provider being taken over/bought out by another organisation. This should include ensuring the ownership, access rights and protection of any data the organisation owns cannot be lost when cloud service provider ownership changes.

There are several data protection acts, and a few important ones are mentioned below:

Data Protection Act 1884 and 1998

The Data Protection Act 1998 controlled the use and protection of personal data and specified the duties a corporation had to protect that data. It supplanted the Data Protection Act 1984 and the Access to Personal Files Act 1987. This law controls how personal data can be maintained and utilised.

Freedom of Information Act 2000

The freedom of information Act 2000 gives the general public the right to request data that public services keep on them. This could be government, school, college or university that keeps data of individuals.

Computer Misuse Act 1990

The Computer Misuse Act 1990 is a law that makes certain activities illegal, such as hacking into other people's systems, misusing software, or helping a person to gain access to protected files of someone else's computer. The Act is relevant to electronic records because it creates three offences of unlawfully gaining access to computer programmes.

GDPR

GDPR stands for General Data Protection Regulation. The General Data Protection Regulation (EU) 2016/679 (GDPR) is a regulation in EU law on data protection and privacy for all individual citizens of the European Union (EU) and the European Economic Area (EEA). It also addresses the transfer of personal data outside the EU and EEA areas.

Cloud Data Management Essentials

To meritoriously manage your data without shuttering it and blocking legitimate requests for access, you need a reliable cloud data management strategy that begins with five important considerations.[38]

Inactive Data

As data sits in its storage, it's often behind firewalls and other layers of security, which it should be, but it's also vital to ensure that your data is encrypted. It should always be encrypted, even when you think it's safely tucked up in your vault.

Accessing Data

It's imperative that your employees can access the data they need to do their jobs whenever and wherever they want, but access must also be controlled. Start by analysing which people lack access to what data and create tailored access rights and controls that restrict unnecessary access. Any person requesting access to data must be authenticated, and every data transaction should be recorded so you can audit later if necessary. Active Directory is the most common place to manage and control such access today

Data in Transit

It's crucial to create a secure, authenticated and encrypted tunnel between the authenticated user and device and the data they're requesting. You want to make the data transfer as swift and painless as possible for the end-user without compromising security. Ensure data remains encrypted in transit so no interceptor can read it.

Arriving Data

When the data comes at its destination, you want to be confident that it is authentic and hasn't been tampered with. Can you prove data integrity? Do you have a clear audit trail? This is key to effectively managing data and reducing the risk of any breach or infection. Phishing attacks often show up in the inbox as accurate data to fool people into clicking somewhere they shouldn't and downloading malware that bypasses your carefully constructed defences.

Defensible Backup and Recovery

Even with the first four pillars solidly implemented, things can and do go sideways from time to time when least expected. Most companies recognise the importance of proper backup hygiene today and have implemented backup and recovery processes. Be sure to test and validate your ability to restore the backups and recover periodically.

In the cloud, there's another critical area to consider carefully: to ensure that you do not put all your data eggs in one basket. Do not store your backups in the same cloud account where your production data resides. That's a formula for disaster you may not recover from should a hacker somehow gain access to your network and delete everything.

That is, leverage multiple cloud accounts to segregate your backup data from your production data. Be sure to back up your cloud infrastructure configuration information as well in case you ever need to rebuild it for any reason.

DevOps

Probably an entire book could be written on this topic as it deserves to be. In this book, until this chapter, I have talked about DevOps at least 34 times. I described cloud-native technologies managing elastic infrastructure through agile DevOps processes and continuous delivery workflows. In implementing the digital transformation strategy, we saw how innovation could be galvanised with predictive analytics and DevOps adoption. How can a more straightforward and faster development cloud be achieved with DevOps by doing Continuous Delivery and Continuous Integrations (CD/CI). We have also discussed in detail in the cloud toolchain section different kinds of DevOps toolsets. The Managed Cloud Service Providers are proving DevOps to deliver new features quickly through automation and enable a DevOps and Agile approach to provide services in the cloud. They are helping in automating repetitive processes with full DevOps adoption. With the cloud target operating model, we also discussed the definition of DevOps. We also looked into ITSM processes and how they interact with DevOps entities in cloud service management.

So, organisations need to move swiftly and respond to consumer demands to stay competitive in today's business environment. DevOps approach breaks down silos to enable collaboration that delivers applications faster, with higher quality and reduced cost and risk; hence it is a culture that needs to be ingrained in the organisational DNA. It's not a one-time change but a change that will need to be adopted from the highest level of the CEO to the most basic workforce member.

According to Gene Kim[39] - "DevOps and its resulting technical, architectural, and cultural practices represent a convergence of many philosophical and management movements (including): Lean, Theory of Constraints, Toyota production system, resilience engineering, learning organisations, safety culture, Human factors, high-trust management cultures, servant leadership, organisational change management, and Agile methods."

In this chapter on DevOps, my principal focus is on streamlining cloud service management and governance. Most of the upcoming innovations will take 1-3 years to become a part of the mainstream, but if one can start building capabilities in the same direction, such companies can be fully prepared when needed, while others would be lagging. The preparedness can be in terms of exhaustive knowledge about DevOps implementation and resources skilled to use technologies, tools and techniques facilitating DevOps and a database of challenges with their solutions.

Cloud is not about disassociation of capital, getting rid of operational activities or moving things to Ether Sphere or somewhere and making things disappear; it's about a new operational model that allows us to be more agile, allowing us to be closer to our customers, closers to the challenges that they face, so the cloud operational model is everywhere, doesn't matter if you are running public cloud, doesn't matter if you are starting to deploy private cloud inside of your organisation, doesn't matter if you are to maintain legacy applications inside of the traditional data centre driven organisation, everyone is trying to adopt cloud operational model that allows them to be more agile and move faster to meet the needs of their customers to support the digital transformation.

Cloud enables digital transformation. To transform, organisations are employing application modernisation, hybrid and DevOps. Its supporting agility at scale requires managing increasing data growth, complexity and a dynamic environment. Organisations need things faster, how fast they can get them. When we talk about DevOps, we talk about changing the operations model. It's all about meeting your end-user expectation and competing with more competitive applications rapidly developed. To get there, we find that application development needs to shift right, into more production stands and think about ways to iterate through application development happening faster. Operations, the traditional infrastructure, and operations centralised team, which remain relevant, to shift left and work more closely with the development team in their experience.

You began your DevOps journey, the day the infrastructure operations team will stop saying, oh no, you can't deploy the application until you show me everything is perfect and starts asking how I can help you to use your application faster so that we can complete better in the business environment that we are facing, so to join the forces cross operations and applications, hence the development, DevOps, that allows us, to meet forward towards delivering our solutions faster.

Moving from the traditional to the agile model will help to be more responsive to the customer. The whole transformation is about customer responsiveness, about being able to move quickly to meet customer needs. Getting rid of capital are a side effect of adoption but not a huge gain. Agile is less centralised and helps to move faster. Make sure we are running more modular processes linked together at the end of the day.

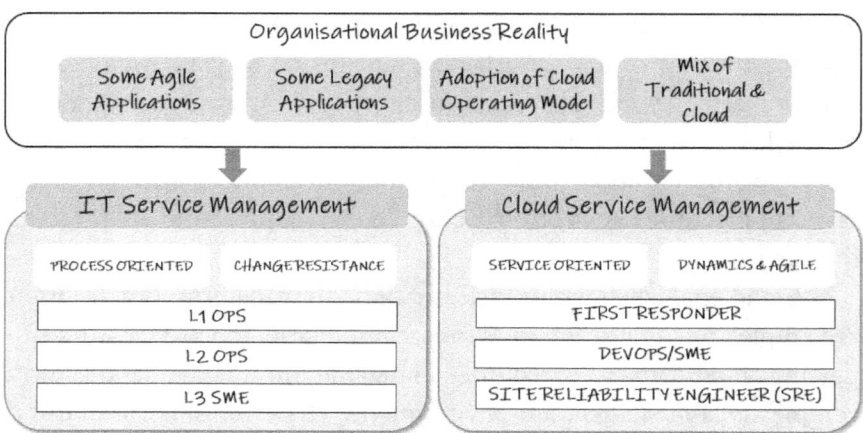

Figure 67 - DevOps adoption

People, Processes and tools – the three interrelated things I mentioned a few times before, would allow you to move forward. But here I want to talk about process, tools and culture. Culture has replaced people because culture and how people interact drive what people can do. So, in the DevOps world, the tools are moving forward tremendously. The introduction of tools from machine learning, introducing experience based on analytics, introducing better topological functions, and more effective identification tools, they are all great, but they are all incremental unless you adjust the process, culture, and embrace the changes. You can't do that until you know how the tools and processes can be involved and how culture drives it. If there are no cultural challenges, you haven't' taken DevOps seriously. That is very true in every customer I saw; they all have different things going on, and accommodating those is the challenge of operations today.

With the traditional service model – which can be managed with ITIL processes, the CAB, reviewing problems, doing RCAs, and change management processes are all designed to move slowly. That's very good and necessary to ensure BAU does not impact changes. So that model can stay there. ITIL also has different layers of operations, e.g., L1 (simple things), L2 (advanced support), and L3 SMEs to get the red light turned off etc.

In cloud service management, there is still the need to identify incidents, problems, changes, etc., but you approach them in a slightly different way with DevOps. What we see evolving is the idea of the first responder, and the first responder is less like a level one operator and more like a fire brigade coming to your house when you have a fire. When a fire bridge comes to your home, the first person at your door doesn't go and look around and goes to the kitchen and says, oh, it's a kitchen fire; let me go and call the kitchen guy but instead he gets in and finds how to get the light out. And that is what we are seeing in many more organisations today, where the first responder isn't' a traffic routing engine but a person with pretty good skills, and he can attack what's the problem and establish context quickly and address them because every time a problem handed off, that means more time.

So, traditionally it could be up to seven persons until the issue is resolved, but in DevOps, that could be a full-stack first-class engineer or at least the person that knows the application entirely. They still have many SMEs. And increasingly, enterprises are introducing a new resource in the operations team, which came from Google, the Site Reliability Engineer (SRE). SRE is a hybrid operations programmer who lives for problem management. If you think about ITIL, they live to understand why the problem is occurring, and to get rid of the root cause of the issues, whether that means changing the way the application interacts with the cloud infrastructure to make it more scalable or rewriting part of the application or re-homing / re-basing bits of process and activity. The duty of the SRE is not to sort an incident but rather to take the incident out of the equation. So, from L1, l2 and L3, we moved to the first responder, SME, SRE model.

SRE and DevOps

Although SRE didn't emerge from DevOps, it is aligned with DevOps. DevOps has the underlying philosophy of full lifecycle responsibility for DevOps teams and of iterating based on that experience. "You build it, and you run it."[40] The values of SRE are:

- Reduction in the meantime to repair (MTTR) and mean time between failures (MTBF)
- Faster rollout of version updates and bug fixes
- Reduction of risk through automation
- Enhanced resource retention by making operations jobs attractive and interesting
- Alignment of development and operations through shared goals
- Separation of duties and compliance
- The balance between functional and non-functional requirements

"A successful man is one who can lay a firm foundation with the bricks others have thrown at him."
- David Brinkley

Reskilling

Many new roles have emerged because of digital transformation and cloud adoption in different organisations. As a result, reskilling has become compulsory. Reskilling is the process of learning or training someone on new skills that will help them do a different job.

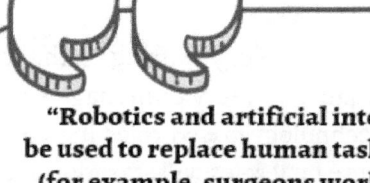

"Robotics and artificial intelligence systems will not only be used to replace human tasks, but to augment their skills (for example, surgeons working with advanced robotics systems to perform operations). This, too, will provide challenges for businesses, which will need to reskill employees so they can work effectively with new technology. Reskilling will be critical to realising the full potential of technological augmentation, both through boosting productivity and mitigating job losses from automation"
World Economic Forum

Emerging roles

Cloud Service Architect: This role is fundamental in determining how a private cloud is built-in support of the goals established for the investment. This is a professional responsible for overseeing organisational Cloud Computing strategy.

Cloud Orchestration Specialist: Cloud orchestration is typically used to provision, deploy, or start servers; acquire and assign storage capacity; manage networking; create VMs; and gain access to specific software on cloud services. The Cloud Orchestration Specialist is responsible for defining and maintaining high-level workflows that are needed for the automation of cloud services.

Cloud Service Manager: The cloud service manager will ensure the cloud service management is "fit for purpose". It will look after service levels, policies and rules associated with each private cloud service. Some organisations will call this a "Cloud Success Manager".

Cloud Infrastructure Administrator: The cloud system administrator will provide daily operational support for several infrastructure components that form a cloud service.

Emerging Roles

There is a collective impact of the technology shifting on the roles in IT. The traditional roles like project managers, service managers or business analysts will decrease as new technology-based roles increase. The below table will explain the areas where new roles will start dominating:

Agile/DevOps

- Scrum Master
- Agile Coach
- Product Owner
- DevOps Engineer
- Automation Architect

Cloud

- Cloud Architect
- Cloud Service broker
- Cloud Security Specialist
- Cloud Vendor manager
- Onboarding Architects

Digital

- Chief Digital Officer
- Digital Product Manager
- UX Designer

- Customer Experience Specialist
- Social Software Specialist

Data:

- Chief Data Officer
- Data Scientist
- Data Integration Specialist
- Data Architect

AI / IoT / Robotics

- AI / Machine Learning Specialist
- IoT Architect
- Robotics Engineer
- Technology Innovator

Emerging Skills

Connecting to emerging roles, we can understand the areas where expertise would be required. The most demanding competencies are everything around digital transformation, automation, machine learning, and IoT. The critical problem is many organisations, and IT professionals are not equipped with the skills to deal with this level of change required for such transformation. Below are my best picks:

1. Architecture
2. Artificial Intelligence
3. AWS Proficiency
4. Business of Technology
5. Cloud Computing
6. Cybersecurity
7. Data Science
8. Design Thinking
9. DevOps
10. HR Management Systems Proficiency

11. Infrastructure and Networking
12. Integration/API
13. IoT
14. Machine Learning Techniques
15. Quantum Computing
16. Robotic Process Automation and Software Engineering

Learning and Development

Companies need to create a global curriculum framework with innovative learning solutions to cope with this change and allow the employees to increase their capabilities with the modern world. It is essential to plan the learning and development carefully for the organisation to keep up with the digital transformation's velocity and move to Cloud Computing. Some training could be made mandatory on digital transformation, and Cloud Computing, like most organisations, will have on company standards, policies, and functional areas. Cloud training providers and virtual learning modules could also be deployed internally with significant advantages.

Recommended upskilling courses

AI For Everyone: https://www.coursera.org/learn/ai-for-everyone
Data Analysis with Python: https://www.coursera.org/learn/data-analysis-with-python
Deep Learning Specialisation: https://www.coursera.org/specializations/deep-learning
Advanced Machine Learning Specialisation: https://www.coursera.org/specializations/aml
Data Science Specialisation: https://www.coursera.org/specializations/jhu-data-science

Best Cloud Certifications

For professionals, some of the most demanding cloud certifications would include:
- AWS Certified Solutions Architect – Professional
- CompTIA Cloud+ Certification

- Microsoft Certified Azure Solutions Architect Expert
- Google Cloud Certified – Professional Cloud Architect
- CCNA Cloud: Cisco Certified Network Administrator Cloud
- CCNP Cloud: Cisco Certified Network Professional Cloud
- VCP7-CMA: VMware Certified Professional 7 – Cloud Management and Automation
- Certified Cloud Security Professional (CCSP)

Free Online Training

There is much free online training currently available that companies can benefit from. I have taken a few of them and some that I found very useful; I am listing them here:

- ***Elements of AI provided by Helsinki University***: Reaktor and the University of Helsinki have partnered to offer a free online course series called The Elements of AI. They advocate for a large audience to become educated on what AI is, what it can achieve, and how to get started developing AI approaches. The courses blend theory with practical tasks and may be completed at your own pace. To access the course, you need to go to this link -elementsofai.com

- ***edX: Digital Transformation Strategy created by Boston University***: This online digitalisation course allows you to explore the world of digital ecosystems in light of your organisation's needs. You'll be introduced to three phases of transformation businesses face on their way to digital reinvention and essential steps that will guide you to success. After the course, you'll understand how machine learning can amplify your employees' talent. Enrolment link: www.edx.org/course/digital-transformation-strategy.

- ***Free AWS digital training and new cloud Practitioner Certification***: I have used this free service of AWS and took a few of them. Very useful for starters, for learning the basics. You can also access previews of more advanced training on Machine Learning and Storage. Digital courses are generally 10 minutes long and designed to help you build foundational knowledge for dozens of

AWS services and solutions. To access this, you need to go to AWS training site: https://www.aws.training/

Recommended Competency Development

Based on market research and job requirements in digital transformation and Cloud Computing areas, I have below suggestions for competency development:

1. **AI/ML/DL** – This is going to be the most demanded skill. If you know this, you are a desirable candidate for any company looking forward to making big money. Machine learning and deep learning are subsets of AI. For the next five years, many job opportunities in this field will be available; if you have not started learning about it, please do so immediately. Also, it can be applied in every sector.

2. **Big Data** - Big data was there for a more extended period, but today big data is used more efficiently than ever before. So, data engineers and data scientists will have significant career opportunities.

3. **Edge and Cloud Computing** – While Cloud Computing can involve creating latency, edge computing can remove the latency; we discussed this before in this book. So definitely, if you are competent in this area, that would be a great trademark for you.

4. **Blockchain Technology** – 2018 and 2019 were tremendous growth of blockchain projects, but due to specific rules in different companies, it did not go very well in 2020 and beyond; there will be lots of new projects on this technology. This will connect to the Internet of Value.

5. **AR and VR** – Augmented Reality and Virtual Reality – are becoming extremely popular, especially in entertainment, education, and medical science. It is now heavily used in medical science. Also, in engineering education, AR and VR are highly demanded. When we talk about AR and VR, they provide you with a virtual environment, which is similar to the real-world environment. It is now the best thing to have and vital for medical science. In medical science, doctors can perform surgery in virtual reality to improve their learning process. So, in this sector, there is a potential requirement.

Training Needs Analysis (TNA)

To start with a Training Need Analysis (TNA), it should be created based on the different roles that you have in your organisation. It should start from top to bottom.

TNA Methodology

The TNA assesses precisely what is required to develop the organisational learning process, adds an outline for each training module and education session, and refines the training development and delivery plan. It is organised in seven steps, and they are described below:

- **Training Strategy** - Agree on the overall strategy in terms of approach, learning objectives and success factors.
- **Identify Skills** - Identify required skills and processes; collate knowledge and skill level requirements by role/person; produce skills matrix.
- **Evaluate Training Environment** - Define and agree on the training system and data requirements; agree on procedures and responsibilities for aligning to the development system, data refresh, and setup of user login IDs.
- **Design Training Solution** - Agree on training programme structure by module, including objectives, topics, prerequisites, delivery method, and duration (if relevant).
- **Design Evaluation Methods** - Determine how learning outcomes, training materials and trainers are to be evaluated; if applicable, design methods for collation.
- **Produce Training Plan** - Produce a detailed plan covering the development of training materials; resource requirements (classroom(s), course schedule, PCs, environment logons); availability of trainees based on shift patterns and so on.
- **Risks, Assumptions, Review, Sign Off** - Confirm risks and assumptions, review and sign off-plan with stakeholders.

Business Impact Analysis (BIA)

A business impact analysis (BIA) aims to systematically identify and assess the likely consequences of a disruption to mission-critical business processes.

Organisations have independent business units with accountability to deliver the strategy, and due to cross-functional processes and operational dependencies, one cannot thrive without the other. Due to this, the usage of classification is superlative essential to ensure consistent prioritisation of applications. The first step is to understand the criticality of each workload in the IT portfolio. Organisations must prioritise planning and delivering what is required since we are not living in a perfect world of unlimited resources and time. To manage the challenge of prioritisation, the following baseline is provided.

The most critical input to balanced prioritisation understands the term criticality. The term "critical" is used in this context as it underlines the importance of the asset and resources allocated to manage this subject. The classification is based on the relative level of business impacts and severity in case of interruption, disruption or incident in the assets associated with the business process. It is highly recommended to align these classifications during the cloud assessment phase and mutually align with the cloud service provider and managed cloud service providers.

Criticality classification is divided into three sub-classifications: Mission, Business and Task critical. I know there are other naming conventions (e.g., mission-critical, unit-critical, high, medium, low unsupported etc.), so these are my generic suggestions only:

Mission Critical

Interruption, disruption, or incident in the assets associated with the business process would stop the workflow or endanger business objectives where failure would cause:

- Direct mass impact on consumers attempting to use the

company's services or support.
- Significant loss of sales, profits or market share.
- Delays of invoicing or critical financial reporting.
- Though the impact level is high throughout the year, high seasons increase the criticality and multiply the negative impact on the business objectives.

Categorically Digital and Physical Delivery Processes related to Sales and Marketing, Supply Chain and Location and Commerce applications are often defined as mission-critical when they directly impact customers (consumer/ business). This also includes supporting platforms and infrastructures that inherit classification from the top.

Business Critical

Interruption, disruption, or incident in the assets associated with the business process would cause delays or errors with the high-cost corrective actions in:
- Payments to externals.
- Organisation's people compensation.
- Decreased customer satisfaction.
- The apparent negative impact on brand image.
- Liabilities to fulfil compliance requirements, e.g., Safety of Products, Legal, Privacy, Digital Trade and SOX (Sarbanes-Oxley Act).
- It is very characteristic that there is a certain "point in time" or "time frame" when failure to meet objectives would cause more severe damage than at any other time.

Categorically Customer Engagement, Management, and Support processes-related applications having high business impact belong to the business-critical class. This also includes supporting platforms and infrastructures that inherit classification from the top.

Task Critical

Interruption, disruption, or incident in the assets associated with the business process would cause:

- Significant delays to the strategic programs.
- Decreases the creative capabilities to respond to new demands.
- Lost business opportunities.
- The window of opportunity is the chance to provide unique and desired solutions to customers at a certain time. Failure to advance from the situation means the competitors will close the window.

Categorically, Product Creation processes-related applications are considered as Task Critical. New business applications with higher classification characteristics are considered Task Critical until fully operational. This also includes supporting platforms and infrastructures that inherit the ranking from the top.

CHAPTER 6:
Cloud Computing Pragmatisms

"Cloud computing is often far more secure than traditional computing because companies like Google and Amazon can attract and retain cyber-security personnel of a higher quality than many governmental agencies."
- Vivek Kundra

Example of Cloud Services

Some example cloud services available to a cloud consumer are listed below[41]:

SaaS services

- *E-mail and Office Productivity*: Applications for e-mail, word processing, spreadsheets, presentations, etc.
- *Billing*: Application services to manage customer billing based on usage and subscriptions to products and services.
- *Customer Relationship Management (CRM)*: CRM applications that range from call center applications to sales force automation.
- *Collaboration*: Tools that allow users to collaborate in workgroups, within enterprises, and across enterprises.
- *Content Management*: Services for managing the production of and access to content for web-based applications.
- *Document Management*: Applications for managing documents, enforcing document production workflows, and providing workspaces for groups or enterprises to find and access documents.
- *Financials*: Applications for managing financial processes ranging from expense processing and invoicing to tax management.
- *Human Resources*: Software for managing human resources functions within companies.
- *Sales*: Applications that are specifically designed for sales functions such as pricing, commission tracking, etc.
- *Social Networks*: Social software establishes and maintains a connection among users tied in one or more specific types of interdependency.
- *Enterprise Resource Planning (ERP)*: Integrated computer-based system used to manage internal and external resources, including tangible assets, financial resources, materials, and human resources.

PaaS Services

- **Business Intelligence:** Platforms for creating applications such as dashboards, reporting systems, and data analysis.
- **Database:** Services offering scalable relational database solutions or scalable non-SQL data stores.
- **Development and Testing:** Platforms for application development and testing cycles, which expand and contract as needed.
- **Integration:** Development platforms for building integration applications in the cloud and within the enterprise.
- **Application Deployment:** Platforms suited for general-purpose application development. These services provide databases, web application runtime environments, etc.

IaaS Services

- **Backup and Recovery**: Services for backup and recovery of file systems and raw data stores on servers and desktop systems.
- **Compute:** Server resources for running cloud-based systems that can be dynamically provisioned and configured as needed.
- **Content Delivery Networks (CDNs):** CDNs store content and files to improve the performance and cost of delivering content for web-based systems.
- **Services Management:** Services that manage cloud infrastructure platforms. These tools often provide features that cloud providers do not provide or specialise in managing certain application technologies.
- **Storage:** Massively scalable storage capacity that can be used for applications, backups, archival, and file storage.

Cloud Service Management Definitions

1. **Cloud Service Management and Operations** - Cloud Service Management and Operations entails all an organisation's activities to plan, design, deliver, operate, and control the IT and Cloud services it offers to customers.[42]

2. **Service Management** - Service management includes the operational aspects of your applications and services. Applications are monitored to ensure availability and performance according to service level agreements (SLAs) or service level objectives (SLOs). After an application is pushed to production, it must be managed.

3. **Site Reliability Engineering (SRE)** - Site Reliability Engineering (SRE) is an approach to operations that ensures that continuously delivered applications run efficiently and reliably using software engineering and automation solutions. An SRE takes operational responsibility for supporting applications and services running globally in the cloud using a highly automated service management approach. The SRE pays particular attention to removing toil, which is repetitive manual labour that doesn't add real value to a project.[43]

4. **Error Budget** - The error budget limits how much time the system is allowed to be down, defined by the contracted service-level agreement (SLA) or the intended service-level objective (SLO). Error budget goes a step further and encourages testing and releasing only if downtime is left in the SLA. The error budget is how much time you're willing to allow your systems to be down, and it depends heavily on the SLA you've defined with the product team. Everyone would like to have systems with 100% uptime, but you need to be realistic.[44]

5. **Post-mortem**: A post-mortem is a written record of an incident, its impact, the actions taken to mitigate or resolve it, the root cause(s), and the follow-up actions to prevent the incident from recurring.[45]

6. **Microservices** - Applications or services are broken down into multiple microservices that provide the functionality required. All the microservices have standard interfaces that allow them to work together correctly but are developed independently. This allows a more modular and agile environment that has automated and regular

release and test cycles. This contrasts with traditional monolithic applications that have elongated development, testing and upgrade cycles. For example, the whole Amazon store is built on microservices.

7. **The Twelve-Factor App** - The 12-factor app manifesto describes a methodology for building applications that can scale without significant changes to tooling, architecture, or development practices.[46]

8. **Containerisation** – Applications run inside dedicated virtual 'containers' housed on a single operating system instance instead of a virtualised operating system running on a hypervisor. This is meant to simplify environments by removing the need to set up and pay for multiple operating systems to cater for application separation. This technology initially focused on deploying modern specifically architected applications (or microservices). Still, this technology is being used more recently to containerise legacy applications to manage portability, scalability, and security (e.g., Docker MTA).

9. **Kubernetes** - Kubernetes is an open-source system for automating containerised applications' deployment, scaling, and management. Kubernetes provides functionality for many operational tasks:
    a. Placement of workload based on resource requirements
    b. Automated rollouts and rollbacks
    c. Service discovery and load balancing
    d. Horizontal scaling
    e. Self-healing

10. **RPO - Recovery Point Objective** - To protect from disasters and meet regulatory needs, backups must be done regularly based on RPO (recovery point objective), which is the maximum targeted period in which data might be lost.

11. **RTO - Recovery Time Objective** - RTO (recovery time objective) is the targeted duration of time and a service level within which a business process must be restored after a disaster.

12. **Prometheus** - Prometheus is an open-source monitoring framework, and Fluentd is a logging data collector. Both tools work with

Kubernetes. They provide some level of HealthCheck API natively, easing the path for developers to take advantage of it.

13. **Correlation Identifiers** - Using correlation IDs not only helps to identify the execution path for a given transaction but also supports visualisation that adds the context of the time, such as latency; the hierarchy of the services that are involved; and the serial or parallel nature of the process or task execution.

14. **OpenTracing** - OpenTracing is a vendor-neutral open standard for distributed tracing.

15. **First Responder** – A first responder is a person with pretty good skills, and he can attack what's the problem and establish context quickly and address them, because every time a problem handed off, that means more time.

16. **Subject Matter Expert (SME)** - A subject-matter expert or domain expert is a person who is an authority in a particular area or topic. The term domain expert is frequently used in expert systems software development, and there the term always refers to a domain other than the software domain.

17. **ChatOps** - The term ChatOps describes this process, where people use an instant-messaging communication platform to collaborate among SMEs. Through the ChatOps platform, all interaction is logged in a central place, and you can browse through the log to see what actions were taken.

18. **Dashboards** - Dashboards visualise topology, deployment activities, and the operational state, showing availability and performance metrics. A dashboard should also visualise the key service indicators from a user perspective.

19. **Five Hows Approach** - The 5 Hows approach, as this method, helps to surface the issue that was ultimately responsible for an incident. This investigation must be operated in a blameless culture; only through that approach are people willing to share their insights and help others to learn from the experience.[47]

20. **Squads** – Squads are operations professionals know that the best protection for production is to accept no changes, and developers are

encouraged to provide new functions quickly, sometimes at the expense of quality. In a DevOps culture, squads are responsible for delivering new capabilities quickly and safely.

21. **Autonomous** - In autonomous squads, "autonomous" means that the squads are responsible for figuring out how best to do the work that needs to be done.

22. **Culture of Meritocracy** - Establishing a culture of meritocracy, where employees are recognised for their achievements, dissolves the formal hierarchy of an organisation. Meritocracies thrive on trust, transparency, and consistency.

23. **Tribes** - While autonomous squads must be able to do their work their way, they also fit in a larger organisation. Delivering an enterprise-grade application requires work from multiple squads, each of which is responsible for a microservice. When those microservices are combined, the entire product is created. Spotify uses the word tribe to describe a set of squads, and people from disciplines such as Marketing and Finance, that are aligned around the goal of delivering a product or service.

24. **Guilds** - Autonomous squads consist of diverse squad members who have a wide variety of skills. Sometimes, it's essential for people who share ordinary skills to discuss ideas and solve problems within their speciality. Guilds gather people from multiple squads around a common discipline. For example, each squad has one or two people who are familiar with the continuous delivery tools used to build, deploy, and manage the product the squad is delivering. A Continuous Delivery guild brings together people who do that job from each squad. The guild drives best practices in continuous delivery and acts as a forum where people who are struggling with a problem can find answers from fellow guild members.

25. **Conway's Law** - Static structures are often ill-equipped to respond to the new business world's constant change, chaos, and confusion. Where squads are trying to design, build, and operate many microservices instead of a single monolithic application, they must similarly organise into decentralised, independent, loosely coupled

squads. Otherwise, as Conway's Law suggests, a monolithic organisation is constrained to create monolithic software.[48]

26. **DAD** - Disciplined Agile Delivery (DAD) - DAD is focused on the end-to-end life-cycle of products, from inception to delivery. Seven principles drive it: delight customers, be awesome, pragmatism, context counts, the choice is good, optimise flow, and enterprise awareness.

27. **LeSS** - Large-Scale Scrum (LeSS). LeSS focuses on getting all teams seeing the entire product rather than taking the view from a "my part" perspective.

28. **The proliferation of Shadow IT** – The proliferation of shadow IT (Proliferation = rapid increase, growth). Shadow IT is the proliferation of information technology (IT) that remains largely unknown and unseen by a company's business IT department, which is concerning from both a security and a management perspective. ... They are often hosted on external platforms such as Amazon

"Own the outcome."
Ryan G Wright, CEO,
DoHardMoney

Cloud Taxonomy Terms and Definitions

1. **Cloud Consumer** - A person or organisation that maintains a business relationship with, and uses service from, Cloud Service Providers.
2. **Cloud Provider** – Person, organisation or entity responsible for making a service available to service consumers.
3. **Cloud Carrier** – The intermediary that provides connectivity and transport of cloud services between Cloud Providers and Cloud Consumers.
4. **Cloud Broker** – An entity that manages cloud services' use, performance and delivery and negotiates relationships between Cloud Providers and Cloud Consumers.
5. **Cloud Auditor** – A party that can independently assess cloud services, information system operations, performance and security of the cloud implementation.
6. **Cloud Distribution** – The transporting of cloud data between Cloud Providers and Cloud Consumers.
7. **Cloud Access** – To make contact with or gain access to Cloud Services.
8. **Service Deployment** – All of the activities and organisation needed to make a cloud service available
9. **Service Orchestration** - Refers to the arrangement, coordination and management of cloud infrastructure to provide different cloud services to meet IT and business requirements.
10. **Cloud Service Management** – Cloud Service Management includes all the service-related functions necessary for the management and operations of those services required by or proposed to customers.
11. **Security** – Refers to information security. "information security" means protecting information and information systems from unauthorised access, use, disclosure, disruption, modification, or destruction in order to provide:

a. Integrity, which means guarding against improper information modification or destruction, and includes ensuring information nonrepudiation and authenticity;

b. Confidentiality, which means preserving authorised restrictions on access and disclosure, including means for protecting personal privacy and proprietary information;

c. Availability means ensuring timely and reliable access to and use of information. (Source: [SOURCE: Title III of the E-Government Act, entitled the Federal Information Security Management Act of 2002 (FISMA)])

12. **Privacy** - Information privacy is the assured, proper, and consistent collection, processing, communication, use and disposition of personal information (PI) and personally identifiable information (PII) throughout its life cycle. (Source: adapted from OASIS)

13. **Software as a Service (SaaS)** - The consumer can use the provider's applications running on a cloud infrastructure. The applications are accessible from various client devices through a thin client interface such as a web browser (e.g., web-based e-mail). The consumer does not manage or control the underlying cloud infrastructure, including network, servers, operating systems, storage, or even individual application capabilities, except for limited user-specific application configuration settings. (Source: NIST CC Definition)

14. **Platform as a Service (PaaS)** - The capability provided to the consumer is to deploy onto the cloud infrastructure consumer-created or acquired applications created using programming languages and tools supported by the provider. The consumer does not manage or control the underlying cloud infrastructure, including network, servers, operating systems, or storage, but has control over the deployed applications and possibly application hosting environment configurations. (Source: NIST CC Definition)

15. **Infrastructure as a Service (IaaS)** - The capability provided to the consumer is to provision processing, storage, networks, and other fundamental computing resources where the consumer is able to deploy and run arbitrary software, which can include operating systems

and applications. The consumer does not manage or control the underlying cloud infrastructure but has control over operating systems, storage, deployed applications, and possibly limited control of select networking components (e.g., host firewalls). (Source: NIST CC Definition)

16. **Service Consumption** – A Cloud Broker in the act of using a Cloud Service.

17. **Service Provision** – A Cloud Broker in the act of providing a Cloud Service.

18. **Security Audit** - Systematic evaluation of a cloud system by measuring how well it conforms to a set of established security criteria.

19. **Privacy-Impact Audit** - Systematic evaluation of a cloud system by measuring how well it conforms to a set of established privacy-impact criteria.

20. **Performance Audit** - Systematic evaluation of a cloud system by measuring how well it conforms to a set of established performance criteria.

21. **Service Intermediation** - An intermediation broker provides a service that directly enhances a service delivered to one or more service consumers, essentially adding value to a given service to enhance some specific capability. (Source: Gartner)

22. **Service Aggregation** - An aggregation brokerage service combines multiple services into one or more new services. It will ensure that data is modelled across all component services and integrated as well as provide the movement and security of data between the service consumer and multiple providers. (Source: Gartner)

23. **Service Arbitrage** - Cloud service arbitrage is similar to cloud service aggregation. The difference between them is that the services being aggregated aren't fixed. Indeed, the goal of arbitrage is to provide flexibility and opportunistic choices for the service aggregator, e.g., providing multiple e-mail services through one service provider or providing a credit-scoring service that checks various scoring agencies and selects the best score. (Source: Gartner)

24. **Private Cloud** - The cloud infrastructure is operated solely for an organisation. It may be managed by the organisation or a third party and may exist on-premise or off-premise. (Source: NIST CC Definition)

25. **Community Cloud** - The cloud infrastructure is shared by several organisations and supports a specific community with shared concerns (e.g., mission, security requirements, policy, and compliance considerations). It may be managed by organisations or a third party and may exist on-premise or off-premise. (Source: NIST CC Definition)

26. **Public Cloud** - The cloud infrastructure is made available to the general public or a large industry group and is owned by an organisation selling cloud services. (Source: NIST CC Definition)

27. **Hybrid Cloud** – The cloud infrastructure is a composition of two or more clouds (private, community, or public) that remain unique entities but are bound together by standardised or proprietary technology that enables data and application portability (e.g., cloud bursting for load-balancing between clouds). (Source: NIST CC Definition)

28. **Service Layer** - Defines the basic services provided by cloud providers

29. **Physical Resource Layer** - Includes all the physical resources used to provide cloud services, most notably, the hardware and the facility.

30. **Resource Abstraction and Control Layer** - This entails software elements, such as a hypervisor, virtual machines, virtual data storage, and supporting software components, used to realise the infrastructure upon which a cloud service can be established.

31. **Portability** - The ability to transfer data from one system to another without being required to recreate or renter data descriptions or significantly modify the application being transported. 2. The ability of software or of a system to run on more than one type or size of a computer under more than one operating system. See POSIX. 3. Of equipment, the quality of being able to function normally while being conveyed. [Source: Federal Standard 1037C]

32. **Interoperability** - The capability to communicate, execute programs, or transfer data among various functional units under specified conditions. [Source: American National Standard Dictionary of Information Technology (ANSDIT)]

33. **Provisioning/Configuration** - Process of preparing and equipping a cloud to allow it to provide (new) services to its users

34. **Mobile Endpoints** - A physical device, often carried by the user, that provides a man/machine interface to cloud services and applications. A Mobile Endpoint may use multiple methods and protocols to connect to cloud services and applications.

35. **Fixed Endpoints** - A physical device fixed in its location provides a man/machine interface to cloud services and applications. A fixed endpoint typically uses one method and protocol to connect to cloud services and applications.

36. **Data Portability** – The ability to transfer data from one system to another without being required to recreate or renter data descriptions or modify the application being transported significantly. [Source: Federal Standard 1037C]

37. **Service Interoperability** - The capability to communicate, execute programs, or transfer data among various cloud services under specified conditions. [Source: modified from American National Standard Dictionary of Information Technology (ANSDIT)]

38. **System Portability** - The ability of a service to run on more than one type or size of the cloud. [Source: NIST, modified from Federal Standard 1037C]

39. **Rapid provisioning** – Automatically deploying cloud system based on the requested service/resources/capabilities

40. **Resource change** – Adjust configuration/resource assignment for repairs, upgrades, and joining new nodes into the cloud

41. **Monitoring and Reporting** – Discover and monitor the virtual resources, cloud operations and events, and generate performance reports.

42. **Metering** - Provide a measuring capability at some level of abstraction appropriate to the type of service (e.g., storage, processing, bandwidth, and active user accounts)

43. **SLA management** – Encompasses the SLA contract definition (underlying schema with the quality-of-service parameters), SLA monitoring, and SLA enforcement according to the defined policies.

Acronyms

Term	Description
A & O	Automation and Orchestration
AD	Active Directory
AI	Artificial Intelligence
AMDB	Asset Management Database
ANN	Artificial Neural Network
ARM	Azure Resource Manager
AV	Anti-Virus
BAU	Business-as-Usual
BIA	Business Impact Analysis
BSC	Business Support Centre
CAGR	Compound Annual Growth Rate
CCoE	Cloud Centre of Excellence
CDA	Component Design Architecture
CDO	Chief Digital Officer
CGM	Cloud Governance Framework
CHRO	Chief HR Officer
CIO	Chief Information Officer
CRM	Customer Relationship Management
CMDB	Configuration Management Database
CMO	Chief Marketing Officer
CND	Content Delivery Networks
CNN	Convolutional Neural Network
COBIT	Control Objectives for Information and Related Technology
CoE	Centre of Excellence
CSM	Cloud Service Management
CSB	Cloud Service Brokerages
CSP	Cloud Service Provider
DB	Database
DBA	Database Administration

Term	Description
DDD	Detailed Design Document
DIO	Digitally Integrated Organisation
DLF	Design Lead Forum
DL	Deep Learning
DX	Digital Transformation
EAB	Enterprise Architect Board
ELS	Early Life Support
ERM	Enterprise Risk Management
ERP	Enterprise Resource Planning
FSA	Full System Architecture
GDPR	General Data Protection Regulation
HLA	High-Level Architecture
HLD	High-Level Design
HPOV	Hewlett-Packard Open View
HVAC	Heating, Ventilation and Air Conditioning
IAAS	Cloud Infrastructure as A Service
ISMS	Information Security Management System
ISP	Information Security Policy
OCM	Organisational Change Management
OTP	Online Transaction Processing
IT	Information Technology
ITO	Information Technology Office
KPI	Key Performance Indicator
MCS	Managed Cloud Services
MID	Mobile Internet Devices
ML	Machine Learning
MSI	Multi Supplier Integration
MSP	Managed Services Providers
NFR	Non-Functional Requirements
NIST	National Institute of Standards and Technology
OS	Operating System
QoS	Quality of Service

Term	Description
PAAS	Cloud Platform As A Service
PI	Personal Information
PII	Personally, Identifiable Information
PIM	Privileged Identity Management
POM	Projects Operating Model
RACI	Responsible, Accountable, Consulted and Informed
RNN	Recurrent Neural Network
RPA	Robotic Process Automation
RPO	Recovery Point Objective
RTO	Recovery Time Objective
SAAS	Cloud Software as A Service
SAJACC	Standards Acceleration to Jumpstart the Adoption of Cloud computing
SCM	Supply Chain Management
SDO	Standards Development Organisation
SDM	Service Delivery Manager
SIEM	Security Information and Event Management
SLA	Service Level Agreement
SME	Subject Matter Expert
SOX	Sarbanes-Oxley Act
SPD	System Physical Design
SRE	Site Reliability Engineer
SVC	Service value Chain
SVS	Service Value Systems
TNA	Training Needs Analysis
TOM	Target Operating Model
ToR	Terms of Reference
UAT	User Acceptance Testing
UPP	Unified Provisioning Portal
VM	Virtual Machines
WG	Working Group

Cloud Management Platforms

Here is a breakdown, by vendor, of some of the most prominent available Cloud Management Platforms. It is not intended to be a complete and exhaustive vendor list. Some providers offer a whole suite of services, while others have broken those features up into several packages. Some offerings are built on open source — most situations involve a "freemium" model where the open-source code is provided freely but where the vendor concerned offers support and premium services at a price. To be clear, all trademarks and trade names are the exclusive property of their respective holders. The names of actual companies, products, and services mentioned in this Guide are for no other reason than to help identify them. Use of these names and brands does not indicate sponsorship.

BMC
Cloud Lifecycle Management Cloud Operations Management
http://www.bmc.com/it-solutions/cloud-computing-software.html
Cisco CloudCenter (formerly CliQr)
http://www.cisco.com/c/en/us/products/cloud-systemsmanage-ment/cloudcenter/index.html
CloudBolt Software
https://www.cloudbolt.io/
Cloudify
http://getcloudify.org/
DivvyCloud
https://divvycloud.com/
Embotics vCommander
http://www.embotics.com/
HPE Cloud Service Automation
http://www8.hp.com/us/en/software-solutions/cloud-service-automa-tion/index.html
IBM
Cloud Orchestrator
Cloud Automation Manager

Cloud Brokerage

http://www-03.ibm.com/software/products/en/ibm-cloud-orchestrator

https://www.ibm.com/us-en/marketplace/cognitive-automation

http://www-03.ibm.com/software/products/en/cloudbrokerage

Infosys Cloud Infrastructure Services

https://www.infosys.com/infrastructure-services/

Morpheus

https://www.morpheusdata.com

Red Hat CloudForms

https://www.redhat.com/en/technologies/management/cloudforms

RightScale

Cloud Management Platform Optima

http://www.rightscale.com/

Scalr

https://www.scalr.com/

ServiceNow

https://www.servicenow.com/products-by-category.html

T Systems Cloud Integration Center

http://cloud.t-systems.com/solutions/enterprise-cloud-broker

VMWare vRealize Suite

http://www.vmware.com/products/vrealize-suite.html

Check Lists

The following checklists could be considered for better preparation for any move to the cloud.

Security Checklist
- ☐ Is the security team aware of / knowledgeable about the cloud?
- ☐ Does the organisation have a cloud security strategy with which its auditors would be happy?
- ☐ Has security governance been adapted to include the cloud?
- ☐ Does the team's structure enable cloud security?
- ☐ Has the security team updated all security policies and procedures to incorporate the cloud?
- ☐ Has the security team guided the business on remaining secure within a cloud environment?

Management Checklist
- ☐ Is everyone aware of their cloud security responsibilities?
- ☐ Is there a mechanism for assessing the security of a cloud service?
- ☐ Does the business governance mitigate the security risks that
- ☐ can result from cloud-based "shadow IT"?
- ☐ Does the organisation know within which jurisdictions its data can reside?
- ☐ Is there a mechanism for managing cloud-related risks?
- ☐ Does the organisation understand the data architecture needed to operate with appropriate security at all levels?
- ☐ Can the organisation ensure end-to-end service continuity across several cloud service providers?
- ☐ Can the provider comply with all relevant industry standards (e.g. the UK's Data Protection Act)?
- ☐ Does the compliance function understand the specific regulatory issues concerning the organisation's cloud services adoption?

Operations

☐ Are regulatory compliance reports, audit reports and reporting information available from the provider?

☐ Does the provider have the right attitude to incident resolutions and configuration management, even when services involve multiple providers?

☐ Does using a cloud provider give the organisation an environmental advantage?

☐ Does the organisation know in which application or database each data entity is stored or mastered?

☐ Is it easy to securely integrate the cloud-based applications at runtime and contract termination?

☐ Do you know the location from which the provider will deliver support and management services?

☐ Do the procurement processes contain cloud security requirements?

Technology

☐ Are there appropriate access controls (e.g., federated single sign-on) that give users-controlled access to cloud applications?

☐ Is data separation maintained between the organisation's information and that of other customers of the provider, at runtime and during backup (including data disposal)

☐ Has the organisation considered and addressed backup, recovery, archiving and decommissioning of data stored in a cloud environment?

☐ Are mechanisms in place for identification, authorisation, and key management in a cloud environment?

☐ Are all cloud-based systems, infrastructure and physical locations suitably protected?

☐ Are the network designs suitably secure for the organisation's cloud adoption strategy?

CHAPTER 7:
The Last Few Things

"Just like the way a beautiful butterfly can't come into life without its transformation cycle from egg to larva, caterpillar to pupa and finally to a brilliant creation, to become a successful digitally transformed organisation, similar transformational stages are essential."
- Enamul Haque

Conclusion

Before their extinction 65.5 million years ago, dinosaurs roamed the planet for nearly 160 million years. Extinction is the scientific term for the disappearance of a species. Extinction is an important part of life's evolutionary process because it clears the way for new species to emerge. As stated by the Encyclopedia Britannica, this type of extinction occurs when a species' population declines due to factors such as environmental pressures or evolutionary changes in its members. We've witnessed similar technological phenomena that many business models disappear because of the needs of an emerging market, and new ones begin to replace them. In fact, a business model focuses on creating and capturing the company's value, and it always requires leveraging new technology.

Today, the business is fundamentally different when digital transformation is more urgent than ever. The impact of technology on our lifestyle is closely linked to how the world of business makes profits today. Over the years, technology has successfully attempted to enter our bodies to change the way we think, and indeed the target is human blood and emotions. Technology has changed the way we communicate, and it has changed the way we watch TV. It even has improved our health. Technology has increased awareness, which revolves around digital transformation- the new way of living. It's a survival game for business. And the old ways will not work anymore as interfacing everything is mission-critical these days. Community building is required not to miss out on social selling opportunities but to help you to establish trust and credibility and improve customer loyalty. It will allow you to add value to the customer experience and improve customer service while creating brand advocates who rave about your business or product. Failing to gain a learning advantage leads people to lose relevance.

The pace of digital operations far outstrips that of more conventional organisations. It's easy to be lost in the shuffle of a rapidly evolving strategy without a strong digital footprint. Also, Cloud Computing is the true catalyst for digital evolution. In the same way that a beautiful butterfly cannot hatch from an egg without first developing into a larva, then a caterpillar, and eventually a pupa, an organisation must go through a series of transformative stages in order to successfully undergo digital transformation. In my opinion, this book will provide you with a fantastic in-flight education in digital transformation technology and its planning and implementation, the sum of which provides a secure landing spot in the cloud ecosystem and the practical experience you need to integrate into it instinctively. In this age of mass extinction, "The Ultimate Moder's Guide to Cloud Computing" is a must-read for anybody seeking a safe transition from the fight for survival to the glory of victory.

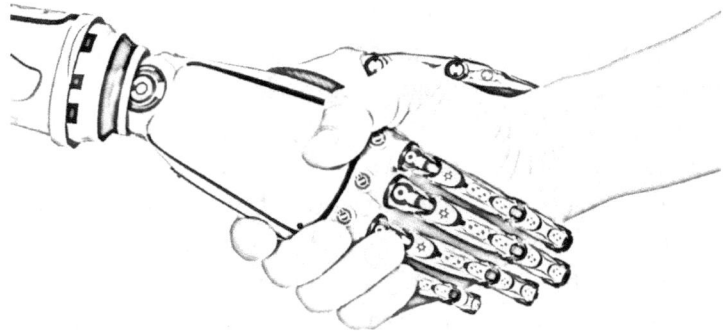

And finally, if you are thinking seriously of a "three days a week", well, it will not be far as digital technology empowered by Cloud computing will bring more vigilance to finish our work quickly. And that way, our future AI-galvanised colleagues will easily be able to continue substituting us so that we can have plenty of time for our family and social life and even relish our hobbies.

Acknowledgements

First, I would like to thank Almighty God for granting me knowledge and wisdom, for which I am truly blessed and grateful.

Secondly, the tremendous inspiration from my family was an asset in writing this book. Family is a foundation that is much more important than wealth and privilege. The love of family is unconditional, and it truly is a support system. I am very thankful to my wife for being extremely patient with me, whether I was staying up late at night to write this book or using the early mornings before setting out for work. She read my first drafts, gave me her opinion, and allowed me to stay focused. A BIG thank you with a lot of love!

I want to thank my three children, Shuaib, Faiyad and Elma. Shuaib Haque is a second-year computer science student at the University of Westminster in London. Faiyad Haque is studying BTEC Level 3 in ICT and is in his second year at the City of Westminster College, London. Both my sons reviewed the manuscripts and helped with the reflective questions. We brainstormed different topics, and they gave me their valuable input. As millennials, their views are essential and make this book more attractive. I believe millennials will drive changes by transforming what businesses think and do – from traditional-led to digital-first. With competence in digital technology, they are the native engineers of the digital world. I thank them for their enormous contribution to this book. I cannot express my appreciation.

I thank my daughter, Elma Inaaya Haque, for helping me to review and edit the material. She is indeed a talented storyteller and presenter. My thanks to her for listening to my stories and offering precious encouragement. I paid great attention to her suggestions; she is an untainted "born digital" – her views were fundamental; I love you all.

Technology and globalisation have created a generation who think a little bit differently, generating masses of transferable life skills, and enabling them to understand the digital and sharing economy at a very early age.

I want to thank all my friends and mentors. My teachers at the Swiss Federal Institute of Technology Lausanne (École Polytechnique Fédérale de Lausanne) that I worked with, during the time of my CMS (Le Cours de mathématiques spéciales). It was an excellent foundation for my IT career. My teachers at the University of Geneva. Especially Professor Paolo Zanella, my favourite teacher of Architecture and Technology of Computer Science. Professor Bertrand Ibrahim and Christian Pellegrini of Structural Programming course. I will never forget them; thanks to them for being inspirational and providing me with the knowledge that later became my stairway to a successful career, resulting in today's ability to share my wisdom. I extend my gratitude and thanks to my friends, Carlos and Hector, who supported my university studies, giving me long hours with lab work and helping with the coursework that we had to prepare, especially in the beginning. At the same time, I struggled with my French language skills. The world is full of beautiful things like you!

I want to thank all my wonderful colleagues in different organisations with whom I developed close relationships during the twenty-six years of my professional life. Because of them, I was able to enhance my knowledge; because of them, I was able to take risks and challenge myself, and because of them, I had opportunities to exercise my creativity and do things differently. I genuinely appreciate each of them. Words are powerless to express my gratitude. Thanks very much.

About the Author

Enamul Haque is a seasoned IT professional with over twenty-six years of diverse experience leading and managing digital transformation and optimisation strategies with sustained operational performance. He has a distinguished track record of leading CIOs, operations, and transformation programs, through advanced digital technologies.

Enamul has a unique style of combining business acumen to evaluate new technologies and develop partnerships at all levels. He can create strategies to generate added value for the business and the stakeholders.

One of the highlights of his career includes his excellent

Figure 68 – Author Enamul Haque

work experience with the United Nations High Commissioner for Refugees (UNHCR) along with the International Telecommunication Union (ITU) in Geneva, Switzerland, following his studies at the Swiss Federal Institute of Technology, Lausanne for a Special Mathematics Diploma (CMS) and later for his licence en sciences de l'informatique, at the University of Geneva.

After eleven years in Switzerland, Enamul moved to Helsinki, Finland, to work in Nokia Headquarters, where he spent over eight years with the immense growth of his career. In 2008, he was able to move to the UK, as he continued working for Nokia and later Microsoft upon their acquisition of the Nokia devices group. After leaving Microsoft, Enamul joined HCL Technologies as an Enterprise Solution Architect. He currently works for Capgemini as a Management Consultant for their Cloud Infrastructure Services.

He also is a collaborative consultant concentrating on creating robust strategies to translate vision into achievements in complex cross-functional matrix organisations. He specialises in helping organisations stay focused and modern in today's digital world by recommending and delivering business and service improvements to assess application and infrastructure landscapes. He assists to re-skill technical workforces creating cost reduction opportunities to ensure business continuity and compliance. He has implemented business transformations across various sectors, including the aviation industry, beauty industry, chemical industry, energy sector, mobile communications, logistics and manufacturing. As a change agent, he works as an effective communicator who is highly adaptable and committed to continuous development.

He is grateful to have considerable industry experience in Cloud Target Operating Model (TOM) Design, Cloud Service Management, Solution Design, Program Management, Contact Centre Operations, Technical Support Operations, Cloud Architecture, Big Data Analytics, the Internet of Things (IoT) and Artificial Intelligence (AI). He has been honoured with ITIL certification in Service Strategy, Service Design, Service Transition, Service Operations and Continual Service Improvement. He also has professional qualifications in Knowledge Management from Edelweiss Connect, Switzerland.

The author also has extensive knowledge in Digital and Cloud Transformation Strategies and Operating Model Development, including Management and Governance Frameworks. Blessed by qualifications in IT4IT, COBIT, ITIL4, KCS, DevOps, ServiceNow, Remedy and many other IT Service Management (ITSM) Systems, Enamul has been inspired to create this book.

His key strengths include Leadership and Management, Business and Information Technology Digital Transformation, Communication and Negotiation, Organisational Awareness, Leading projects in Service Integration and Management (SIAM), ITIL Consultancy, ITSM Process Re-engineering, and ITSM tool Deployments, Adaptability and Flexibility and creativity and Innovation.

Enamul has received many accolades and great recognition for his achievements in the IT industry. Nokia Academy has awarded him a Business Leadership Diploma after a year of a successful business development project. Enamul is an avid enthusiast about sharing his industry knowledge. Additionally, Author Enamul has written various articles published in many newspapers, magazines and social media platforms. He has regularly presented lectures at several universities and colleges in London as a guest lecturer. He's ecstatic to be able to share his expertise with a broader audience through his books, as he believes this is the best way to sustain his many years of work experience for the benefit of the IT industry.

Author Official Website: https://www.enamulhaque.co.uk/
All Books by Enamul Haque: https://enamulhaque.co.uk/my-books
Enamul Haque Blog: https://enamulhaque.co.uk/my-blog
Goodreads Author Profile: https://www.goodreads.com/haquenam
Twitter handle @haquenam: https://twitter.com/haquenam
LinkedIn Profile: https://www.linkedin.com/in/haquenam
YouTube Tutorial: https://www.youtube.com/c/digitaldeepdive
Facebook Author Page: https://www.facebook.com/authorenam

Other Books by the Author

The Ultimate Modern Guide to Artificial Intelligence: ISBN-13: 979-8691930768

Cloud Service Management and Governance: ISBN: 978-1-71678-835-2

Elements of Digital Transformation: ISBN-13: 978-1716762222

The Ultimate Modern Guide to The Internet of Things (IoT) ISBN- 979-8574788950

Digital Transformation Through Cloud Computing: ISBN: 979-8632535090

Book: The Ultimate Modern Guide to The Internet of Things (IoT)

DESCRIPTION

The Internet of Things explained: Simply and Non-Technically. IoT is a computing paradigm in which several technologies connect various devices based on wireless Internet, acquire environmental information through sensors, and control based on this. This book provides a rigorous understanding of the IoT framework, characteristics, architecture, applications, technologies etc., in plain English to improve your awareness. A key objective of this book is to provide a systematic source of reference for all aspects of IoT.

KEY FEATURES

- Fundamentals of IoT
- IoT Technologies & Connectivity
- IoT Architecture and Protocols
- IoT Applications, Platforms and Hardware
- IoT Programming Framework
- IoT Solution Development
- IoT Business development
- IoT Job Market, Skills and Training
- IoT & Emerging Technologies
- IoT Value Creation & Future Developments

WHAT WILL YOU LEARN

- The rise of the IoT – how it all began and where it is heading
- What effect the IoT has on our daily lives
- Architecture and technologies of IoT
- How do you develop IoT business and products
- What are security concerns related to IoT
- IoT & emerging technologies
- IoT-related professions & skill development
- AI, big data, Cloud Computing, Machine Learning & much more

WHO THIS BOOK IS FOR

- Anyone who wants the knowledge about IoT
- Professionals & Researchers
- Designers of smart systems
- Industry specialists & experts
- Solution architects & project managers
- Entrepreneurs of emerging technologies

WHERE TO GET IT

Amazon: https://www.amazon.com/author/enamulhaque

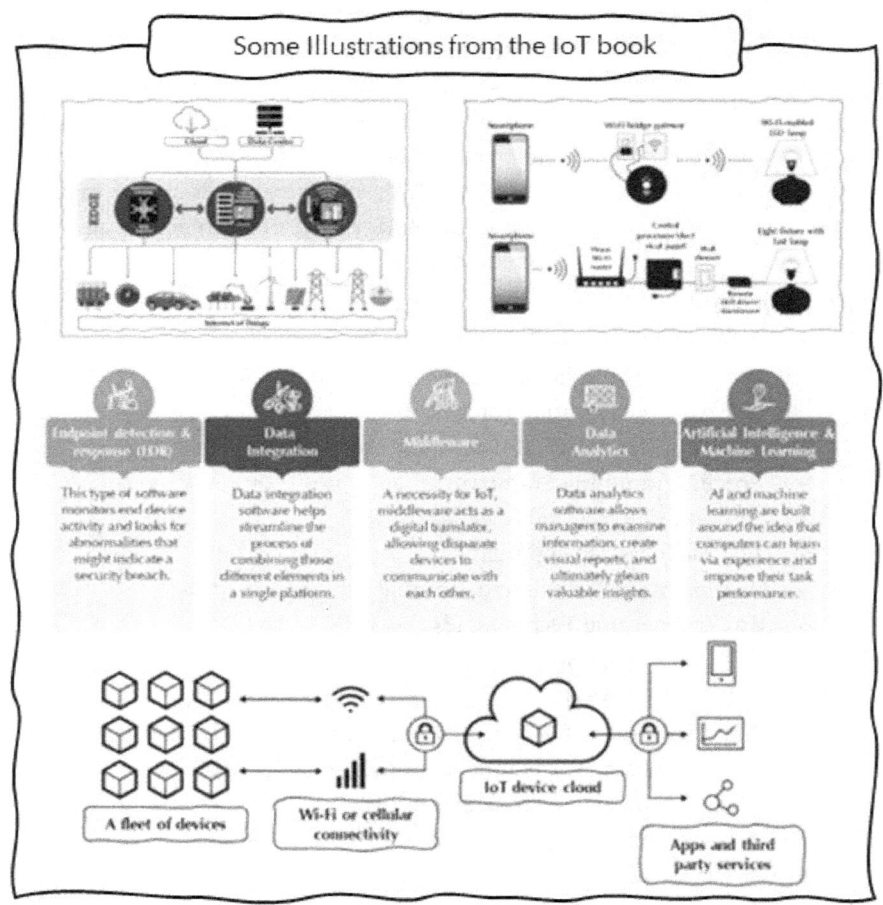

Book: The Ultimate Modern Guide to Artificial Intelligence

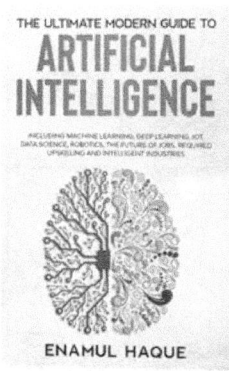

DESCRIPTION

Artificial intelligence will significantly change societal structures and the operations of companies. The next generation of employees need to be trained as a workforce before entering the job market, and the existing workforce is regularly recharged and skilled, there is plenty on this for reskilling too. This book opens your door to the most critical understanding needed of AI and other relevant disruptive technologies. This is the most definitive compendium of AI, The Internet of Things, Machine Learning, Deep Learning, Data Science, Big Data, Cloud Computing, Neural networks, Robotics, the future of work and intelligent industries.

KEY FEATURES

- What is AI and why it matters
- The most common use of AI
- The application of AI
- The history of AI
- Neural networks – human vs machine intelligence
- Data science, AI and IoT
- The philosophy of AI
- AI Programming languages
- AI categories
- Stages of AI
- Robotics (including humanoid robots)
- Voice recognition technology
- Big data, cloud computing
- Machine learning fundamentals
- Deep learning and the use of AI
- AI in the military, agriculture, government etc.
- The use of AI in IT Service Management (AIOps)

- DevOps – CI/CD – RPA and many more

WHERE TO GET IT

Amazon: https://www.amazon.com/author/enamulhaque

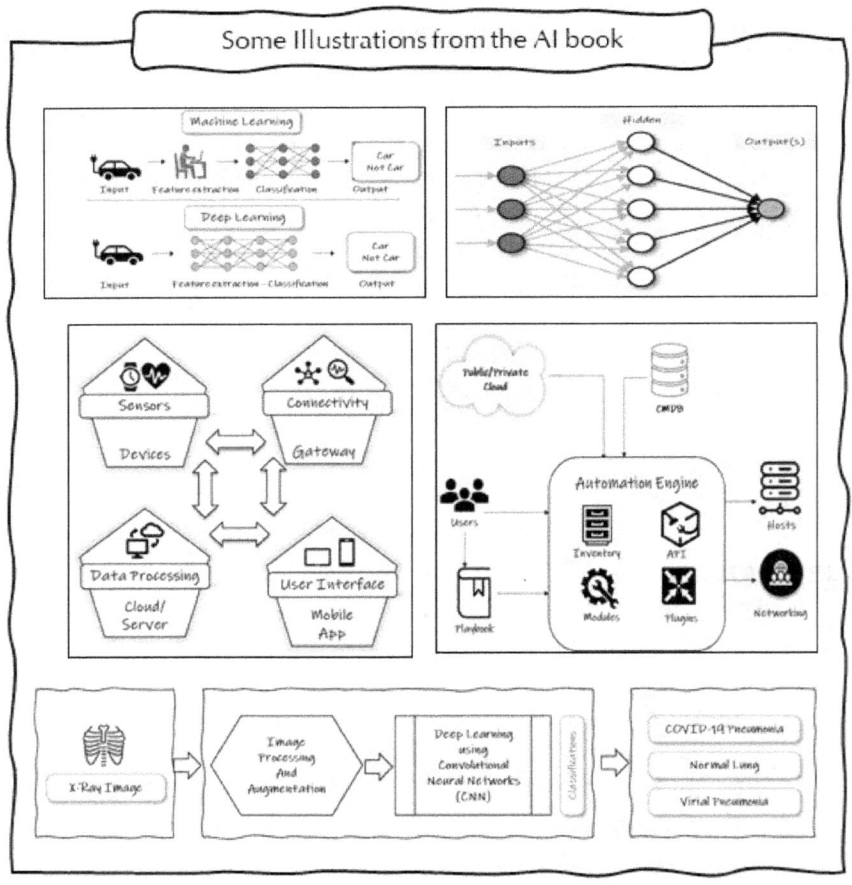

Book: Cloud Service Management and Governance

DESCRIPTION

Once an organisation adopts cloud computing, it quickly becomes apparent that the traditional approaches to IT Service Management processes will need to undergo drastic changes to integrate and run Bi-Modal IT Service Operations.

This book is an alleyway to managing enterprise could services with a framework that consists of progressive Service Management practices to ensure practical, strategic, and modular methodology for the positive transformation of ITSM for cloud delivery models is followed.

KEY FEATURES

- Understanding the enterprise transformation
- Fundamentals of cloud computing
- Understanding the IT service management frameworks
- Understanding cloud service management principles
- ITIL 4 processes and cloud service management
- Cloud service management reference model
- Cloud service management value chain
- Cloud policy management
- Cloud service portfolio management
- Cloud financial management
- Cloud capacity and availability management
- Cloud incident, problem, change, knowledge management
- KPI and critical success factors
- Cloud service governance and operations framework
- Cloud operations and capabilities management and many more

WHERE TO GET IT

https://enamulhaque.co.uk/my-books

Cloud Service Management Process Flows
from the Cloud Service Management Book

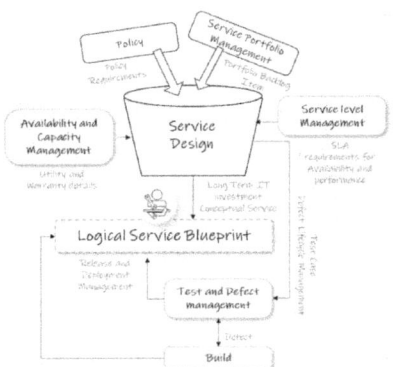

Design Value Stream Workflow

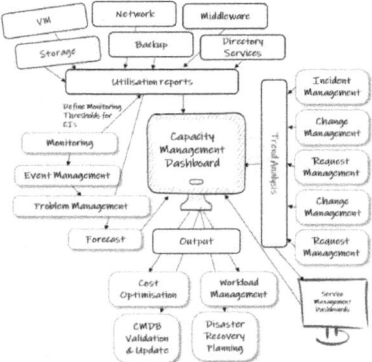

Capacity Management High-level Process

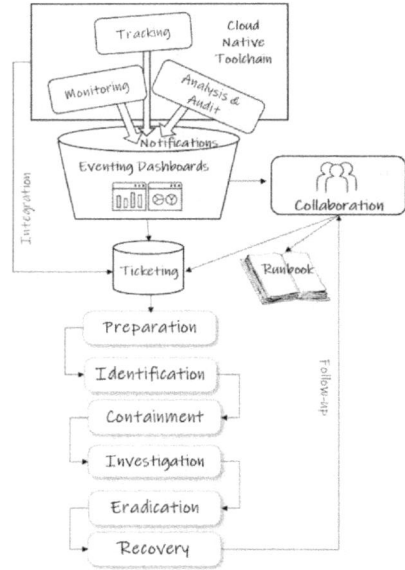

Cloud Incident Management Workflow

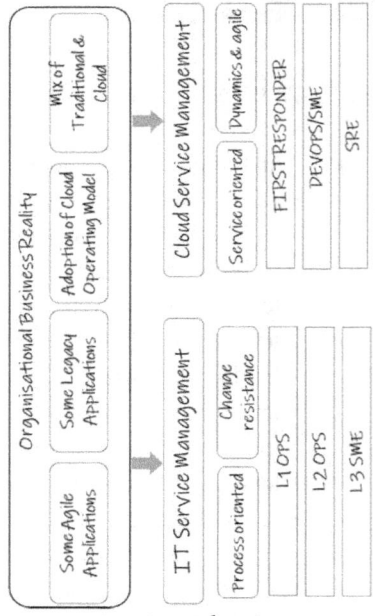

DevOps Adoption

Book Reviews

Industry leaders provided feedback on the "Digital Transformation Through Cloud Computing" book, and here are a few of them:

The most comprehensive and up-to-date publication I have seen on the topic. This book goes beyond the broader technical aspects. It shows how companies can gain a competitive advantage through cloud strategy, which makes it a must-read for IT managers and executives alike.

Dr Thomas Frankl,
Professor and Department Head
International University in Geneva.

With a pragmatic approach and simple language, Enamul Haque has cracked the codes of digital transformation through Cloud Computing as a strategy for sustainable growth for organisations. It is not only a guide for practitioners but also a ready-reference for students who want to conceptualise a complex hypothesis in straightforward terms.

Dr S M A Moin,
Associate Head of Research and Scholarship,
Coventry University

This is a brilliant, rigorous and visionary analysis of the disruptive impact of digital transformation with an influential explanation of how Cloud Computing, when implemented ensuring security, privacy and ethical implications, can revolutionise business transformation.

Lee Bennning,
Managing Architect, Cloud & Edge Services, Capgemini

This book is an excellent summary of relevant and useful frameworks and tools which can be used when navigating through the turbulent seas of digital transformation.

Jiska Druey,
IIOT Expert, Amazon Web Services (AWS)

List of Figures

List of Tables

Notes and References

[1] **Marc Benioff** (Extracted from the article called "What Is Digital Transformation?", published in Salesforce website - https://www.salesforce.com/products/platform/what-is-digital-transformation/

[2] **Big Data Analytics – IBM** - https://www.ibm.com/analytics/hadoop/big-data-analytics

[3] **Christy Pettey** - Build your organization's data and analytics competency for digital transformation success. - https://www.gartner.com/smarterwithgartner/why-data-and-analytics-are-key-to-digital-transformation/

[4] **Jason Hiner** – (September 2017) - https://www.zdnet.com/article/big-data-and-digital-transformation-how-one-enables-the-other/

[5] **Melvin Greer** – (February, 2019) - Data: The Fuel Powering AI & Digital Transformation - https://www.forbes.com/sites/cognitiveworld/2019/02/06/data-the-fuel-powering-ai-digital-transformation/#3c602d92578b

[6] **Cynthia Harvey** - Big Data Use Cases - https://www.datamation.com/big-data/big-data-use-cases.html

[7] **Mate Labs** – (July 2019) - 3 ways AI can aid Digital Transformation - https://towardsdatascience.com/3-ways-ai-aids-digital-transformation-4a5965708c45

[8] **InfoSys** - The revolution isn't just digital. It's human - https://www.infosys.com/human-amplification/

[9] **Mark Hung** - *Leading the IoT* (2017) - https://www.gartner.com/imagesrv/books/iot/iotEbook_digital.pdf

[10] **Chris Middleton** - Five ways the Internet of Things is transforming businesses today - https://internetofbusiness.com/5-ways-the-internet-of-things-is-transforming-businesses-today/

[11] **Inmarsat** - Businesses expect Industrial IoT to boost revenues by $154 million – https://internetofbusiness.com/iiot-adoption-inmarsat-report/

[12] **Chris Middleton** – Cambridge Innovative Institute - https://internetofbusiness.com/5-ways-the-internet-of-things-is-transforming-businesses-today/

[13] **All references and materials** in this book used from NIST are based on written permission obtained from the Department of Public Affairs Office of the National Institute of Standards and Technology

[14] **Microsoft** - What is the Cloud? – https://azure.microsoft.com/en-gb/overview/what-is-the-Cloud/

[15] **Das Projekt GAIA-X** - https://www.bmwi.de/Redaktion/DE/Publikationen/Digitale-Welt/das-projekt-gaia-x.pdf?__blob=publicationFileandv=22

[16] **Ryan** - The Cloud Ecosystem for Dummies - https://blog.shuttle-cloud.com/cloud-ecosystem-for-dummies/

[17] **Gartner definition** – "Shadow IT refers to IT devices, software and services outside the ownership or control of IT organisations."

[18] **Gartner** warns skills shortage could hamper digital transformation efforts - https://www.information-age.com/gartner-skills-shortage-123474620/#

[19] **Gary Thome** (August 2019) How to overcome 4 common challenges to hybrid cloud adoption - https://www.cio.com/article/3432545/how-to-overcome-4-common-challenges-to-hybrid-cloud-adoption.html

[20] **introduction to infrastructure as a service** - https://www.skdav-polytech.ac.in/news_files/3_1586804278.pdf

[21] **Margaret Rouse, Kate Brush; Stephen Bigelow** (2013) - Platform as a Service (PaaS) - https://searchcloudcomputing.techtarget.com/definition/Platform-as-a-Service-PaaS

[22] **Gartner Glossary** – IT Services - https://www.gartner.com/en/information-technology/glossary/it-services

[23] **Sean Spicer** - 10 Benefits of Cloud Managed Services Providers (January 2018) - https://www.agileit.com/news/10-benefits-cloud-managed-service-providers/

[24] **7 Criteria to Select the Right Managed Cloud Service Provider** - https://www.cloudjournee.com/blog/7-criteria-select-right-managed-cloud-service-provider/

[25] **Elias Khnaser**, VP Analyst at Gartner - https://www.gartner.com/smarterwithgartner/6-steps-for-planning-a-cloud-strategy/

[26] **Shadow-Soft Team** (November 2017) Cloud Migration Models: How to Pick the Right Strategy - https://shadow-soft.com/cloud-migration-models/

[27] **Gartner** "Decision Point for Choosing a Cloud Migration Strategy for Applications," Traverse Clayton, 20 November 2018. https://www.gartner.com/document/3893681 (Gartner subscription required)

[28] **Gartner Glossary - It Governance** (itg) - https://www.gartner.com/en/information-technology/glossary/it-governance

[29] **Ian Hutchinson** (September 2017) – What is a cloud centre of excellence and what can it do for you? https://www.rackspace.com/aws-future-insight/aws-insights/helping-customers-build-aws-cloud-centre-excellence/

[30] **Google** - Building a Cloud Center of Excellence - https://services.google.com/fh/files/misc/cloud_center_of_excellence.pdf

[31] **The Open Group** – IT4IT - https://www.opengroup.org/it4it

[32] **A reference architecture** in the field of software architecture or enterprise architecture provides a template solution for an architecture for a domain. It also provides a common language with which to discuss implementations, usually with the aim to stress commonality

[33] **Cloud Availability and Capacity Characteristics** - https://crmtrilo-gix.com/Cloud-Blog/IaaS-and-PaaS/Cloud-Availability-and-Capacity-Characteristics/157

[34] **Cloud Availability and Capacity Characteristics** - https://crmtrilo-gix.com/Cloud-Blog/IaaS-and-PaaS/Cloud-Availability-and-Capacity-Characteristics/157

[35] **Microsoft** (2013) Cloud Services Foundation Reference Model (CSFRM) - https://blogs.technet.microsoft.com/cloudsolutions/2013/08/15/cloud-services-founda-tion-reference-architecture-reference-model/

[36] **BMC** - Cognitive Service Management - https://www.bmc.com/it-solutions/cog-nitive-service-management.html

[37] **SCOPISM** – SIAM Body of Knowledge - https://www.slideshare.net/des-mond.devendran/siam-foundationbodyofknowledge

[38] **Rick Braddy** - Contributor, Network World (July 2018) - https://www.network-world.com/article/3290240/the-5-pillars-of-cloud-data-management.html

[39] **Gene Kim** is a multiple award-winning CTO, researcher and author, and has been studying high-performing technology organisations since 1999. He was founder and CTO of Tripwire for 13 years. - https://itrevolution.com/faculty/gene-kim/

[40] **IBM – SRE** - Site Reliability Engineering, the cloud approach to operations - https://www.ibm.com/cloud/blog/site-reliability-engineering-cloud-approach-opera-tions

[41] **Cloud Taxonomy** - http://cloudtaxonomy.opencrowd.com/

[42] **IBM Garage** - Cloud Service Management and Operations - https://www.ibm.com/cloud/architecture/courses/csmo

[43] **IBM Garage** - Cloud Service Management and Operations - https://www.ibm.com/cloud/architecture/courses/csmo

[44] **Kaja Polachowska** – September 2018 - Error Budget - https://neo-teric.eu/blog/what-is-an-error-budget/

[45] **Gary O' Connor** - Postmortem Culture: Learning from Failure - https://land-ing.google.com/sre/sre-book/chapters/postmortem-culture/

[46] **Adam Wiggins** - The Twelve Factors - https://12factor.net/

[47] **IBM** - Problem analysis by using the 5 Hows - https://www.ibm.com/gar-age/method/practices/manage/five-hows

[48] **Wikipedia** - https://en.m.wikipedia.org/wiki/Conway%27s_law

This book has the most simplified explanations of Enterprise Service Management with little technical jargon.

Enterprise Service Management (ESM) describes how organisations aim to maximise value creation in line with the organisation's mission. It provides a source of elegance and structure when the world becomes more chaotic, with new techniques and technology vying for our attention.

In this book, we explored some key trends driving ESM adoption across industries today. These include cloud computing, DevOps workflows, AI, blockchain, metaverse and many other collaboration tools, which have become increasingly popular with IT organisations over the past few years.

You will find step-by-step guidelines for streamlining your ESM journey along with other corporate objectives. You will understand business disruption and digital transformation – all influencing such adoption for an enterprise to function today.

The main features include setting up your ESM strategy, ESM implementation methods, ESM operating model, and future trends in ITSM. We looked into the metaverse, blockchain, ESG etc., their ways of shaping the ESM platforms, and many more features that the ESM roadmap would require.

Buy it from here: https://www.lulu.com/spotlight/authorenam

www.ingramcontent.com/pod-product-compliance
Lightning Source LLC
Chambersburg PA
CBHW071400170526
45165CB00001B/127